Memorials of the Huguenots in America

with Special Reference to Their Emigration to Pennsylvania

Rev. A. Stapleton, A.M., M.S.

Life Member of the Pennsylvania Historical Society—Member of the Pennsylvania German Society,—Author of "Natural History of the Bible,"—"Compend of Church History,"—and "Evangelical Annals."

"Sir, it is the part of the Church of God to endure blows, and not to deal them; but your Majesty will please remember that it is an anvil which has already worn out many a hammer."
—Theo. de Beza to the King of Navarre.

HERITAGE BOOKS
2008

HERITAGE BOOKS
AN IMPRINT OF HERITAGE BOOKS, INC.

Books, CDs, and more—Worldwide

For our listing of thousands of titles see our website
at
www.HeritageBooks.com

A Facsimile Reprint
Published 2008 by
HERITAGE BOOKS, INC.
Publishing Division
100 Railroad Ave. #104
Westminster, Maryland 21157

Originally published:
Carlisle, Pennsylvania
1901

— Publisher's Notice —
In reprints such as this, it is often not possible to remove blemishes from the original. We feel the contents of this book warrant its reissue despite these blemishes and hope you will agree and read it with pleasure.

International Standard Book Numbers
Paperbound: 978-0-7884-2260-7
Clothbound: 978-0-7884-7532-0

AUTHOR'S PREFACE.

IT must be apparent to the reader that the gathering of material for this work was immeasurably difficult because of the scanty and scattered sources of information. With the exception of the excellent work of Prof. Charles W. Baird (1) and several monograms by the American Huguenot Society, no work on the Huguenot emigration to America has hitherto appeared. True, the Virginia Historical Society has published a small volume on the emigration to that Province, and chapters devoted to the settlements in New England and South Carolina are to be found. Still the reader will find that, with the exception of a few newspaper articles, the history of the Huguenot emigration to Pennsylvania has hitherto remained unwritten. It is chiefly on this account that our resources have been specially devoted to their emigration to this Province.

The question may be pertinently asked why so much pains have been taken to gather particulars concerning so small a portion of our Colonial immigrants as the French Protestants? The answer is found in their *character*. The Huguenots were something *more* than immigrants seeking a home in a new land. They were *refugees*, stripped of all human rights, both civil and religious, by the Revocation of the Edict of Nantes in 1685, and not until the Edict of Toleration, in 1787, could they claim a right to full liberty of conscience in their home land.

In the industrial arts, learning and religious thought the Huguenots were of the most advanced and enterprising type of civilization, and the impressions they have made on the institutions and character of the lands of their exile were more profound and far reaching in proportion to their numbers than that of any other class of immigrants.

This is pre-eminently true of America, as we believe this work will abundantly demonstrate, and we believe that the study of this element of our Colonial population will be pursued with greater interest by future historians as their mighty influence in shaping the character and destinies of our country is more fully recognized.

---

(1). "The Huguenot Emigration to America."

With the passing years they disclose the original virility of their character by continually adding new names to America's roll of honor. To such imperishable names as *Jay, Boudinot, Bowdoin, Marion* and *Laurens*, of the Provincial period, they have added others of equal greatness, and whose force of character and sterling worth is in no small degree attributable to their Huguenot ancestry.

In later years Presidents *Tyler* (1), *Garfield* (2) and *Roosevelt*, *Alexander Hamilton*, the *Bayards* of Delaware, Commodores *Stephen Decatur* and *W. S. Schley*, and Admiral *George Dewey*, then also the poets *Whittier* (3), *Thoreau, Lanier* and *Emily Bouton*, have all contributed largely to make America great.

Although, as already indicated, the literature pertaining to the subject of this work is very scanty, we may state that considerable data was found in county histories, especially in the works of Prof. I. Daniel Rupp and General W. H. M. Davis. The Pennsylvania Archives, "Notes and Queries" by Dr. Egle, "Documentary History of New York" "Baird's Huguenot Emigration to America," besides the publications of the Pennsylvania Historical and Pennsylvania-German Societies, have all yielded valuable materials. We are under very great obligations to a large number of local historians and private individuals for clues and suggestions that in many instances led to important results. We are specially indebted to the following gentlemen for valuable assistance: The late Hon. John Blair Linn, of Bellefonte; Mrs. Cora Weber Lindsey, of Pittsburg; Henry S. Dodderer, Editor of "The Perkiomen Regeon," Prof. Julius F. Sachse, author of several works of great value on the emigration to Pennsylvania, John W. Jordan, of the Pennsylvania Historical Society, all of Philadelphia; deB. Randolph Keim, of Reading, and Editor of "The Keim and Allied Families;" James B. Laux, of New York; Rev. P. C. Croll, Editor of the Pennsylvania German, and lastly, the lamented Dr. W. H. Egle, of Harrisburg, late State Librarian, and Editor of the Pennsylvania Archives, to whose valuable assistance we are deeply indebted. As a matter of mournful interest we may state that one of the last acts of his busy life was to furnish the introduction to this work a few days before his death.

If we have in a measure succeeded in rescuing from oblivion the memory of a people who have been such a potent factor in shap-

(1). President Tyler descended from Dr. Louis Contesse, an eminent physician, who fled from France to Virginia after the Revocation (Va. Hist. Col.).
(2). President Garfield descended from Maturin Ballou, a refugee to New England.
(3). The ancestor of Whittier was a refugee named Fouillevert, who fled to England from Brittagne in the early stages of the persecution (vide Am. Meth. Ill. Monthly, vol 11, p. 229).

ing the character and destinies of our land, and preserved to posterity the names of many from whom it is an honor to claim descent, we shall consider ourselves well rewarded for our many years of toil.

REV. A. STAPLETON.

CARLISLE, PA.

INTRODUCTION.

By Dr. W. H. Egle, M. D., M. S., Late State Librarian of Pennsylvania, Etc.

*"Sit at the feet of History—through night
Of years the steps of virtue she shall trace,
And show the earlier ages, where her sight
Can pierce the eternal shadows o'er her face."*
—*Bryant.*

THE Huguenot emigration to America is a subject of abiding interest to the historian, as well as to the general reader. The Frenchman's love for his home-land exceeds that of any other nationality, and the causes leading to the extirpation of any considerable number of them must be dire in the extreme. These causes, and their far-reaching consequences, are brought out in a remarkable manner in these "Memorials of the Huguenots."

There is a peculiar charm clustering around the relations of France with the American Colonies during their struggle for freedom in the dark days of the Revolution. The Colonies were intensely *Protestant* in faith, and France just then awakening from her stupor, brought on by ages of priestcraft and misgovernment, sprang to the rescue of the Colonies at the period of their darkest peril. Many of her noble sons enriched the soil of freedom with their blood, for which America will always be grateful ; and many of her chief citizens to-day are proud to wear the insignia of "The Society of the Cincinnati" (1) as a memorial of the time when the infant Republic of the New World and the future Republic of the Old World, together, lit the torch of freedom that still shines with increasing lustre across the dark waters of time. Thus has France, the pioneer Republic of Europe, derived hope and inspiration in her lofty aims from the new Nation, which her exiled sons assisted to build !

The Huguenot emigrants as a class, we may safely say without fear of successful contradiction, have furnished a larger number of

---

(1). A patriotic and benevolent society, organized by the American and French officers in 1783 to perpetuate their friendship and raise a fund for relieving the widows and orphans of those who had fallen during the war. The noted French Colonel LeEnfant designed the badge of the order. General Washington was for many years its President.

men of eminence, in proportion to their number, than any other nationality. So strongly marked were their characteristics that neither time nor amalgamation with other races has as yet extinguished the traces of their high moral sentiments and love of liberty from the character of their descendants. This character is still a dominating force in our national life. The extremes of Huguenot theology may be modified by modern criticism. Its mistaken notions of a religio-civic government may give way to broader views, but its lofty spirit and high ideals can never perish because they are the basic elements of human progress. Its spirit has been perpetuated on canvas (1) and in the drama (2) as well as in history, song and story, but its most abiding features are incarnate in the noble life and deeds which has given a new value to human effort and has cast new light on the path of human progress. In the fire of the pulpit, in the eloquence of the legislative hall, in the various fields of learning and research the Huguenot spirit still leads the van. On the field of battle and on the trackless seas they have not only maintained our Nation's honor but have opened new eras in the world's history. The naval glories of Stephen Decatur, the epoch making achievements of Admiral Dewey (3) at Manilla, and of Commodore Schley at (4) Santiago, are compliments to the Huguenot origin of these heroes.

The reader will find elaborated in this work a phase of history relating to the Huguenots which has hitherto been either slighted or overlooked by writers on our Colonial history, namely, its intimate relation with the great Palatine exodus to Pennsylvania. The latter movement had its origin in much the same causes which led the Huguenots to flee from their homes and seek a new destiny in unknown lands. Hence both Huguenot and Palatine, with an almost identical faith, tired of murder, rapine, fire, sword and spoilation under the guise of the Christian religion, seem to have joined in heart and purpose in working out a common destiny in the New World.

In view of the fact that the Palatine emigration has received so much attention at the hands of many historians, the scant reference to the considerable Huguenot element among them seems remarka-

---

(1). "Les Huguenots," a famous painting by J. E. Millias, P. R. A., 1852, representing a trysting couple.
(2). "Les Huguenots," an opera by Meyerbeer, still quite popular.
(3). Admiral George Dewey is a descendant of Thomas Dewey who, at an early day, emigrated to Vermont from England, whither his ancestor had fled from the Huguenot persecutions. ("Notes and Queries," 1898, p. 76).
(4). Admiral W. S. Schley derives his Huguenot ancestry from Madame Ferree, whose great grand-daughter, Rebecca Ferree, wife of David Shreiber, moved to Frederick County, Maryland. (Rupp's Hist. Lanc. Co., p. 112).

ble. In this work we have this missing chapter in our Colonial history, and its rescue was made possible only by a long and profound study of the personality of the immigrants.

The student must not expect to find in this work every name that belongs there. The subject is not exhausted. There are many more Huguenot names among us with a very thin Teutonic veneer over it and which the keen eye of genealogical research will yet uncover There are yet many German family names with Huguenot traditions which still remain to be differentiated from present encumbrances and reinstated on its proper page of a glorious history.

WILLIAM HENRY EGLE, M. D., M. A.

IN MEMORIAM.

Dr. William Henry Egle, M. D., A. M.

Dr. W. H. Egle, the distinguished historian, was born in Harrisburg, Pa., September 17, 1830, and died in that city February 20, 1901. His ancestor, Marcus Egle, was a Swiss who came to Lancaster county, Pa., prior to 1740. Another ancestor was Francis Mentges, a French Huguenot, and the father of Col. Francis Mentges, of the Revolution. In 1859 he graduated in medicine in the University of Pennsylvania, after which he established himself in that profession in his native city. In the Civil War he served with distinction as a surgeon. In 1887 he was appointed State Librarian by Governor Beaver, and was reappointed to that office by Governor Pattison in 1891 and by Governor Hastings in 1894. His life was an exceedingly busy one and the result of his labors immense. He was the author of scores of historical works of great value, among them "History of Pennsylvania," Histories of Lebanon and Dauphin counties, Archives of Pennsylvania, over twenty volumes, "Notes and Queries," some twelve volumes, "Pennsylvania Genealogies," etc. He was a member of many learned societies both in America and Europe, and the first president of the Pennsylvania German Society, of which society he was one of the founders. He was a most amiable and approachable Christian scholar of the highest rank, whose great delight it was to place his immense stock of historical knowledge freely at the disposal of his fellow men. His sudden death amid his many unfinished literary enterprises was a great loss and called forth universal regret.

Memorials of The Huguenots.

CHAPTER I.
Extending From the Beginning of the French Reformation to the Promulgation of the Edict of Nantes--1510--1598.

*"Great truths are dearly bought,
Not found by chance;
Nor wafted in the breath of summer dream,
But grasped in the great struggle of the soul,
Hard buffeting with adverse wind and stream."*
—*Anon.*

THE sixteenth century is one of the most notable periods of all history. The discovery of America, the invention of the art of printing and other elements had awakened a spirit of universal inquiry and independence of thought throughout the world. The great masses began to realize that their consciences were dominated by the priests, while their lords regarded them as vassals and mere chattels.

No particular country can be said to be the cradle of the Reformation. The time for which Providence paved the way was ripe, and, like a mighty torrent, broke away from human restraint and flooded the world with the blessings of the pure gospel.

When Martin Luther nailed his ninety-five propositions on the *Schloss Kirche* at Wittenberg in 1517, the gates of the reservoir were opened, where before the waters had, so to speak, only overflowed the banks.

Our aim will be simply to trace, in brief, the Reformation in France, leaving the reader to seek information concerning the work in other countries from other sources.

Reformation Begins at Meaux.

The Reformation in France first established itself in the department of Meaux, and from thence spread rapidly. The leading spirit of this movement was *Jacques Lefever* who, with a fiery zeal and restless energy, proclaimed the Reformation in many places.

Francis I had, from the beginning of his reign, condemned the excesses of the Church of Rome, and when the Reformers of Meaux decried the evils of the Papacy it was not without countenance from the King of France. He even went so far as to join the Protestant princes in the Smalkaldic League (1). Margaret, Queen of Navarre, a sister to Francis I, embraced the Reformed doctrines and, unlike her vacillating brother, she boldly identified herself with the cause. Had the King followed her example France would have been won for the Protestant cause.

Perhaps a majority of the nobility and many of the leading ecclesiastics were ready for reform. Even the great Sorbonne (2) looked with favor on the movement. The chief reason why France was lost to the Reformation was because the sovereign and his civil and ecclesiastical dignitaries regarded the Roman Church as the true body of Christ and favored the reform of abuses *in* the church. This was impossible in a body so corrupt. As the Reformation advanced it became necessary for its adherents to form organizations of their own with pastors and leaders distinct from the church. The Reformed people of France were called "Huguenots." The origin of this term is uncertain, so that a discussion of the term in this connection would be useless. The Reformation in France was somewhat unfortunate in assuming a political aspect. It early counted many of the greatest statesmen of the Kingdom on its side. Besides the House of Navarre, the members of which figure conspicuously in this history, the Huguenot party counted among its leaders the celebrated Gaspard de Chatillon, Count de Coligny, Admiral of France, and also his brothers Odet, Cardinal de Chatillon, and Francois de Chatillon, Sire d'Andelot, the Captain-General of the French infantry, also the Dukes de Rohan, the La Rochefoucaulds, the Grammonts, the Princes de Porcien, the Lords of Piennes, of Soubise, of Genlis, of Mornay, of Esternay, and many others who, under various titles, figured in the history of the times.

John Calvin.

The great spiritual leader of the Huguenots was *John Calvin*, born at Noyon, in Picardy, 1509, and died in Geneva, Switzerland, in 1564. Calvin easily ranked with Luther as a great reformer. With great eloquence and profound learning he expounded and defended the Reformed doctrines. After laboring for a number of years in France, removing from place to place because of opposition, he at last established himself in Geneva, where for many years

---

(1). A defensive alliance of Protestant European Powers. formed in 1631 for mutual protection against Charles V and the Catholic Powers.
(2). The Theological Faculty of the University of Paris.

he was the virtual head of the French Reformation. His theological works are numerous and profound. His "Institutes of the Christian Religion" was probably the greatest work of the Reformation period, and continues to exercise a strong influence on Protestant theology, even to the present day.

An important factor in the religio-political struggle of the French Reformation was the *Guise* family, or House of Lorraine. The Guises were in close affinity with the Roman See, and were considered foreigners by the French. Francois, Duke of Guise, however, made himself popular by his success at arms against the enemies of France, and attained a high station in the army. His brother, the Cardinal de Lorraine, was an ecclesiastic only in name, and with the duke arose to political prominence. The Guises, together with Catharine de Medici, mother of the king, and herself a foreigner and a bigoted papist, were the controlling spirits of the opposition against the Reformation. Such are a few of the ecclesiastical and political elements of the great struggle.

The First Martyr.

It is impossible to even refer to the many struggles of the Huguenots through the dark centuries embraced in their history. We can only in a general way point out some of the leading events. *Jean Le Clerk*, one of the earliest reformers of Meaux, permitting his zeal to exceed his discretion, entered several Catholic churches, broke the images and posted placards denouncing the corruptions of the Pope and church. For this he was apprehended, condemned as a heretic, and burned at the stake in the city of Metz in 1525. He was the first conspicuous martyr of the Huguenots. Notwithstanding the great persecutions which were now instituted the Protestants continued to increase in numbers and influence.

Armed Resistance.

The year 1560 marks the period of armed collision between the Papists under the Guises and the Huguenots under the Prince of

Conde. One dreadful feature of the conflict was the massacre of twelve thousand Huguenot prisoners at Amboise. The Reformation also lost the noble Baron de Castlenau, who was condemned to death on the pretext of treason.

Foreign complications ameliorated the struggle. On August 21, 1560, there was an assembly of notables held at Fontainebleau for the consideration of the national difficulties, at which time the Duke de Coligny presented to the King a petition coupled with an eloquent plea for religious toleration. The King and many of his party inclined to the petition, but were violently opposed by the Guises. It was agreed to defer the matter until the assembly of the States General, but before it convened Francis II. died, December 5, 1560. Francis had been a mere tool in the hands of his uncles, the Duke and Cardinal of Lorraine. In order to preserve the interests of her house, Catharine de Medici, the Queen Regent, was compelled to repress the Lorraines and court the favor of the Huguenots. The King, her son, Louis IX., was at this time but nine years old.

States General Favorable.

The States General met at Orleans December 13, 1560. The Chancellor de l' Hopital, who had always exercised moderation toward the Protestants, spoke strongly against Romish excesses. The Duke de Coligny, as the leader of the Protestants, was a tower of strength and greatly distinguished himself. The liberation of France from Papal tyranny seemed near at hand. Even the Queen Regent lent encouragement by opening the pulpit of the Palace of Fountainebleau to the Bishop Montluc, who boldly preached the doctrines of the Reformation. The tide running so high in favor of the Huguenots at this assembly, was turned against them by the Lorraines, who formed what is known as the Triumvirate for the upholding of the Catholic Church. At the head of this league was the Duke of Guise.

Great Debate at Possey.

It was then arranged to convene a great assembly at Possey, where the religious differences should be discussed in the presence of the notables by a representative from each side. The conference met September 9, 1561. The Catholics were represented by the Cardinal of Lorraine and the Protestants by Theodore de Beza. The Chancellor was again the benign L'Hopital, whose opening address was most favorable to the Reformation.

The great Huguenot theologian, de Beza, with nothing but the

Bible as his text-book, completely swept away the Romish traditions and dogmas of the Cardinal. The Assembly drew up a documant defining the position and rights of both parties, which was in the main satisfactory to all but the Lorraines and the Sorbonne, which branded it as in the highest degree heretical. Thus terminated the famous council October 9, 1561.

The Huguenots strenuously insisted on civil and political rights. The Queen Regent, desiring information concerning their strength, the Count de Coligny furnished her a list of two thousand one hundred and fifty churches that petitioned for religious toleration. In January, 1562, the Assembly of Notables issued regulations which, in a very narrow measure, granted toleration. The discontent of the Reformed was somewhat quieted by a request of the Queen Regent for loyal submission. The Guises now sought to counteract the advantages of the Protestants by isolating their nobles from the cause. Antoine de Bourbon, the King of Navarre, was the first to fall in the snare by flattery and the insidious allurements of promised power and greatness. Despite the entreaties of Calvin and Beza, and his noble wife, Jeanne de Albret, who was the only daughter of Margaret de Valois, Navarre renounced the Protestant faith. It is a sad chapter in the history of this noble woman that, upon her remaining firm, she was forced to leave her home and children and retire to her estates in Bearne. Notwithstanding the attempt of the Pope to bring her before the Inquisition she remained faithful to the Protestant cause.

Calamities Multiply.

The defection of the King of Navarre brought immediate calamity to the Huguenot party. The Duke de Coligny and his brothers left the court but remained firm in the faith. The Guises now having a free field sent a troop to Vassy and made a descent upon a Huguenot assembly numbering about twelve hundred, who were engaged in worship, a great number of whom were massacred in the most horrible manner. Great was the indignation caused by this unprovoked butchery and led to a protest to the Queen Regent against the assumption of power by the House of Lorraine.

Some time later, at a meeting of the notables, the King of Navarre in a manner justified the attack on Vassey, when Theodore de Beza, who was present, replied in these words, which have become historic: "*Sir, it certainly becomes the Church of God, in whose cause I speak, to endure blows, and not strike them; but may it please your Majesty also to remember that it is an anvil, which has worn out many a hammer.*"

Civil War.

The aggressions of the Guises at once plunged the country into civil war. The Huguenots were led by the Prince of Conde and the Duke de Coligny. The Papists were led by the King of Navarre and the Duke of Guise. Both armies were swelled by thousands of recruits from foreign lands. The Huguenots were assisted by the Protestant States of Germany, the Catholics by heavy bodies of troops from Spain. The war raged with indifferent success to both sides, and resulted in terrible loss. The Papist leader, the Duke of Guise, and also Marshal de St. Andre, were slain. The Prince of Conde, the Huguenot leader, who was virtually a prisoner, concluded at Ambois, March 19, 1563, a treaty of peace with the Queen Regent, Catharine de Medici. This treaty was far less advantageous to the Protestants than the edict of January, 1562, and did not meet the approval of Coligny. By its very elements it lacked the conditions of permanent peace. The Queen Regent, Catharine de Medici, at the instigation of Papal emissaries, renewed her intrigues against the Protestant nobles, and on August 4, 1564, she gave an interpretation to the edict of Ambois wholly detrimental to Protestant rights. To strengthen her position she imported six thousand Swiss mercenaries, which was rightly taken by the Huguenots as a renewal of hostilities, and they at once flew to arms, under the leadership of the Prince of Conde and the Duke de Coligny. On November 10, 1567, an indecisive battle was fought near Paris, in which Montmorency, one of the Triumvirate, was killed. The success of the Huguenots induced Catharine de Medici to sue for peace, on condition that the edict of pacification should be permanently established. To this the Prince of Conde, on behalf of the Protestants, assented, and the treaty of Longjumeau was signed March 20, 1568.

Protestant Faith Betrayed.

Never was a solemn treaty more shamefully violated. Scarcely had the Protestants laid down their arms when the priests, doubtless instigated by the higher authorities, inflamed their people against the defenseless Huguenots and the most frightful atrocities were committed. In three months upward of 10,000 were put to death, many in the most horrible manner. The Protestant leaders, the Prince of Conde and the Dukes de Coligny and de Andelot, fled to their stronghold, La Rochelle, where Jeanne d' Albret, Queen of Navarre, and sister to the Prince of Conde, joined them with 4000 men.

No decisive action took place until March 16, 1569, when the two armies met at Jarnac, resulting in disaster to the Huguenots.

The noble and pious Prince of Conde, being severely wounded, surrendered himself, after which he was cruelly assassinated and his body dragged about on an ass.

Coligny now took the chief command of the Huguenot forces. After gaining a few minor advantages he was overwhelmingly defeated October 3, 1569, at Moncontour, where he lost two-thirds of his army and was himself dreadfully wounded. The faith and courage of the great Duke never shone with greater lustre than amid this crushing misfortune. In a short time he had gathered another army, gained important advantages and marched in triumph towards Paris. This speedily brought Queen Catharine to terms and a treaty of peace, more favorable than any previous, was signed August 8, 1570, at St. Germain-en-Laye.

Massacre of St. Bartholomew.

THE MASSACRE OF ST. BARTHOLOMEW constitutes one of the darkest blots on the fair history of France. The only redeeming feature is the fact that most of the instigators were not Frenchmen, but foreigners, who, hissed on by the Papal powers, succeeded in causing their deluded and subservient subjects to strike this diabolical blow. The Protestant leaders had again been deceived when, on August 8, 1570, a supposed honorable peace was concluded. The verdict of history is that the Papacy never surrenders to a dissenter the right of conscience, hence what cannot be done by force must be done by intrigue and assassination.

Charles IX. and his mother, Catharine, with the House of Guise, now feigned the greatest friendship for the Protestant nobles. Jeanne d'Albert, the Queen of Navarre, upon the most pressing invitations, was induced, in the month of May, 1572, to pay court to the reigning house. While partaking of their supposed hospitality she fell sick and in five days died, June 9, of poison.

The Duke de Coligny, who had in 1571 taken his place in the Court of the King as one of his most influential advisers, was shot on August 22, 1572, by a page of the Duke of Guise. This assault was rightly interpreted by the Huguenots as a fresh attack upon them. Numbers of the Protestant leaders hastened to the quarters of the Duke, who, although severely wounded, was still able to converse.

The fateful hour at last came, and on Sunday morning, August 24, the signal was given by the tolling of the great bell, and the slaughter began. The Duke de Coligny was stabbed to death by a servant of the Duke of Guise, for which he was rewarded by the

Cardinal of Lorraine. The Protestant Princes, Henry de Navarre and the Prince of Conde, to save their lives professed Catholicism.

The massacre of St. Bartholomew was the most horrible tragedy of the Reformation period, and we may well say, with an illustrious statesman, "Let it be erased from the memory of man." The number of the slaughtered Huguenots has been variously estimated, but the best authorities agree in placing the aggregate at many thousands.

The news of the massacre was received at Rome with great joy, and the Pope had a medallion struck in commemoration of the event, while the Protestants all over the world were steeped in mourning. The Papists, however, utterly failed to stamp out the Protestant faith.

> *" Truth crushed to earth shall rise again,*
> *Th' eternal years of God are hers."*

A number of Protestant cities made a stout resistance, especially La Rochelle. After the death of Coligny the leadership passed to Francis de Lanau. Many of the influential Protestants fled to La Rochelle, where a successful defense was maintained under de Lanau.

The horrible outrages of 1572 had so shocked the world that a strong revulsion of feeling set in in favor of toleration.

France itself felt the reaction of sentiment so strongly that a new edict was issued August 11, 1573, permitting Protestant worship in La Rochelle, Nismes and Montauban.

Death of Charles IX.

Charles IX. died May 30, 1574, bitterly bewailing the part he bore in the terrible massacre. He was succeeded by his brother, Henry III., who, instead of heeding the good counsel of his contemporary sovereigns to use moderation in his dealings with his Protestant subjects, rather heeded the solicitations of his fanatical mother, Catharine, and the foreign Papists by whom she was controlled. The result was a civil war against the ultra Catholics on the one hand, and the Huguenots and Liberals on the other. After varying successes by both parties, a treaty of peace was concluded at Chastenoy May 6, 1576, which professed to guarantee enlarged privileges to the Huguenots. The stipulations, however, were soon discovered by the Protestants to be invalid, and they resumed the war. In this struggle they were left to themselves by the Liberals, and the leaders of the Huguenots concluded hostilities by the Peace of Bergerac. On October 8, 1577, was issued the edict of Poitiers, which pretended to grant certain privileges to the Huguenots. On February 28, 1579, was issued the explanatory edict of Nerac.

A considerable number of the nobility still remained faithful to the Protestant cause and consequently a new order of warfare was instituted by the Papists, namely, to corrupt by flattery and promises of preferment the leaders of the Huguenots. These tactics succeeded to a melancholy degree, and from henceforth the nobility bore a very inconspicuous part in the religious conflicts. Having won over many of the nobility the rights of the Protestants were more and more restricted.

The League of the Holy Union.

"The League of the Holy Union," of which Philip of Spain was the General, having as its object the extirpation of Protestanism throughout the world, made inroads in France. The Duke of Guise, a leading factor of this league, brought such influence to bear upon Henry III. that he, by the treaty of Nemours in 1585, deprived the Huguenots not only of the right of worship but also of the liberty of conscience. Orders were given to all ministers to leave the kingdom within a month, and all the laity to abjure their faith or emigrate within six months under penalty of confiscation of property.

This wanton violation of sacred guarantees was the signal for war. The Prince of Conde again espoused the cause of the Huguenots and succeeded in collecting a considerable army. No serious conflict occurred until October 20, 1587, when the two armies met at Contras. The Huguenots, before going into battle, bowed in prayer and chanted the 118th Psalm. The result was the complete rout of Henry III. and the loss of one-half of his army. Henry had been very unpopular with the Duke of Guise, who was now at the head of the League and a willing tool of the Pope and foreign party. His defeat therefore precipitated a crisis that had been pending for years. The Duke of Guise, supported by the League, was borne in triumph to Paris and made demonstrations for the throne. His triumph was brief, as he was assassinated, by order of Henry, on December 23, 1588. This act naturally widened the breach between the League and the King, and he was compelled to resort to arms in order to maintain his throne. In his extremity he sought the support of his late opponents, the Huguenots. The King of Navarre, as their head, held a conference with the Sovereign April 30, 1589, at which time a basis of operations against the League was agreed upon. The combined forces were very successful and repulsed the Leaguers at every point and finally invested Paris.

Scarcely had they achieved this triumph when Henry died at the hands of an assassin, August 2, 1589. The murderer, Jacques

Clement, was eulogized by the Romanists for this bloody deed, and commended by Pope Sextus "as an act comparable for the salvation of the world with the resurrection of Christ."

The Protestant House of Navarre now succeeded the Catholic House of Valois to the throne of France, and Henry of Navarre, the Huguenot leader, took his place on the throne of France as Henry IV.

The path of Navarre was beset with difficulties, the most powerful dignitaries of his realm as well as the majority of his subjects were Catholics, and bitterly hated his religion, while on the other hand many of his chief supporters and advisers were Protestants, among whom was the talented and pious Duke of Mornay, who may well rank with such noble Huguenot spirits as the Duke de Coligny and the Prince of Conde. The Protestants, headed by Mornay, brought pressure to bear on the King to mitigate their religious condition, and accordingly, in July, 1591, an edict of toleration was issued, which restored to them the privileges of 1577, but this was still far from religious liberty.

While the Protestant cause in France had now every reasonable prospect of triumph, it was doomed to disappointment through the instability and duplicity of Henry. For several years Mornay was able to keep him nominally in line with the Protestants.

CHAPTER II.

Extending From the Promulgation of the Edict of Nantes, in 1598, to its Revocation in 1685.

> *"Ours is the seed-time; God alone*
> *Beholds the end of what is sown;*
> *Beyond our vision, weak and dim,*
> *The harvest time is hid with Him."*
> —*Whittier.*

ALTHOUGH the abjuration by Henry IV. of Protestantism and its toleration at the same time created considerable dissatisfaction, yet by a combination of circumstances the Huguenots at last reached the highest point of religious freedom they ever enjoyed until the complete triumph of the cause in the eighteenth century. The country was beset with perils. Spanish forces were at his doors. Henry must do something to rally once more his brave Huguenot generals to his side. By according some measure of protection he hoped to quiet his subjects of the Reformed faith.

The Edict of Nantes.

Accordingly, in the month of April, 1598, he promulgated the famous Edict of Nantes, which was irrevocable in its character. Although it granted but limited toleration, it nevertheless put an end to the terrible wars which had already cost France over a million of her subjects, reduced many of her towns to ashes, ruined her industries, and brought her to the verge of destruction.

The contest between the Reformed and Catholic faith was now removed from the field of battle to the arena of theological discussion. Public debates between the champions on both sides were common and the country was flooded with controversial literature. One by one the House of Navarre fell into the snares of Popery. Catharine de Navarre, the King's sister, alone remained faithful to the religion of her mother, the noble Jeanne d'Albret. She died in 1604, the last Protestant Bourbon.

After the promulgation of the edict the National Synod of the Reformed Church met regularly. Seven hundred and sixty churches were reported, some of which had thousands of members. General tranquility prevailed until May 14, 1610, when a sad event took place which was a great disaster to France but more especially to the Protestants. This was the assassination of the King by a Jesuit because of his defiance of the Pope and toleration of Protestants.

The death of Henry was the signal for new troubles for the Huguenots. The Queen Regent, Mary de Medici, and the new King, Louis XIII., who was then but eight years old, were wholly under the influence of Papal intriguers. A collision between the Protestant nobles, headed by the Duke de Rohan and the King, was narrowly averted in 1615. This was the first dark cloud that presaged the reopening of the religious wars.

The Principality of Navarre, which was annexed to France upon the accession of Henry IV., was almost wholly Protestant. Yet in this Province all church properties which, since 1569, had been appropriated for religious purposes by the Protestants, were ordered to be restored to the "Church." This, of course, meant confiscation by the government of all places of worship of the Huguenots. The non-compliance with these orders induced the King to lead an army thither in 1620. Pillage and robbery by the soldiery became rampant and a veritable reign of terror prevailed.

The Last Civil War.

These outrages naturally aroused all the Protestants of France. Their rights, guaranteed by the edict of Nantes, were more and more infringed and the limit of endurance was reached. They called a political assembly to meet in December, 1620, at La Rochelle. The Huguenot nobility, however, were not so ready as formerly to appeal to arms for their religious convictions. The Duke de Bouillon remained neutral; Marshal de Lesdiguieres, the Dukes de la Tremoille and the Marquis de Chatillon—the latter a grandson of the great Coligny—the Marquis de la Force, the Duke de Sully and Mornay were either vacillating or undecided. But two distinguished noblemen, the Duke de Rohan and his brother, the Duke de Soubise, sons of Sully, were ready to draw sword in defense of Protestanism. Armed resistance was agreed on May 10, 1621.

The first triumph of Lonis XIII. was his obtaining possession of the town and stronghold of Saumur, held by Mornay. This he accomplished by false promises. The aged Mornay, who had so long and valiantly battled for religious freedom, refused all offers of preferment and bribes to forsake his religion, but repaired to his castle, where he died in 1623. He was one of the noblest of the political leaders of the Huguenots and a worthy compeer of Calvin and the great Coligny. The progress of the King was unsuccessfully resisted until Montauban was reached. This great Protestant stronghold was held by the Marquis de la Force, with the Duke de Rohan as support. After a siege of two months and a-half the King withdrew. The war was, however, resumed the following year with terrible fury. The Papists perpetrated many horrible outrages, especially in the vicinity of Montauban, where many Huguenots were put to the sword in cold blood. De la Force, to save himself, made an inglorious treaty with the King. Montpellier, however, under the Duke de Rohan, held out, and the King was glad to conclude a treaty of peace in October in which the Edict of Nantes was confirmed.

This, however, did not end the trouble. The reader should understand that in France, above all other countries, the Reformed were a political as well as an ecclesiastical power. The Papists of the Reformation period held that only *one* religion could be *true*, and that, of course, was their own, and that it was the duty of the State to suppress all innovations against the established religion, not only as an ecclesiastical but also as a civil necessity. From this standpoint it is apparent that all edicts of toleration to the Protestants were mere subterfuges and temporary makeshifts, and as soon as opportunity afforded the conflict was again renewed.

To break up the political power of the Protestants and at the same time begin a systematic extirpation of the "Pretended Reformed Religion," as it was officially termed, was determined on by Cardinal Richelieu, who was the virtual power behind the throne of France.

The first step to this end was to capture La Rochelle, a city of great commercial importance and the stronghold of Protestanism. The Huguenot merchants of La Rochelle were the most enterprising in the Kingdom, and by their maritime interests were connected with the commercial centers of the world. The city had for centuries been a semi-independent municipality, and during the religious wars had successfully resisted every attack. The siege of La Rochelle began in 1627 and continued for more than a year. A relief expedition from England failed to render the needed assistance and the Huguenots were left to their fate. Finally, after two-thirds of its inhabitants had perished, the city capitulated October 28, 1628. This was virtually the downfall of the Huguenots as a political power. In vain did the Duke de Rohan attempt to rally the Protestants to a continuance of the struggle. Calamities multiplied; at Privas the Huguenot garrison, eight hundred in number, were put to the sword under the most atrocious circumstances.

In July, 1629, the King issued an edict of pardon which, in effect, was an abridgement of the Edict of Nantes. On August 21 Montauban, the last Huguenot stronghold, surrendered, and the struggle of the French Protestants to maintain their guaranteed rights by force of arms was at an end. The gallant Duke de Rohan, the last great Huguenot military leader, laid down his arms. Dispirited and almost heart-broken, he forsook his native country and died in the service of a foreign land. Although attempts were made in later years by enemies of the Sovereign to incite them to armed resistance, they never again, as a body, took up arms to assert their rights.

The political power of the Huguenots being broken up the process of corrupting the ecclesiastical heads of the church by the Papists was next attempted but without success. The greatest difficulties were thrown in the way of holding the National Synods, consequently but three were held between 1631 and 1645.

In 1652 was issued a proclamation which re-established the Huguenots in their rights under the edicts, of which they had been deprived, and from this period until 1656 they enjoyed comparative tranquility. The rest, however, was brief, as in this year a new crusade was instituted against them, and which did not cease but grew in fanatical virulence under the direction of Papal agents until it culminated in the revocation of the Edict of Nantes in 1685.

In 1656, at a convocation of Catholic clergy, there was made a violent attack on the growing influence of the Protestants. Many evils were laid at their doors, and even treasonable designs were imputed to them. This charge was of course made to incense King Louis XIV. against them. As an immediate consequence many of their privileges were abridged, and when, in 1658, the Provincial Synods sent ten deputies to Paris to lay their wrongs before the King, he compelled them to wait four months before granting them an audience and then curtly dismissed them with an indefinite promise.

The Last National Synod.

On November 10, 1659, was convoked the National Synod, which had been permitted by the Prime Minister Mazarin only after the most persistent entreaty. At the opening of the Assembly the Commissioner of the King announced that His Majesty would not tolerate any complaints, which consequently made any petition or representation to the Sovereign of violated rights impossible. It was also intimated that the National Synod would not be permitted to meet hereafter, and when they adjourned on January 10, 1660, the ecclesiastical organization of the Reformed Church of France was virtually destroyed after an existence of about one hundred years.

Although the Prime Minister Mazarin was no friend of the Huguenots, yet his moderation kept the hatred of Louis IV. against them in check, so that his death in 1661 may be regarded as a misfortune to the cause of the Reformation.

The general course of events from this time on was more and more disastrous to the Huguenots; the Jesuits were everywhere and all the time busy, and with tireless energy worked for the complete eradication of the "Pretended Reformed Religion." Many places of worship were now interdicted, charitable institutions were confiscated and churches destroyed under the most frivolous pretexts and the sufferers were denied all legal remedies against their oppressors and despoilers. Thus was the way gradually paved for the final revocation. Infractions of the edicts were made under the guise of ordinances which invaded the most sacred rights of the Protestants—even the privacy of the home was no longer respected.

In May, 1665, was passed the ordinance authorizing the priests, in company with an officer, to appear before the sick and induce them to abjure heresy and die in the faith of the church. In October of the same year a decree was issued that male children at the age of fourteen and females at the age of twelve were capable of embracing Catholicism.

The force of this decree may well be imagined when the susceptibility of youth is considered and the nature of the inducements that were held out for their abjuration. Protestant burials were made permissible only at daybreak, and funeral corteges exceeding ten persons were prohibited except in a few cities. They were not allowed to marry except at set times and nuptial assemblies were limited to twelve persons. Poor churches were prohibited from receiving aid. Ministers were prohibited from receiving titles, etc. In 1666 a new set of regulations comprising fifty-nine articles was issued, the provisions of which so invaded all the rights of humanity that they evoked a remonstrance from several Protestant Sovereigns in whose continued friendship Louis XIV. was interested. This had some effect, and in 1669 several of the most inhuman articles were revoked and others were modified.

The Regulations of 1666 was the occasion of the first emigration of the Huguenots, and in a short time thousands of the better class had sought refuge in foreign lands. In 1669 Marshal Turenne, one of the former military leaders of the Huguenots, abjured the Reformed faith and became a confidential agent of the King to bring the Protestants back into the Catholic fold, promising that the gross abuses of the church should be corrected. Many of the Protestant nobles yielded, but the clergy, whose piety and devotion to principles was of a higher type and uninfluenced by political motives, remained firm.

Louis XIV., whose immoralities had greatly scandalized his court, professed in 1676 to have reformed, and in order to signalize his devotion to the church undertook anew the complete extirpation of heresy in his Kingdom. This was the beginning of the end of the horrible tragedy under the guise of the Christian religion. A well regulated system of "Conversion" was established under Pellison, who had formerly been a Huguenot but was now a most bigoted Catholic. This system provided for bribing the consciences of the Protestants with money and other rewards; the procurers were also rewarded according to the rank and importance of the converts. Records were kept of the so-called "converts." As may be supposed, thousands of the weak and ignorant gave way to this new crusade. In this diabolical business great frauds were perpetrated against the government by the procurers, causing the most outrageous scandals.

After the peace of Nimegue in 1679 Louis reached the climax of his power. It was apparent that he was now fully bent on making short work of his intractable Protestant subjects. Accordingly all his courtiers and subordinates vied with each other in anticipating the designs of the King. Among these was Madame de Maintenon, with whom the King contracted a secret marriage. Her grandfather, Agrippa d'Aubigne, was one of the great Huguenot leaders in the days of their strength. The most shocking atrocities were committed.

The Dragonades.

Among the means of extirpation was the introduction of the *Dragonades*. This consisted of quartering the soldiery upon the Huguenots and they were compelled to support them. The Dragonades were considered the most dreadful infliction that could be imposed. The privacy of the home was broken up, all valuables were taken, defenseless women ravished and all manner of horrors perpetrated by the brutal soldiery. Any remonstrance on the part of the Huguenots was regarded as resistance against the authorities and was met by the most inhuman punishment, and even death. Such were the Dragonades!

The Protestant courts of Europe again protested against this inhumanity, but their protestation were met by the King's declaration that the Edict of Nantes was duly observed and that only lawlessness was punished. More and more dreadful became the regulations of suppression. All Huguenots were debarred from holding any public office; they were virtually stripped of all civil rights. Even Protestant midwives were prohibited.

The new regulations on marriage created scandalous situations for Protestants—in fact thousands awoke to the fact that they were not legally married. Children at the age of seven years were given the right of abjuration which resulted in wholesale transfers to Catholic charges and guardians, while their Protestant parents were compelled to support them. All converts to Catholicism were given exemption from taxes and military services for a certain time; three years' grace for the payment of debts was granted them. Beneficiary funds for schools and church purposes were seized, property was confiscated under color of law, no new Protestant converts were allowed to connect themselves with churches. The privileges of worship were so narrowed down that it was almost impossible to have public services at all, while the pastors were not allowed to make mention of any of these hardships imposed upon them.

Protestant Churches Destroyed.

One by one the great Protestant churches were demolished; in many cases the wretched Huguenots were compelled to perform the work of demolition themselves at the point of the bayonet.

The situation was now terrible; thousands sought relief by flight which the authorities sought to prevent, but in vain. All Protestant Europe was aroused in behalf of the sufferers. By official proclamation England, Holland, Switzerland and Denmark offered asylum to the refugees. Many of the nobles and literary men who had escaped to foreign lands exerted a powerful influence in their adopted countries in behalf of their oppressed countrymen. Great pressure was brought to bear on the King to modify his harsh measures but in vain. Petitions were ignored and eminent deputies were turned away. The heart of the grandson of Henry of Navarre, the Promulgator of the Edict of Nantes, was rendered callous by the corruption of his court and the influence of a fanatical priestcraft.

CHAPTER III.

Extending From the Revocation of the Edict of Nantes, 1685, to the Edict of Toleration, 1787.

"Hope looks beyond the bounds of time
When what we now deplore,
Shall rise in full immortal prime
And bloom to fade no more."

THE time for the revocation of the great charter of religious liberty in France was now ripe and Louis XIV. was ready to perpetrate an act that should forever blight his memory and place an ineffaceable blot on the history of France. His cruel blow, aimed at a class of his own subjects for no other reasons than that they differed from him in their views and practice of Christianity, simply rebounded upon himself. Illustrious France failed to interpret the signs of the times and turned away from the light of her own bright star of destiny! The pall of night settled down upon her. Her expatriated sons enriched the literature, built up the commerce and brought prosperity to other lands, and by the true nobility of the Huguenot character and its influence upon the nations in which they found asylum they illustrated to coming generations what France *might* have been had she listened to the voice of reason instead of a corrupted and bigoted priestcraft.

The Revocation.

On October 18, 1685, the King signed the Revocation of the Edict of Nantes for the reason, as he says in the preamble, that his subjects of the " Pretended Protestant Religion" had in the main returned to the Catholic fold and hence there was no occasion for its statutory existence. The world stood aghast at the stupendous falsehood. By the terms of the Revocation it became unlawful to exercise in the Protestant religion. Pastors were ordered to leave the country in fifteen days. Parents could no longer instruct their children in the Reformed faith, but were compelled, under heavy penalty, to have them baptized and instructed by the priests. They were forbidden to emigrate, and those who had done so must return in four months or suffer the confiscation of their property. A cry of agony went up from every Huguenot home of France and resounded throughout the world. The Revocation had the immediate effect of alienating the Protestant powers from France, while at home it sowed the seeds of infidelity and anarchy that culminated in the terrible French Revolution a century later.

Flight of the Huguenots.

Notwithstanding the most strenuous efforts to prevent it there was a stampede of the Protestants to leave the Kingdom. The most unheard of and astonishing methods of disguise in order to escape were resorted to. The knowledge of secret pathways to the borders and the best methods of eluding the vigilance of the guards was communicated from one to another in a marvelous manner. Proclamations were issued by nearly all Protestant Sovereigns welcoming the fleeing Huguenots to their realms. They comprised all classes of people. Conservative estimates places the number of refugees at half a million while other writers make the number a million. The latter estimate is also supposed to cover previous emigrations; among this number is included about fifteen thousand of the nobility. From twelve to thirteen hundred refugees were seen to pass Geneva in Switzerland in a week. Many thousands lost their lives by exposure or violence in their attempts to escape. The details of their sufferings are so sickening that we will spare the reader a recital of the same.

Thousands of the refugees entered the military service of other lands. England alone organized eleven regiments of Huguenot soldiers and one brigade under the Count de Shamburg, fought under the Prince of Orange at the battle of the Boyne in Ireland in 1690. French Protestant congregations were formed in very many places. London alone had twenty-two societies (1). Some colonies drifted to the uttermost parts of the earth. The Huguenot colony at Cape Town, South Africa, is a notable example. The Revocation, however, did not crush Protestantism in France. Louis XIV. was self-deceived.

The horrible atrocities committed against the best citizens of the realm led to a revulsion of feeling among the most intelligent classes. Nearly a million of French remained at heart Protestants. Thousands had gone through a mere formulary of abjuration, which was "official" and which the "convert" did not consider binding upon his conscience. The fury of persecution having somewhat spent itself many pastors returned to the remnants of their flocks in a few years and services were secretly held in many places.

The King was not insensible of the shadow that fell upon his name by the Revocation and became somewhat indifferent to the war of extirpation. Sometimes, however, when importuned by the highest ecclesiastical councils, his old-time hatred against the Protestants asserted itself in new orders and regulations which resulted in the suppression of reviving churches, the execution of prominent leaders, and the condemnation for life to the galleys of many others. This vacillating policy continued until his death in 1715.

Among the elements that ameliorated the situation of the Protestants was the disastrous effect of the Revocation on the material prosperity of the country. The Bishops of Grenoble and St. Pons, in episcopal letters, discouraged *forced conversions* as against the principles of the holy religion. The leading statesmen in memorials regretted the loss of so many skilled artisans. The minister of marine complained that the persecutions had robbed the navy of thousands of its best sailors. The poet Racine in 1689 dared to express sentiments against religious intolerance, and Fenelon, one of the greatest and noblest of Catholic ministers, sent a strong plea to the King for toleration.

The Church of the Desert.

The severities of the persecutions relaxing somewhat in the course of years, the Huguenots, bleeding and despoiled, began again to assemble themselves. True, the old church organization was destroyed, their pastors were driven away and all religious exercises declared unlawful, still the true spirit of vital Christianity survived

---

(1). Many of the Huguenot refugees to England, and their descendants, have been an honor to the land of their adoption. Among the many we may mention *Droz*, who founded the first public library and literary newspaper in Dublin, Ireland. General *Thelluson*, who was ennobled for distinguished services in the Peninsular War, and Generals *Ligonier*, *Prevost*, *de Beaguiere* and *Boquet*, all of

all calamities. The people began to gather in secret places and organized themselves into small societies. Pastors they had none, but pious laymen conducted the services and sought to give religious instruction and impart encouragement and consolation. Such was the beginning of the "Church of the Desert," which represents a distinct phase of French Protestantism. The chief instrument in this revival was *Antoine Court*, born of humble parentage in 1696. He at the age of seventeen began to take the lead of assemblies in the "Desert." The movement grew stronger from day to day, and the small societies, meeting in secret, became quite numerous. On August 21, 1715, was convened the first Synod after the Revocation at Cevennes, after which they were held for years in secret places, the participants using every precaution to prevent detection by the authorities.

Gradually Protestantism arose from the ashes of her seeming ruin like the fabled Phœnix of old and attracted public attention. On May 14, 1724, was issued a new code of oppression exceedingly severe, but only to elicit declarations of disapproval from many distinguished officials of both Church and State. The public conscience was fully aroused and many leading men felt that the country had been sufficiently disgraced in the eyes of the world, and thus the decrees of 1724, after several displays of their brutality, succumbed to popular disfavor. There were, nevertheless, many local outbursts of persecution, and in some localities the atrocities continued until the publication of the Edict of Toleration in 1787. The most serious of these persecutions was in the Province of Languedoc, beginning in 1754 under the instigation of Cardinal Richelieu, and was of great severity.

Among the pastors of the revived church who suffered martyrdom were the following : At Montpelier *Pierre Durand*, a coworker with Antoine Court in 1732 ; *Disubas*, 1746 ; *Jacques Roger*, 1745 ; *Francois Benezet*, 1752 ; *Etienne Lafarge*, 1754 ; also *Louis Ranc* at Die in 1745. These were all prominent and their loss was a terrible blow to the struggling Huguenots. No Protestant leader after the Revocation wielded a greater influence than *Paul Ribaut*. He was born near Montpelier in 1718, and was one of the few who, having endured the hardships and perils as a pastor "in the Desert,"

---

whom shed lustre on the British arms. *Le Fever*, speaker of the House of Commons, who was elevated to the peerage as Lord Eversly, *Roumilly*, the great barrister, was likewise honored. *Saurin*, the great jurist and Attorney General of Ireland, *Majendie*, Bishop of Chester, *Labouchere*, the publicist and member of the British Cabinet, and who was also ennobled, *Layard*, the scholar, diplomat and excavator of ancient Nineveh, and *Punshon*, the eloquent divine, are all distinguished names in English history.

survived to see his countrymen in the enjoyment of religious freedom. He was educated at the Huguenot Seminary at Lausanne under the tutelage of Antoine Court, and in 1743 began his ministry at Nismes, and continued to labor incessantly in that capacity as a minister, writer and organizer for the Protestants until his death by violence in the civil disturbances of 1795. Although under sentence of death he managed to perform his arduous duties, living for many years in caves and huts in desolate places known only to his faithful people. It should be here remarked that nearly all the ministers of the "Desert" bore assumed names for prudential reasons. During his long career Ribaut bore a number of assumed names which disguised his identity in the eyes of the law. He was on intimate terms with the Protestant leaders in foreign lands, and even with high officials of his own country who favored toleration.

The Synod Re-established.

In August, 1744, was convened the first National Synod of the re-established church. It met in an obscure place in Lower Languedoc so as not to attract attention. Michel Viala was its president. By scrupulously avoiding all publicity, and especially open conflicts with the civil authorities, they safely rounded the rocks on which so many had grounded before them. From 1755 it was comparatively easy to ransom the Protestant galley slaves ; foreign dignitaries secured the release of many persons of rank, while foreign money assisted in the release of the poorer classes.

In 1762 *Francis Rochette*, a Huguenot pastor, suffered martyrdom in Toulouse, having been apprehended as a robber while on a journey. In the courts he easily cleared himself of the charge but was immediately remanded by his enemies for heresy. Public sentiment was much divided. The old laws were still on the statute books, according to which he would fall under the severest penalty known to the courts. It seems that the officials purposely offered him opportunities of escape but for some unaccountable reason he failed to improve them and accordingly suffered. Amid the excitement three brothers named *Grenier*, of noble rank, hastened to the scene, armed to the teeth, in the expectation that a massacre would occur. To go armed was a fatal mistake. The laws were against them and they were accordingly condemned and executed February 19, 1762. On March 9 following *Jean Calas*, a father of 69 years of age, was broken on a wheel in a most horrible manner. Thus Toulouse, where blazed one of the first martyr fires in 1532, also witnessed the *last* legal execution in France for the sake of religion.

These executions aroused the country against the power of the priests and the unjust severity of the laws. Three years later the Parliament, by a unanimous vote, annulled the decrees of the court against Calas. These last executions greatly inured to the advantage of the Protestants by arousing a general sympathy. Although the barbarous laws against the Huguenots were still in force yet so strong had the spirit of toleration grown that they were almost a dead letter.

In 1763 we see the Protestants supporting a representative in close relation to the Government. This responsible trust was reposed in Court de Gebelin, a son of Antoine Court, who as a civilian became a pillar in the Protestant cause.

The Edict of Toleration.

We cannot follow the rapidly increasing agencies that led to the final victory of religious freedom in France. The spirit of liberty was, so to speak, "*in the air*" as a reaction against the spirit of intolerance. Many able Catholic statesmen by pen and voice advocated toleration and the undoing of the terrible wrongs committed. The Catholic clergy were equally active in their efforts to prevent this but in vain.

Perhaps the strongest individual agent in effecting the Act of Toleration was the Marquis de Lafayette (our own Lafayette of the American Revolution). In the National Assembly of Notables in 1787 he proposed a scheme for toleration and reform in the civic laws with special reference to religious delinquents. The propositions were favorably considered by the King, and in November, 1787, Louis XVI, signed and promulgated the *Edict of Toleration*. In 1789 the Constituent Assembly broke down the few remaining barriers by publishing a Declaration of Rights. Art. XI. declared all citizens equal before the law, which made Protestants eligible to all offices. Art. XVIII. guaranteed liberty of conscience in religion. The complete emancipation of the Huguenots may be inferred by the fact that in March, 1790, Rabaut, Saint Etienne, the son of the fugitive pastor of the Desert, was appointed President of the Constituent Assembly, one of the highest offices in the realm. It is sad to chronicle that this great man died on the scaffold in 1793 during the dreadful political upheavels of the French nation at that period. His aged father, of whom prominent mention has been made, died in 1796. Another son, Rabaut Dupuy, also became an eminent statesman and presided over the Constituent Assembly in 1802, and by his integrity and broad-minded statesmanship shed lustre upon his Huguenot antecedents.

Here we close our brief recital of the struggles of the Huguenots of France for religious freedom ; a struggle which lasted longer and raged with greater severity than any other in Europe, and was fraught with greater consequences to human progress and civilization than perhaps any other movement of modern times.

Distinguished Clergymen and Literary Institutions of the Huguenots.

As has already been shown, the first great leading spirit of the French Reformation was *John Calvin*, who directed the work from Geneva, Switzerland. It is questionable whether any other modern writer has left a more profound impression on theology than Calvin (B. 1509, D. 1564). Next to Calvin *Theodore de Beze* wielded the greatest influence. For many years he personally shared the struggles of his coreligionists in his native land. Born of noble parentage at Vezelai, 1519, died 1605. Then also *William Farrell*, a most able coadjutor of Calvin. In later times we note the following : *Andre Rivet* (1572–1651), a noted preacher, teacher and author who ended his days in Holland ; *Edeme Aubertin* (1595–1652), author of a great work on the Eucharist, who suffered martyrdom ; *Benjamine Besnage* (1580–1652), a great preacher and author and grandfather of the famous Jacques Besnage ; *David Blondel* (1595–1655), the great historian ; *Samuel Bochart* (1599–1667), pastor at Cæn, and a profound historian whose works are of enduring merit ; *Michael Le Faucheur* (D. 1657), whose published sermons are still of literary value ; *Jean Mestrezat* (1591–1657), pastor of Charenton Temple, Paris, an able preacher, writer and disputant ; *Charles Drelincourt* (1595–1689), also a pastor of Charenton Temple, whose great work, "*Consolations Contre la Mort*," passed through fifty editions and was translated into almost every European language ; *Jean Dille* (1595–1670), colleague of Drelincourt and noted author ; *Pierre Dubose* (1623–1692), pastor at Cæn, considered one of the greatest preachers of his times, who died in exile ; *David Ancillon* (1617–1692), a great preacher and poet at Metz who fled to Berlin at the Revocation ; *Jean Claude* (B. 1619,   ), one of the last famous pastors of Charenton Temple ; *Matthieu de Larogue* (1619–1684) ; *Pierre Jurieu* (1637–1713), a most eminent author and controversialist, whose work made a deep impression throughout Europe ; *Pierre Alix* (1641–1717), the last pastor of Charenton Temple, who fled to London at the Revocation where he won great distinction, being honored with degrees from Oxford and Cambridge Universities.

Jean La Placette (1639–1718), "the Nicole of the Huguenots," fled to Copenhagen at the Revocation where he was pastor of the refugees for thirty years. *David Martin* (1639–1731), the famous commentator and lexicographer; *Jacques Besnage* (1653–1723), who became the head of the French church at The Hague after the Revocation. His services to Protestantism in Europe were very great. *Jacques Abbadie* (1654–1724), one of the greatest writers and apologists of the Huguenots, died an exile in Ireland. He was the author of several very valuable works. *Elias Benoit* (1640–1728), was not only a great preacher but also an able historian. His "History of the Revocation of the Edict of Nantes" is the greatest authority on that subject. *Jacques Saurin* (1577–1730), ranks as the greatest pulpit orator of the Huguenots. He was for many years pastor of a French church in London. His published sermons are still considered masterpieces. *Jacques Lenfant* (1661–1728), and *Isaac Beausobre* (1659–1738), who linked their labors and fortunes in Berlin, were both pastors of refugee churches there. Their historical and biblical works were justly celebrated.

Gladly would we give at least a reference to the noble and illustrious Huguenots in other walks of life—the famous artisans who founded great industries in foreign cities, the men noted in literature, art and science; the soldiers and sailors who brought glory and renown to the land of their adoption—but the limits of this work forbid further notices.

By the terms of the Edict of Toleration the Huguenots were permitted to maintain a limited number of institutions of learning, several of which attained a considerable celebrity.

The Academy of MONTAUBAN, founded in 1599, had in the height of its glory the celebrated *Daniel Chamier*, who assisted in drawing up the Edict of Nantes. In 1600 he conducted a famous discussion with the confessor of Henry IV. He was killed on the ramparts of Montauban while ministering to the troops in the siege of 1621. *Michael Berauet* and *Antoine Grissoles*, of the same institution, added lustre to the cause. This academy was ruined in 1661 by the intrigues of the Jesuits, but was restored a century and a-half later (1808–10) by the creation of a faculty of Protestant theology by Napoleon.

SAMUR was founded by the celebrated Mornay. Some of its great teachers were *Jean Cameron* (1579–1625), and his famous disciples *Moise Amyrault* (1596–1664), who enriched Protestant literature by producing nearly forty works. His colleague, *Louis Cappel* (1585–1658), was one of the foremost Hebraists of the age. *Josue de la Place* (1596-1655), and *Etienne Gaussen* (died 1675), were likewise noted professors in this academy.

In the Academy at SEDAN was *Pierre Damoulin* (1568–1678), who in more than seventy years of public life, amid many perils and difficulties, gave to the world seventy-three theological and devotional works. *Louis Leblanc de Beaulieu* (1615-1675), was also a teacher and writer of note connected with this school.

The college at LA ROCHELLE, founded in 1565 and endowed by *Jeanne d' Albret* and other members of the House of Navarre, was also justly celebrated, and its faculty were noted for their wide range of talent and excellent work. In addition to its fine college LA ROCHELLE was also the seat of many great printing and publishing establishments where enormous quantities of Protestant literature were issued and scattered broadcast over Europe.

The Academy of NISMES had the celebrated *Samuel Petit* (1594-1643). All the Protestant institutions of learning having been destroyed at the Revocation it became necessary to establish a training school for the pastors of the "Desert." This was done by *Antoine Court*, the leader of the Church of the Desert. Owing to the dangers such an institution would be subject to in France it was established at Lausaune in Switzerland. 1731 *Antoine Court* took personal charge of the institution. Here were educated and trained nearly all the ministers of the Re-established Church, and it continued in this grand work until, as we have noticed, the authorization by the Emperor Napoleon of a Protestant Faculty of Theology.

CHAPTER IV.
Huguenot Settlements in America.

COLIGNY'S COLONIAL SCHEME ; SETTLEMENT AT RIO DE JANEIRO ; FAILURE ; PORT ROYAL ; LA CAROLINA ; DISASTER FOLLOWS ; CHARLESTON ; ON THE SANTEE AND TRENT ; VIRGINIA ; NEW NETHERLANDS ; NEW ENGLAND ; RHODE ISLAND ; NEW FRANCE ; THE ANTILLES.

> "*Amidst the storm they sang,*
> *And the stars heard, and the sea—*
> *And the sounding aisles of the dim wood rang*
> *To the anthems of the free—*
> *The ocean eagle soared*
> *From his nest by the white waves' foam,*
> *And the rocking pines of the forest roared—*
> *This was their welcome home.*"

THERE is, perhaps, no people in Europe less disposed to emigrate than the French. They are naturally much attached to their country. No great masses of French are found in the United States as is the case with other European nationalities, and the greater number of those who are here have descended from

Colonial ancestors. This fact illustrates the benefit of religious toleration to France at the present day. Her people, both Protestant and Catholic alike, now delight to stay in their own sunny clime, while intolerance drove away, as we have seen, over a million of her best people to swell the population and build up the industries of foreign and hostile countries.

Even the remotest quarters of the earth were enriched by her expatriated children who fled thither in order to enjoy religious liberty. As is well known the Huguenots, in connection with the Dutch, founded the settlement at the Cape of Good Hope and were an important factor in building up the States and commerce of South Africa.

Duke de Coligny's Scheme.

The great leader of the Huguenots, the Duke de Coligny, conceived the idea of establishing colonies of his persecuted countrymen in America. In 1555 a settlement was made through his instrumentality in Brazil, near the present city of Rio de Janeiro. In the following year Pierre Richer and Guillaume Chartier were sent to minister to the colony and were the first Protestant preachers to cross the Atlantic ocean. Unfortunately in the course of a few years Villegagnon, the Governor of the Colony, renounced Protestantism, and by connivance with the home government proceeded to destroy the Protestant character of the colony by deporting the ministers and chief men. In 1558 he caused the death by drowning of Pierre Bourdon, Jean du Bordel and Mathieu Verneuil, who were the first martyrs to the Protestant cause in the New World.

Thus through the perfidy of its leader the first Huguenot colony failed.

Port Royal.

Notwithstanding this failure the Duke de Coligny was not discouraged but still resolved to carry out his cherished plans. In 1562 he sent out the second expedition under the supervision of Jean Ribaut, an experienced officer of the army and a staunch Protestant. On May 1 they entered the mouth of the St. John's river and took possession in the name of France. Continuing their course northward they settled Port Royal, in South Carolina. The first civil war between the Protestants and Catholics breaking out, Ribaut hastened home to join the forces of the Prince of Conde, and the small colony at Port Royal soon went to pieces. When the peace of Amboise closed the war Coligny sent another expedition in 1564 which settled on a bluff on the St. John's river, and called the place La Carolina. The Governor, Laudonniere, however managed the colony very indifferently and it did not prosper. In 1565 Jean Ribaut appeared at the mouth of the river with seven vessels and nearly a thousand men, many of whom were of the nobility. The Spaniards, who claimed the country by right of discovery, also sent a fleet which arrived a few days later. Ribaut put to sea to engage the Spaniards but his vessels were wrecked off the coast. The Spaniards then sent an expedition to La Carolina and took it by surprise, putting to the sword nearly all the inhabitants.

Meanwhile Ribaut gathered his shipwrecked party on the coast and marched to the relief of La Carolina only to find it in the possession of the Spaniards upon his arrival. Ribaut agreed to terms of surrender under promise of quarter, but no sooner had he done so when the Spanish fell upon them and nearly all were massacred. Thus the hopes of Coligny were again doomed to disappointment.

Charleston, S. C.

Notwithstanding the disasters to the settlements under Ribaut and others, the project of establishing Huguenot colonies in Carolina was not abandoned. When the Carolinas were erected into an English Province over a hundred years later, Huguenot pioneers already appear among the colonists. Their number was so large in 1681 that when the city of Charleston was laid out at that time they established the first church (1) and are generally credited with being the founders of the city. A large number of refugees arrived after the revocation of the Edict of Nantes (1685). One of the early pastors of the Huguenot Church in Carolina was Rev. Elie Prioleau (2) who had been a minister at Pons, in Saintonge, France. His church being destroyed and congregation scattered at the revocation he fled to England, and later came to Charleston where he died on his estate in 1690.

A considerable number of Rev. Prioleau's former parishioners eventually made their way to America and found repose under the fostering care of a Protestant government.

Reader, let us here pause a moment and reflect. What a tragic story, rivalling the dreams of fiction, clusters around the Huguenot congregation of Charleston, S. C.! Heartless dragonades, fire, sword, confiscation, ruin, bloodshed, heartrending separations, and the final gathering of a remnant of the flock in the wilds of the New World, many thousand miles distant! This is but one of many similar scenes.

---

(1). See "Ravenal Record," page 264.
(2). Ibid., page 101.

The old family ties, welded together in the fire of persecution over 200 years ago, still hold firmly, hence we find the original congregation still in existence, and is, in fact, the only distinctively Huguenot church in America to-day.

Santee.

After the influx caused by the Revocation three additional congregations were formed, "one on the eastern bank of the Cooper River known as Orange Quarter; one on the western bank known as St. John's, Berkely, and one at Jamestown on the Santee" (1). The latter soon became a large and important settlement.

It is a notable circumstance that many of the refugees to Carolina were of distinguished antecedents, and not a few of the nobility. Among the latter was Pierre de St. Julien and his brother Louis, their brother-in-law, Rene Ravenal, and Samuel Bordieu, all from the town of Vitre in Bretagney. They came to America in 1686, several leaving considerable estates behind them which were confiscated by the King (2). Their descendants in America have amply *proven the excellency* of their ancestral character and have given many names to the aristocracy of personal worth.

Virginia.

A very large number of Huguenots found asylum in Virginia, and their descendants have borne a conspicuous part in the development of that great State. The first arrivals were by way of England under the patronage of the King in 1690. The second expedition arrived in 1699 under the leadership of Philip de Richebourg, a French nobleman of considerable note. This expedition, numbering about 600 members, was the largest colony of refugees ever landed in America. Most of them were located on the south side of the James River, near the present site of Richmond.

The settlement was called "Manikintown," which, in the course of a few decades, lost its original character. A great number of the emigrants removed farther south, many settling on the river Trent, a branch of the Neuse, in North Carolina, where a colony was established in 1707.

New France.

For many years the enterprising merchants of La Rochelle had sent fishing vessels to the regions contiguous to the mouth of the St. Lawrence River. French commerce being mostly in the hands

---

(1). "Ravenal Records," page 89.
(2). Baird, Vol. II, page 85.

of the Protestants, their efforts to establish a Huguenot colony in this part of the New World was quite natural.

In 1602 de Monts, a French Protestant nobleman, secured from Henry IV. a grant of all the territory between the fortieth and forty-sixth degrees of north latitude for the purpose of founding a French colony. This territory was called New France and its charter secured religious liberty for the colonists. A settlement was made at Port Royal, in Nova Scotia, in 1604. In 1608, in company with the noted navigator, Champlain, de Monts founded Quebec. These and other settlements were, however, soon doomed to pass from Protestant to Jesuit control. In 1610 Henry IV., the friend and patron of the colony, fell at the hands of an assassin, and in a short time thereafter de Monts was compelled to relinquish his office as Viceroy of New France. From force of circumstances, not necessary to relate here, he transferred his rights to the territory to Madame de Guercheville, a devoted Catholic. Under the new regime the Protestants were more and more restricted until 1633, when they were entirely suppressed. The Jesuits, with fanatical zeal, were ever busy making New France a Catholic country. In suppressing the Huguenots as colonists France committed an irreparable blunder. By introducing her policy of repression in her American colonies she checked the emigration to them, while a great number of the best colonists removed to the neighboring New England settlements.

The settlements of Acadia (Nova Scotia) had some immunity from the harsher persecution prevalent on the St. Lawrence. Claude de la Tour, of the noble house of Bouillon, and his son Charles, who were early leaders of the Port Royal colony, were the chief factors in this amelioration, which continued until the death of Charles in 1666.

New Netherlands (New York).

The city of Leyden, in Holland, early became the refuge of great numbers of Huguenots who introduced various industries which made the city highly prosperous. The greater number of these refugees were Walloons, who established a strong congregation in 1584. Most intimate relations existed between these Walloons and the English Separists or Puritans, who were then living there in voluntary exile.

Walloons and Puritans alike directed their eyes towards America as the best field in which to realize their hopes of founding colonies in which to enjoy their religious faith unmolested, and hence Leyden became a center from which emanated several movements most potent in shaping the destinies of the New World.

The Puritans accordingly obtained a colonial patent from the Virginia Company, and on August 5, 1620, left Delft Harbor, the seaport of Leyden, for America. Several Huguenots were in their number. The landing of these "Pilgrims" at Plymouth Rock and the momentous influence of the colony in the history of this country, is familiar to the reader. Meanwhile the Walloons followed the example of their Puritan brethren. In July, 1621, the English ambassador to Holland was petitioned by them for a place of settlement by his government, their desire being to go to Virginia. The promoter of this movement was Jesse de Forrest, a prominent Walloon of Leyden. This petition and list of signers is still preserved among the British archives. The negotiations with the English did not proceed very satisfactorily. Meanwhile the Dutch West India Trading Company was chartered by the Government of Holland. When the designs of the Huguenots were brought to the notice of the company they were accorded most excellent terms of settlement. Early in March, 1623, the emigrants, comprising about thirty families, embarked in the little ship "New Netherlands," which, after a propitious voyage, arrived at the mouth of the Hudson (1).

A settlement was made on Manhattan Island, now New York city. A number of families proceeded up the river and formed a settlement called *Orange*, while four couple, who had been married at sea, proceeded to an island in the Delaware River. The names of the passengers on the New Netherlands have unfortunately been lost, but a comparison with the original list presented to the British ambassador, already referred to, shows that many of them appear as among the first citizens of New Netherlands, hence it is probable that most of them eventually came to America. Although the New Netherlands was under the control of the Dutch, a very large portion of the colonists were Huguenots whose exact numbers can never be known.

In 1656 a vessel laden with Waldensian refugees (Vaudois), sailed for New Netherlands, which was stranded at the entrance of New York harbor. Many of these unfortunates located on Staten Island, which eventually became the home of many fellow-Huguenots.

New Paltz, N. Y.

In 1660 Louis du Bois, who had sojourned a number of years at Manheim in the Palatinate, came to New Netherlands, and with a number of others established the colony of New Paltz, near the

---

(1). Documentary Hist. of N. Y., Vol. III p. 35.

present site at New Kingston, in Ulster County (1). This region was called "Esopus," and was a favorite place of settlement for the Huguenots, and from whence many came to Pennsylvania in later years.

New Rochelle, a short distance up the Hudson, was likewise a Huguenot colony and named in honor of the French city of that name, and from which many of the colonists had come.

In New York the Huguenots worshipped in connection with the Dutch, but so numerous did they become that in 1652 the Consistory of the Reformed Dutch Church found it necessary to make special provision for them. About the time of the English occupation (1664) the French and Waldensians were constituted a separate charge under the supervision of the Dutch Church. In 1683 Rev. Pierre Daille took charge of the Huguenot congregations of New York, New Paltz, etc., and remained their pastor until 1696, when he took charge of the congregations in Boston, being succeeded by Rev. De Bon Repos.

New England.

Among the earliest arrivals of Huguenots in New England were a number of families who settled in Salem perhaps as early as 1660. They were for the most part from the Channel Islands, whither they had fled from France. In 1662 Dr. John Touton, of La Rochelle, France, directed a petition to the Governor of Massachusetts for permission for himself and a large number of others who were expelled because of their religion, to settle in that Province (2). This petition was favorably received and we accordingly find that a considerable influx of refugees took place. In 1680 agents from La Rochelle arrived in Boston to gain permission and make arrangements for the settlement of their persecuted people there, and during the next few years many families arrived in an utterly destitute condition; collections were taken up in the churches for their benefit in 1682.

When finally the Revocation of the Edict of Nantes (1685) extinguished the last vestige of their civil and religious rights, a very large number, aggregating hundreds, came to Boston prior to 1690. From this point many scattered to various colonies.

---

(1). The company were twelve in number, all of whom were Huguenot exiles. The fac simile of their signatures, as also that of the Indian Sachems, may be seen in Vol. III p. 506 Doc. Hist. N. York. The names of the patentees were Louis du Bois and sons Abraham and Isaac, Abraham Haesbroucq, Christian Deyoe and son.in-law, Simon Lefever, Peter Deyoe, Andreas Lefever, Anthony Cespel, Jean Brocq, Hugo Frere and Louis Bevier. Treaty signed May 26, 1677.

(2). Mass. Archives, Vol. X page 208.

The Huguenots organized a congregation in Boston as early as 1685, permission being given them to worship in the public school buildings. In 1705 a site for a church was procured but the edifice was not erected until 1715. The ministers of the congregation were Rev. Laurent du Bois, who was succeeded in 1686 by Rev. David de Bonrepos, a refugee minister from St. Christopher in the Antilles. In 1696 de Bonrepos was succeeded by Rev. Pierre Daille, who, since his arrival in America, had ministered to the congregations in New York. In 1715 this excellent and distinguished exile died in the sixty-seventh year of his age. Prior to his flight he had been a professor in the famous Huguenot Academy of Saumur. Daille was succeeded by a talented young graduate of the Academy of Geneva, Andre Le Mercier, a native of Cæn in Normandy. Le Mercier died in Dorchester, Massachusetts, in 1765. The society maintained its separate existence until about 1748, when nearly all the original refugees were dead, while the younger generation became affiliated in language and religion with the populace.

In 1687 a company of Huguenots, led by Rev. Daniel Bondet, made a settlement in the "Nipmuck" country about seventy-five miles west of Boston. There were about fifteen families in the party, which number was much increased in the course of a year. They founded the town of New Oxford, built a fort, mill, etc., with every promise of a permanent establishment. Being on the frontier of the Province it was exposed to the ravages of the Indians, and after suffering considerably from their savagery it was deemed best to abandon the settlement, which was done in 1696 and the inhabitants scattered to other colonies. The ruins of their fort may still be seen. In 1884 a magnificent monument was erected as a memorial to the colony on its ancient site. In 1686 an extensive settlement was made by the Huguenots near the western shore of Narragansett Bay. The locality was in (now) East Greenwich. They were accompanied by an able minister, Ezechiel Carre, and a physician, Pierre Ayrault.

The colonists were very unfortunate in their selection of this locality for the reason that they could obtain no satisfactory title to their land, and also that they were surrounded by an element very unfriendly to them. In 1691 they concluded to abandon the colony, a large number of the settlers going to New York.

The Antilles.

The French Islands in the Caribbean Sea, and known as the Antilles, became at an early day a landing place for the Huguenots. In St. Christopher there was a very considerable number of them, and their church there was a large and influential one. For many years they had comparative immunity from persecution. All this was changed, however, in a short space of time. During the Revocation period a large number of Protestants were transported thither from the home land. Upon arrival they were sold to the planters and subjected to the most rigorous servitude by their Catholic masters.

In a short time the condition of the Protestants in the French Antilles was as miserable as that of their brethren in the home land, and soon a general flight to the English colonies of North America was begun. Hundreds effected their escape and made their way, through almost incredible hardships and sufferings, to Charleston, Philadelphia, New York, Boston and other Huguenot centers, and many names have been enrolled on our National history whose ancestral records come to us from France by way of the Antilles.

CHAPTER V.
The Emigration to Pennsylvania.

THE PROVINCE AS A PLACE OF REFUGE—PENN'S OBJECT REALIZED—QUAKERS—MENNONITES—GERMAN-BAPTIST BRETHREN—PALATINES — COVENANTERS — SCHWENKFELDERS — MORAVIANS—FRENCH REVOLUTIONISTS—JOSEPH PRIESTLY, ETC.—CHARACTER OF THE HUGUENOT EMIGRATION—THEIR EMINENT PUBLIC SERVICES.

"From Delaware's and Schuylkill's gleam,
Away where Susquehanna twines,
And out o'er Allegheny's stream
In places distant fell their lines.

By river and by fountain,
Where'er they touched this strand,
In wood and vale and mountain
They found a fatherland."

[ARMS OF PENNSYLVANIA].

PENNSYLVANIA stands unique in the history of the Colonies of the New World as a place of refuge for the persecuted and oppressed of the Old. Its establishment had, in fact, its inception in the earnest desire of its founder to provide an asylum, not only for the people of his own faith, but all other Protestants as well.

The "Holy Experiment" of William Penn constitutes an epoch in the civil and religious advancement of the human race which will be sure of more thorough study by future historians as its importance and far-reaching significance is more fully realized. The literature of this great movement is somewhat scanty and its elements and character obscure, and must be worked out, in a measure, from the visible results. It is a fact too generally overlooked that the founding of Philadelphia by the Quakers in 1682 and Germantown by the Mennonites under Francis Daniel Pastorius in 1683, was contemporaneous so far as the original plans of emigration was concerned.

In June, 1694, arrived the famous band of Pietists (Rosecrucians) under the leadership of Baron Johannis Kelpius, and formed their community on the Wissahickon, near Philadelphia, so graphically described by Julius F. Sachse in his "German Pietists of Pennsylvania."

Scarcely was the success of these initial settlements assured when began the flocking in of thousands and tens of thousands of Palatines from the blood-stained fields and smouldering ruins of the Valley of the Rhine. The same period witnessed the incoming of thousands of Covenanters (Scotch-Irish) who made New Castle their chief landing place, and from whence they pushed northward and founded the settlements of Octorora, Donegal, Paxtang, Marsh Creek, the Cumberland Valley, etc. In 1719 about twenty families of the German Baptists (Dunkards) arrived at Germantown, followed ten years later by the entire parent organization under the leadership of their founder, Alexander Mack, from Schwartzenau, Germany, to Pennsylvania, as the result of great persecution. In 1734 there arrived in Philadelphia from Silesia, after a wearisome journey on foot through Holland (where they embarked), the scattered remnants of the Schwenkfelders to start anew the work of their beneficent faith among the hills of eastern Pennsylvania (1). In 1741 the advance guard of the Moravians arrived as the result of disquietude in their new settlement in North Carolina, and founded at Bethlehem the largest colony of these excellent people in America. During the dark days of the French Revolution, in 1793, a large number of political exiles, mostly of noble rank, came to Pennsylvania and founded the town of Asylum, on the North Branch of the Susquehanna River. Among its promoters was the Viscount, Louis de Noialles, the brother-in-law of Lafayette. Among the distinguished visitors to this place in 1795 was

---

(1.) Adherents of the Reformer Casper Von Schwenkfeld, of Silesia (1490–1561).

Prince Louis Phillipe, himself an exile then, but who later ascended the throne of France, and that greatest of French diplomats, Talleyrand, Prince of Benevento, and also the Count de la Rochefoucauld. Many of the exiles returned to France when quiet was restored, others remained and gave to us a worthy posterity, among whom may be mentioned the late Hon. John Laport, one of the foremost men of the State. In 1774 the last refugee party arrived from England with the distinguished Dr. Joseph Priestly (1) at their head.

About the close of the Provincial period a small but exceptionally brilliant coterie of French people graced the city of Philadelphia. Many of them were of the highest nobility who had fled hither from the horrors of the French Revolution. Inasmuch as they were political refugees a further notice of them would not be germane to this work. Another class, however, must not be passed by. Among the French allies who came to assist in the achievement of our Independence were many who remained in America to enjoy its freedom. Among the prominent men of this class were *Dr. Felix Bruno*, a foster brother to Lafayette, an account of whom is elsewhere given in this work. *Major Peter S. Duponceau* (2) *Louis Crousillat* (3) *Simon Vallerchamp* (4) *Pierre Javin*

---

(1). Dr. Joseph Priestly was born in 1733 and was one of the greatest men of his times. By his discovery of oxygen in 1774 he laid the foundation of modern chemistry. In consequence of his religious and political views a mob wrecked his house and destroyed his laboratory and valuable library in Birmingham, England. Soon after this sad event he emigrated to Northumberland, in Pennsylvania, being accompanied by a number of his friends. He continued his scientific and theological labors here until his death in 1804.

(2). *Duponceau, Pierre S.*, was born on the Isle of Rhe, France, in 1760, his father being an officer then stationed at that place. He was given an excellent education, and when still a youth was fired with an ambition to come to America and assist the struggling Colonies. He took a position as an aide on the staff of Baron Steuben and served in that capacity from 1777 to 1779 when, becoming an American citizen, he accepted a position as a secretary in the Foreign Office of the Colonial Government. He was a great student and became celebrated as a lawyer, linguist and scientist, and was the President of the American Philosophical Society many years. He died in Philadelphia in 1844.

(3). *Crousillat, Louis Martial Jacques*, was born at Salon, France, 1757. Came to Philadelphia in 1780 and entered the Continental service. After the war he entered the mercantile business and amassed a fortune. He was noted for his benevolence, and died in Philadelphia in 1836.

(4). *Simon Vallerchamp* was born in Lorraine June 29, 1751. His father, who was wealthy, died when his only son Simon was but fourteen years of age. The youth, who was left to shift for himself, finally drifted to Paris. He joined the expedition of Lafayette in aid of the American colonies and served throughout the war as an officer. He was wounded seven times, which eventually caused his death. Upon his return to France he found that his only sister had been put into a convent against her will, and he having imbibed Protestant principles found it unsafe to remain, and so returned to America. In Philadelphia he married a daughter of General Thomas Bond. She died early, and he then married Hannah Dodson and removed to Huntingdon, in Luzerne county. While preparing to return to France to settle up the family estate one of his wounds, which had never healed, became suddenly worse, and he died in consequence July 12, 1825.

(1) and *Frederick de Sanno* (2).

Pennsylvania may also pride herself in the citizenship of such renowned Frenchmen as *Stephen Girard* (3) *Pierre du Simetere* (4) and *John James Audubon* (5) who not only left the fruits of their industry but also the example of a noble life as enduring legacies to posterity.

A considerable number of Huguenot names may be traced to the heroes of the Duke de Shomburg, who fought with William, Prince of Orange, at the battle of the Boyne (1690). Some of these soldiers (or their descendants) came to Pennsylvania with the Scotch-Irish. Of such immigrants came the families *Brevard, de Cesna, Douthett, Lamont, Lilou, Pickens* (6) *de Armaud* and *Pierie.*

In all those incoming bodies of immigrants, expatriated from their native land by the mailed hand of religious intolerance, were a considerable number of Huguenots, as will be seen in succeeding

---

(1). *Pierre Javin* was born of wealthy parentage in Paris in 1757, and was given a good education. He served with distinction with Lafayette in the American Revolution and was severely wounded by a sword thrust. Becoming a Protestant he concluded to remain in America. He married in Reading, Pa., and was one of the pioneer settlers of Crawford county, where he died about 1821, leaving an honored posterity.

(2). *Frederick de Sanno* located in Bucks county. His son, Frederick Jr., was a Lutheran minister and author of note. In 1805 he became pastor of the Lutheran Church in Carlisle, Pa. Later he removed to Philadelphia and died there. Major William de Sanno, another son of the immigrant, served with distinction in the war of 1812 and was severely wounded at the battle of Lundy's Lane. Through General Scott he was made commandant of the Carlisle Barracks in 1826, a position which he retained until his death in 1865.

(3). *Girard, Stephen*—1750–1831. Was born at Bordeaux, France, and established himself in Philadelphia as a merchant in 1777. He amassed a vast fortune as a shipping merchant and was identified with all the leading enterprises of his adopted city. At his death he bequeathed his fortune to various charities. His greatest monument is Girard College, which he established for the education of orphans with an endowment of several millions of dollars.

(4). *Du Simetere, Pierre Eugene*, was born of Huguenot parentage at Geneva, Switzerland. He was a man of rare talents and excelled in many arts. Among his accomplishments was that of a naturalist, botanist, mineralogist, antiquarian, annalist and artist. About 1750 he went to the West Indies where he occupied himself in various researches. He came to New York in 1764 and to Philadelphia in 1766, making the latter city his home. His paintings and drawings of eminent men of his times are justly celebrated.

(5). *Audubon, John James*, born in America 1780, was a son of Admiral Audubon, who served in the American Revolution. In 1798 he came to possess an estate near Philadelphia, purchased by his father, and where he lived many years. He died in 1851. As a naturalist he has probably never been excelled, and his works on American ornithology and zoology were regarded as stupendous productions.

(6). *John* and *Andrew Pickens* were early settlers at Paxtang, in now Dauphin county. Here was born September 19, 1739, Major General Andrew Pickens, of the Revolution War. He was a son of Andrew. About 1741 the brothers migrated to Augusta county, in Virginia, and in 1752 Andrew removed from thence to the Waxhaw settlement in South Carolina.

chapters. Their emigration to Pennsylvania was somewhat different from that of their coreligionists in other parts of America, as most of them came with the German speaking Swiss and Palatines with whom they, or their fathers, had sojourned after their flight from France. Many had already exchanged their French names for a German equivalent and also adopted the language of their German friends.

We have, however, reason to believe that by far the greater number of them still clung to the faith for which they and their fathers suffered, as a considerable number of the names given in this work occur in the Reformed Church records of the Provincial period.

Galley Slaves.

In this connection we record a circumstance which has doubtless a vital connection with the emigration of many Huguenots to America. In 1896 when Henry S. Dodderer, of Philadelphia, was making researches in the archives of Dortrecht, in Holland, he discovered a printed list of Huguenot galley slaves who had been released by order of Louis XIV. of France on condition that they leave the realm (1). It may be inferred from this that many of these unfortunates were deported to Holland.

Besides the name of the victim there was also given his official number and the term of years he had suffered. This list is not only a silent witness of the many years of suffering but also of the great numbers of the Huguenot galley slaves.

In addition to those released there was also a list of many who were not released. The reasons why this list, which comprises but a small fraction of the entire number was made, we may never know. The highest number appearing was Jean Guillaume (John Williams) 39,336. A number had already served a period of twenty-seven years. Does the reader fully comprehend what the foregoing number and years means? No, we cannot at this late day realize its full significance! The recent persecution of the Armenians and the onslaught of the Chinese on the missionaries, which recently shocked the whole civilized world, are insignificant incidents compared with the persecution of the Huguenots. This list is of vital interest to us as many of the names are identified with some that appear in this work, and we are irresistibly led to infer, as already said, that some at least are identical as to persons.

As a striking example we herewith append a few names, all of which are represented in the emigrant list of this work: *Barree*,

---

(1). See " Historical Notes," Vol. I by Henry S. Dodderer.

Blanc, Boyer, Bourell, Bertrand, Bouchee, Bertow, Chapelle, Corbier, Clevel, Dasser, Durand, de Mars, Folquier, Gachon, Gautier, Guillaume, Mallet, Martiel, de Marcellin, Melon, Mariler, Perrier, Peritier, Prunier, Peret, Reneau, Reno la Roue, Sauvet, de Turk, Valet, Vincet, etc.

The Piedmontese.

The persecution of the Protestants in Piedmont was of the most terrible character, and the most shocking and unheard of methods of torture were adopted by their enemies. A large number escaped and found refuge in Protestant countries. Holland seems to have given asylum to a very large number. Public measures for their relief were adopted as late as 1710. Amsterdam and other cities of the Low Countries were congested with Piedmontese and other Huguenot refugees, and from these countries doubtless came a large number of emigrants to Pennsylvania and whose ancestors are said to have "fled to Holland and from thence came to America."

We herewith give the names of a few Piedmontese martyrs who perished for their Protestant faith in consequence of the Edict of 1655: *Marie de Armand* was flayed alive; *David de Armand* was compelled to lay his head on a block when a soldier crushed it with a hammer; his brother *Paul* was also killed; aged *Jacob Perrine*, an elder of the church at Villars, and his brother *David* were flayed alive; *Bartholomew, John,* and *Ludwig Durant, Daniel Nevel* and *Paul Renaud* (Reno) met a shocking death by having their mouths filled with gunpowder which was exploded; *Jacob Birone*, a teacher, met a death too horrible to relate; *Lucia du Bisson*, wife of Peter who was killed, fled to the Alps with two small children. In the forest alone she gave birth to another child. Owing to cold and hunger all her children perished, while she alone, of all her family, reached a place of safety.

Daniel Rambaut (Rambo), an aged elder of Villaro, suffered death in a way too shocking to relate; *Baptist Utre, Paul Garnier, Magdalena Pierre, Joseph Pont, Paul Clement, Daniel Benech*, all met death in a dreadful manner. The reader will find all these Piedmontese names represented in our immigrant list to Pennsylvania. In the city of Nismes, in another part of France, and at a much later period, *Oliver Desmond*, a minister eighty years of age, was killed; also *Louis Le Char* (now Lesher), and a family named *Chasseur*.

As already said, we are irresistibly led to the conclusion that there is in many instances a connection between these martyr families here and elsewhere noted, and immigrants of a similar name who have traditions of persecuted and martyred ancestors.

A study of the Huguenot emigration to Pennsylvania indicates that in many instances large and well organized parties came together with the evident purpose of contiguous settlement. This fact presupposes conferences and maturing of plans before their departure from Europe. Doubtless in many instances there were family ties and bonds of friendship formed in their own native France which were continued during their exile in various Protestant countries and contributed largely to the reuniting of the many connectional links that are so frequently met with in America.

The first distinctively Huguenot colony to come to Pennsylvania was that of Madame Ferree, for whom a large body of land was surveyed in Lancaster county in 1710. Her party came with many others under the leadership of Rev. Joshua Kocherthal (1) landing in New York in 1709. Most of these, after a brief stay in Ulster county, came to Pennsylvania. Madame Ferree, with her family, including her son John and son-in-law, Isaac Lefever, with their families, came to Pequea. Hubert Hubertson came to the Schuylkill Valley as early as 1709 (2) while Isaac de Turk and others went to Oley in 1712. Both places immediately became centers of emigration.

An examination of the emigrant lists in Volume XVII. Penna. Archives (2d series), very readily discloses a large number of Huguenot parties. As an illustration of this we subjoin a number of lists of names compiled from a few shiploads of "Foreigners." Many more such lists as follow might be given:

In ship "*Princess Augustus*," September 16, 1736—Jean Comer, Sebastian and Dietrick Coquelin, Pierre Delon, Nicholas Gerard, Jean Francois Christean, Collas Drasbart, Joseph and David Noel, Francois and Nicholas Orth.

In ship "*Loyal Judith*," November 26, 1740—Conrade Douay, John Conde, Fred Laurans, Bernett Saye, John H. Leshire, John Angell.

In ship "*Neptune*," October 25, 1746—Jean Duestro, Francois Conreau, Pierre Vintvas, Arenne Consul, Pierre and Joseph Gerro, Saul Ruibec, Alexander Gibbo.

---

(1). See Rev. Joshua Kocherthal's petition to Queen Ann, of England, for relief for himself and his party, distressed by the invasion and ravages of the French army (Documentary Hist. of N. Y., Vol. V. p. 44. List of his party see p. 52). Kocherthal was pastor of a church near Lindau, Bavaria. Queen Ann gave them substantial aid and they were naturalized before leaving England. Kocherthal died in Esopus, N. Y. in 1719.

(2). This year he signed a petition for a road to Manatawny. See "Perkiomen Region," Vol. II p. 135.

In ship "*Phœnix*," September 15, 1749—Daniel Duvall, Francois and Adam Grandaden, Humber Benoit, Joseph Coutour, Abraham Chedron, Jean La Motte, Nicholas Daton, Joseph Charlier, Jacob and Herman La Tour, Andre De Grange, Francois Hognon.

In ship "*Brotherhood*," November 3, 1750—Joseph and Peter Fahrne, Paul Tomel, Pierre and Isaac Paris, Pierre Delabach, Henri Jeune.

In ship "*Patience*," September 9, 1751—Isaac Reno, Michael Harcourt, Christian Galle, Jean Henri Pierre, Pierre Balmas, Matthieu Morrett, Eberhart Chapelle.

In ship "*Phœnix*," November 22, 1752—Jean Jacques, Adam Le Roy, Daniel and John La Wall, Jean Lanblene, Pierre Gulliame, David Jochnal, Gulliaume Sebrick, Jean Botisman.

In ship "*Patience*," September 17, 1753—Pierre Armeson, Jacques Balme, Jean Bennett, Jacques Berger, Jacques Bach, Etienne Brun, Jeremie and Jean Pierre Chapelle, Pierre Rochon, Paul Caffarel, Jacques Gourier, Pierre Gautier, Mattieu Ture, Lorie Neron, Charles Shownet, Jean Jaques Servier, Jean Richardson, Jaques Sanguinet.

In ship "*Nancy*," September 14, 1754 (Lorraines)—Abraham and Charles Huguelot, Simon Keppler, Fred Showay, Antoine Hogar, Jeannia Quipic, Peter Ramie, John Seyser, Abram Joray, Abraham Gobat, Christian Cally, Pierre Vautie, Jean Pierre Monin, Sr., Jean Pierre Monin, Jr., David Marchand, Abraham and Alexander Zuille, Pierre, Jean Christian and J. N. Pechin, Phillip Sponseller, John Geo. Steubesant, Abraham and Adam Le Roy, Abram De Die, Abram Bouthert, Jean Periter, Sr., Jean Periter, Jr., Francois La Mar, Jaques Barberat, Pierre Greine, Jean Mathiot, Jean Jaques Allemand, Alphonse Louis Willeman, Frantz Philip Weis.

In the Public Service.

There is perhaps no aspect of the history of the Huguenots in America that impresses the historian more profoundly than the record of their public service. In the present instance we will confine ourselves to the consideration of their distinguished services in Pennsylvania. In the study of this subject we meet with astonishing results, which can only be accounted for on the assumption of exceptional excellency of character and patriotism. Although the weakest of the recognized elements of our Provincial population we have the following marvelous record of public service:

In the War of the Revolution Philadelphia furnished in the person of Elias Boudinot a President, and in Michael Hillegas the first Treasurer of the Nation; also Major General Daniel Roberdeau, of the same city, and Brigadier General Philip de Haas, of

Lebanon. Besides the foregoing they furnished *fifteen colonels* for the Revolution besides a proportionate number of officers of lesser rank.

To enumerate we have Col. John Bayard and his nephew, Col. Stephen Bayard, both of Philadelphia but of a Delaware family, Col. John Ferree, Col. Joel Ferree, Col. Francis Mentges, Col. Henry Haller, Col. Adam Hubley (son of Bernard Hubley), Col. Adam Hubley (son of Michael Hubley), and Major Michael Ferree, all from Lancaster; Col. John Hay and Captain Michael Doutel, who led the first Pennsylvania company to the seat of war, were from York; Col. John de Cessna and his brother, Col. Charles de Cessna, were from Bedford; Col. Abraham La Bar, Col. Stephen Balliet and Major Marien La Mar, who fell at Paoli, were from Northampton; Col. Sebastian Le Van, Col. Daniel Utrie, Major George Lorah and Adjutant Philip Bertolet were from Berks county. This same preponderating prominence is shown in other lines of public service of which we will only name the Judiciary.

The closing years of the past and opening years of the present century will illustrate this feature. We may note Judge S. Leslie Mestrezat, of the Supreme, and former Governor James A. Beaver, of the Superior Court; Judge Cyrus L. Pershing, Judge J. W. Bittenger and Judge Dimmer Beeber, all of whom, with the exception of Judge Mestrezat, descend from Alsatians. Then also Judge de Pew La Bar.

CHAPTER VI.
The Lower Delaware.

THE FIRST WHITE RESIDENTS OF PENNSYLVANIA HUGUENOTS—SETTLEMENT OF THE LOWER DELAWARE REGION—FRENCH AND WALDENSIAN REFUGEES—PETER MINUIT, THE GOVERNOR AND OTHER OFFICERS—HUGUENOTS—BOHEMIA MANOR——PHILADELPHIA AND GERMANTOWN.

*" Our boast is not that we deduce our birth
From loins enthroned and rulers of the earth;
But higher far our proud pretentions rise—
The sons of parents passed into the skies."*

IT is a remarkabls fact that the first white residents of Pennsylvania were Huguenots! In May, 1623, Jesse De Forrest, a Walloon, at the head of a large party of his countrymen, arrived in New York Bay under the auspices of the West India

Trading Company, and founded the city of that name. Among this party, composed of about thirty families, were four young couple who were married during the voyage and who, soon after their arrival, were sent to form a trading station on the Delaware River. There is some disagreement among historians as to the location of this station. The best authorities locate it on an island which is now almost washed away and situated on the Pennsylvania side just below Trenton Falls. After a residence here of several years they abandoned the place.

The region ceded to William Penn in 1681 and now known as Pennsylvania, originally embraced the three counties comprising the State of Delaware, and not until 1703 was it erected into a separate Colony. This region, which was successively under Swedish and Dutch occupation, had a considerable population prior to Penn's arrival. Among the settlers were a large number of French and Waldensian refugees who mostly came between 1654 and 1663. The names of many have been irrecoverably lost, while many who were unquestionably Huguenots are erroneously classed as Dutch and Swedes in the early records.

It is a remarkable circumstance that nearly all the officials of the Colony under both the Swedish and Dutch occupation were of Huguenot antecedents. The distinguished list begins with the Governor, *Peter Minuit*, and whose history is invested with a mournful interest. His parents, who were of the French nobility, fled to Holland during the early stages of the Huguenot persecution. Minuit early entered the service of the Dutch Republic and was a very capable officer, serving as the second Director of New Netherlands. When the Delaware Colonies fell under the dominion of Sweden he was appointed Governor, in which capacity he served from April 28, 1638, to January 30, 1640. He founded the town of Christiana in Delaware, and where he died in 1641.

Another Huguenot who shed lustre on his race was *Jean Paul Jacquett* (1) who, in 1654, settled at the "Long Hook," near Wilmington. The Dutch having repossessed themselves of the Delaware Colonies the Governor of New Amsterdam (New York) in 1655 appointed Jacquett as Vice Director of the same. In 1676 he was constituted a Justice. From the various references to him in the histories of the Colonies we are led to infer that he was a man of considerable distinction. He died after 1684 at an advanced age. His great grandson, Major Peter Jacquett (1754-1834), was a gallant soldier of the Revolutionary War.

---

(1). Pa. Mag. of Hist., XIII 271. Later researches show that he was born in Nuremberg of French parentage

Joost de la Grange was also a man of prominence in the Colony. He is said to have been one of "three brothers" who fled from Normandy to Holland, and from whence they came to America in 1656. In 1662 it seems he purchased Tinicum Island. His title thereto being contested after his death his son *Arnoldus* addressed a statement in relation to the matter to Governor Andros in 1678 (1).

Alexander Boyer, a Huguenot, was Deputy Commissary of the Colony in 1648 and a man of great prominence for many years.

Captain John de Haes was one of the most notable officials of the Delaware Colony. In 1673 he was made a Commissioner to receive quit rents and in 1674 Collector of Customs at New Castle, and in 1678 was made a Justice (2).

In the limits of New Castle county, particularly in Red Lion Hundred, the Huguenots formed a considerable element of the population. We herewith give such names as we have recovered, deeply regretting that the identity of so many seems to be irrecoverably lost.

Among the first settlers on the Delaware were the refugee brothers, *Jacques*, *Hypolite* and *Jean Le Fever*. The first named had been an officer in the French army (3).

Gerrit Rutan was a prominent resident prior to 1660 (4). *Daniel Routte* was located in Kent county prior to 1683, and *John du Bois* prior to 1694. In Blackbird Hundred settled *Elie Naudin* in 1698, whose father, also *Elie*, fled from La Tremblade in 1682 with wife and several small children and took refuge in Southampton, England. *Arnold* (5) a brother to the Delaware emigrant, located in New York.

At Murder Creek Hundred, in Kent county, settled *John Gruwell*, whose sons John and Jacob established the family name (6). In West Dover settled the three brothers, *Daniel*, *James* and *William Voshell* (7). *Dr. des Jardines*, who settled in this region prior to 1683, had fled to England where he was naturalized. The *Casho* family came from Jacob Casho, whose father fled to Ger-

---

(1). Penna Arch., VII p. 778.
(2). Penna. Arch.
(3). Biog. Hist. of Del., Vol. I p. 536.
(4). Abraham Rutan, doubtless a relative, in 1682 escaped from France to Germany, from whence he came, to New York. Some of his descendents located in Washington county, Pa., from which branch came the late Hon. James S. Rutan, Ex-Speaker of the State Senate.
(5). Baird's Hug. Em., II p. 35.
(6). Biog. Hist. of Del., II p. 813.
(7). Augustine and Peter Voshell, Huguenots, came to N. Y. with the Palatines in 1700.

many at the Revocation, and from whence Jacob came to Delaware and settled at Wilmington. During the Revolution he was an interpeter on the staff of Lafayette (1).

Laurens Rochia, the founder of a well-known family, fled from France to Ireland and from thence he came to Delaware. Richard Saye, of Nisms, arrived in 1686. Prior to 1677 appear the names of *Philipe Chevalier, Henri Clerq, Albert Blocq, Math. d'Ring, Mosis de Gan, Hubert Laurans, Paul Mincq* (2). To the foregoing may be added the following Colonial families whose names and traditions all point to a Huguenot origin. Nearly all of them were established in Delaware prior to 1700 : *Jean Savoy, Bellevill, Cammon, Bassett, Cazier, Deto, La Pierre, La Forge, Le Compte (La Count), Larue, Sees, Setton, Janvier, Du Chesney (Dushane)* (3) *Vigoure, Tunnell, Le Croix, Hueling* (4).

---

(1). Biog. Ency. of Del.
(2). Penna. Mag. of Hist., III 352.
(3). There was a family of this name ennobled in Picardy ("Science des Armoiries," p. 5).
(4). **The Huling Family in America.**—This family ranks very high in France and several branches belong to the nobility. A large number of this name were of the Protestant faith and were scattered to many lands during the Huguenot persecution. Several fled to England prior to the Revocation, from whence came Abraham and William to New Jersey in 1674. The latter was married in Burlington county in 1680 and died 1713 (vide Lit. Era, Vol. VIII p. 569). James Huling died in Newport, R. I. 1687. Francois Huling and wife Elizabeth were members of the Huguenot Church in New York in 1694 (Coll. Hug. Soc. of Am., Vol. I). Elias Hulin, a French mariner, located at Marblehead, Mass., about 1741. Ambrose Hulin was one of the refugees to South Carolina, while George Hulin came to Pennsylvania in 1750 with the Germans.

Our chief aim has been to trace the so-called Swedish branch of this family, from which a very large number of prominent persons in America descend. The account of this family prior to its arrival here is gathered from dates preserved by widely divergent branches and originally drawn from family records before its dispersion two centuries ago. The genealogical part is derived from official records and therefore correct.

All accounts agree that the ancestor of this family was the Marquis Jean Paul Frederick de Hulingues, a young Huguenot nobleman of the old French Province of Bearn, who was a companion of Henry of Navarre and attached to his court.

During the sojourn of Navarre at the court at Paris the young Marquis became betrothed to Isabella du Portal, a lady in waiting to Catharine de Medici. It was at this period that the awful massacre of St. Bartholomew took place (1572). By a reference to the chapter covering this event the reader will learn that the King of Navarre saved his life by renouncing the Protestant faith. Many of his friends, however, were put to death. The Marquis de Hulingues and his affianced wife, however, made their escape to Dieppe where they were married. Here they took a vessel and put to sea. Adverse winds, however, drove them far beyond their original destination, and they landed in Sweden where they were taken under the protection of the court. The Marquis had but one son whose name is not known. A grandson was Lars, (Laurence), Huling who came with the Swedish immigrants to the Delaware sometime prior to 1640. Only two sons of the immigrant are definitely known. They were Laurans and Marcus (1st), both of whom resided in Gloucester county, New Jersey. In the records of this county is (1) the will of Laurens Hulings dated Aug. 25, 1700. His wife Katharine was the sole legatee. (2) Will of Laurens Hulings, proved June 4th, 1748. Legatees, sons Laurens,

Bohemia Manor.

In 1683-4 arrangements were perfected for the planting of a colony of Labadists (1) in America. The commissioners of the Labadists secured for that purpose a large tract of land situated on the Elk river at the head of Chesapeake Bay in Cecil county, Maryland, but at that time claimed by Penn to be within the limits of his grant. This tract was named after its original owner, Augustine Herrman, a Bohemian, to whom Lord Baltimore had granted it in 1666. Very little information concerning this colony has come down to us. Its members came from various parts of Europe, some of them being French. After a precarious existence of several decades the society dissolved and was absorbed in the general populace, upon the death of their bishop, Petrus Sluyter, about 1726. Among the original grantees of the Labadists tract 1683, were two men of eminent Huguenot antecedents. They were *Arnoldus De la Grange*, whose father as we have seen was a prominent official under the Dutch and Swedish occupation. The other was *Peter Bayard*, the founder of a family from which has come a long line of soldiers, scholars, and statesmen, and who have shed lustre on the pages of American history.

The Bayard family of France was of a noble rank, and in the Reformation period ranged itself on the side of the Protestant Faith. During the period of the massacre of St. Bartholmew (1572), an eminent divine of the Bayard family fled to Amsterdam where the name

---

Michael, Abraham, Israel, Joseph, Marcus and dau. Dinah. Executors, his brother Mich. Hulings of Philadelphia and son Abraham.

Marcus (1st) Hulings second known son of the immigrant died in Gloucester Co. prior to 1700, leaving known sons Marcus (2nd), and Laurens. Marcus (2nd) married Margaret, a dau. of Mouns Jones and with his father-in-law removed to the Swedish settlement of Molatton on the Schuylkill river where the village of Douglassville, in Berks county, Pennsylvania is located. Here the Jones house dated 1716, may still be seen in a good state of preservation.

Marcus Huling (2nd) died here in 1757, aged 70 years. His children were (1) Mouns, who died prior to this father, leaving children John, b, 1743, and Mary, b, 1747, who m. George Thomas in 1767. (2) Marcus (3rd), (3) Bridget, (4) Maudlin, (5) John, and (6) Andrew.

Of the foregoing Marcus (3rd) located prior to 1754 at the mouth of the Juniatti river where he had a considerable estate, including a mill at the mouth of Sherman's creek. He appears prominently in the records of the frontier wars, and died in 1788. His children were (1) Marcus (4th) who erected the first house where Milton now stands in 1772, (2) Mary m—Stewart, (3) Samuel, (4) James and (5) Thomas. The latter was the executor of his will and gained possession of the estates. Among the many distinguished men of the Marcus Huling line is Gen. J. Willis Huling, of Oil City, Pa., who has the distinction of leading into action in Porto Rico the only Pennsylvania regiments engaged in the Spanish-American war.

---

(1). Jean de Labadie, the founder of the order of Labadists, was born in France in 1610, and was reared as a clerical, becoming a Protestant he served for some years as a minister at Montauban. Because of erratic views he was repudiated by the Reformed Communion, whereupon he founded a new and peculiar monastic sect which became extinct in about a half century.

became established, and from whence a number came to America. A descendent became the wife of Peter Stuvesant, the last governor of New York, under the Dutch occupation, and whose brother-in-law, *Samuel Bayard*, established the name in America.

The immigrant had three sons, *Nicholas* and *Balthassar*, who became prominent citizens of New York, and *Peter*, who came to Bohemia Manor, and founded the Delaware branch.

Among the notable descendants of the latter was Colonel John Bayard, of the Revolution. A gallant soldier who was commended by General Washington for bravery in action, and also Colonel Stephen Bayard, (1743-1815), a nephew of the foregoing, and likewise an officer of high merit. In late years came James A. Bayard. James A. Bayard, the diplomat, who negotiated the Treaty of Ghent in 1814, which closed the war of 1812, and also Thomas F. Bayard, Embassador to England under the administration of President Cleveland.

Another distinguished member of the Labadist Colony was *Legide Bouchelle*, who died subsequent to 1700. His widow became the second wife of Bishop Petrus Sluyter. Upon the death of Bishop Sluyter, *Dr. Peter Bouchelle*, his wife's son by her first husband became his sole heir to the extensive interests of Bohemia Manor. Dr. Bouchelle died in North Carolina in 1799, at an advanced age.

Du Pont.

The Du Pont family, of America, is of old and eminent stock, and spring from the nobility of France. The first of the name in America was *Abraham Du Pont* who first fled to England, and from thence removed to the Huguenot Colony on the Santee in South Carolina about 1694. His son, *Gideon*, devised the method of rice culture that has made this industry one of the greatest sources of wealth, and a boon to mankind.

The Delaware branch came from *Pierre Samuel Du Pont Du Nemours*, (a grand nephew of Abraham above mentioned), who was born in Paris, Dec. 14th, 1739, whose people still clung to the Huguenot faith. He was an eminent scientist, political economist and statesman, and in a long career, bore many high and responsible governmental offices.

Owing to the turbulence of the times, he and his *confreres*, including his sons, passed through many vicissitudes, and on several occasions he narrowly escaped death, while many of his associates were less fortunate. He was an ardent supporter of King Louis XVI, and on the memorable Aug. 10th, 1792, with his son *Eluthere Irene*, (1771-1834), engaged in the defense of the person of the King. He escaped the fury of the mob, and was secreted in the dome of the Paris observatory by the astronomer La Land until Sept. 2nd, during which time he wrote "*The Philosophy of the Universe.*"

When quiet was restored he again entered public life, and soon came in conflict with the anarchistic elements, under the leadership of Robespierre. On July 20, 1794, he was cast into prison, and condemned to be beheaded, but escaped that fate by the timely death of Robespierre, on July 28th.

Owing to the continued political disturbances he emigrated to America in 1799, but returned to France in 1802, and again came to this country upon the escape of Napolean from Elbe, and died in Delaware, Aug. 7, 1817.

As an author and statesman, he was one of the foremost men of his times, and when wearied with battling for peace and reform in his own land, he was invited by several sovereigns of Europe, to locate in their realms. He was a great support to the American Colonies in their struggle for freedom. He was Chief of the Secret Diplomatic Service, and through his instrumentality the Treaty of Peace was brought about in 1783, by which the independence of the Colonies was recognized by England. He was also the chief instrument in the sale of Louisiana to the United States in 1803.

His son *Eluthree Irene*, founded the great powder mills near Wilmington, Delaware, in 1801, at which most of the powder used by the United States Government since that time has been manufactured.

Victor Marie Du Pont De Nemours, (1767-1827), eldest son of the statesman was also a man of prominence and for many years in the diplomatic service. In 1800 he resigned his positions and came to Delaware, where he united his interests with the rest of his family.

Several of the family have been very prominent in the affairs of their State and Nation. Among others we may mention Commodore *Samuel Francis Du Pont*, (1803-1865), whose achievements in the Civil War added new lustre to the naval history of our country.

Henry Du Pont, (1812-1889), and *Col. Henry Algernon Du Pont*, (b-1838), a graduate of the National Military School at West Point, a distinguished soldier of the Civil War and prominent in public affairs ever since, have fully maintained the high character of the family.

Philadelphia and Vicinity.

The residence of Huguenots in Philadelphia is coeval with its founding, and it may be truly said that the city has had no more valuable citizens than the expatriated sons of France and their descendants. Some of them came with the Colonists from England where they, or their fathers, were naturalized, others came from older Colonies, while others came directly from France.

Among the original citizens were *Edmund Du Castle*, *John De La Vall* and *Andrew Doz*. The latter was a refugee and was brought over by William Penn as his vine dresser. In 1690 (1) he was granted a plantation of two hundred acres of land, and including the vine yards on the Schuylkill river by the founder, for his services. His grandson, also named Andrew, was a very public spirited citizen and magnificently endowed a number of charitable and religious institutions in his native city.

Gabriel Rappe and *Nicholas Reboteau* of the Isle of Rhe, and *Andrew Imbert* of Nisms, were naturalized in 1683.

Samuel Robinett also appears as one of the first citizens. The Robinetts were originally from the Isle of Rhe, from whence they fled to England.

At the Revocation *Pierre Chevallier* of a noble family of Normandy fled to England. Soon after this date we find a *Pierre Le Chevalier* in Charleston, S. C., and *Jean Le Chevalier* in New York, while Philip Chevalier appears in Delaware as early as 1677. That they were immediate relatives is quite probable. The refugee to England had a son also named Pierre, who married an English lady, and who in 1720 came to Philadelphia where he founded an honorable posterity. (2)

The *Boudinot* (3) family of de la Tremblade bore a prominent part in the French Reformation and suffered terribly in consequence. At the Revocation several branches of the family found their way to America. In 1686 *Elias Boudinot* located in New York, from whence a son, also Elias, came to Philadelphia prior to 1735. The latter was the father of Elias Boudinot, (third of the name), who justly ranks among the great men of his times, and who is elsewhere noticed in this work.

The *Duche* (4) family, one of the most eminent in America, descend from *Jacques Duche*, who fled from La Rochell to London

---

(1). Pa. Arch. XIX, 32-35.
(2). Pa. Mag. of Hist. VII, 483.
(3). Ibid. III, 191.
(4). Ibid. II, 58.

in 1682, with his wife, Mary, and eight children. The founder of the American branch was a son, *Anthony*, who came to Philadelphia near 1700, and died in 1762, at a very advanced age. He left three sons, *Anthony, Jr.*, who died in 1772, *Jacob*, born in Philadelphia in 1708, and died in Lambeth England, in 1788. He was the father of the *Rev. Jacob Duche*, an eminent Episcopal divine, who as rector of Christ Church, Philadelphia, had the distinction of opening the first Continental Congress with prayer. *Andrew*, the youngest son of the immigrant died in Philadelphia in 1778.

The *Benezett* family has an honorable record in the history of the Huguenots, and a number sealed their faith with their lives. Among the last to suffer was the Rev. J. Benezett, a prominent minister of Vigan and who was executed at Montpelier in 1752 (1). In 1731, *John Stephen Benezett* arrived in Philadelphia. He was born of noble and distinguished parentage in 1683 in Abbeville, France (2). At the Revocation period his parents fled to Holland, and from thence to England in 1715. Upon his arrival in Philadelphia, Mr. Benezett became one of the leading citizens and had the distinction of being the first treasurer of the City. He was nominally a member of the Society of Friends, but was strongly attached to the Moravians, and for some time a member of that body, and on terms of intimacy with its leaders. Count Zinzendorf, their great patron, was frequently entertained by him during his visit to America in 1742. He had three sons who worthily represented their distinguished ancestry, *James*, the eldest, who located in Bucks county, *Samuel*, a major in the Revolution, and *Anthony*, a noted philanthropist and anti-slavery advocate, and who is supposed to have written the first anti-slavery work in America (3). Three daughters married prominent Moravian ministers. *Susan* became the wife of Rev. Ch. Pyrlaeus, *Judith* married Rev. David Bruce and another became the wife of Rev. Jacob Lischey, who died in York county.

The *Suplee* family of Pennsylvania derives its origin from *Andros Souplis*, a young officer of the French army and of distinguished parentage. In 1682 he made his escape to Germany where he was married to Gertrude Stressinger. In 1684 he came to Philadelphia. He was a man of great intelligence and ability, and stood high in the estimation of William Penn. He had but one son, *Andrew*, who changed the name to its present form.

---

(1). Browning's Hist. of the Huguenots, p. 321.
(2). Memorials of the Moravian Church, Vol. I, p. 171.
(3). "Considerations on the Keeping of Negroes." (Phila. 1754.)

Isaac Roberdeau, a refugee from fhe island of St. Christopher in the Antilles, arrived in Philadelphia at an early day. His son, *Daniel Roberdeau* (1727-1795), was a most distinguished citizen. He was a member of the Continental Congress, and a major general of Provincial troops during the Revolution. General Roberdeau died at Winchester, Va. His son, Isaac Roberdeau (1763-1829), was a distinguished engineer.

The *Garrigues* family are descended from refugees of that name who fled from Montpellier to England during the Revocation period. The family under the name of "*Garrick*" is still extant in England and has furnished in the person of *David Garrick* (1716-1779), one of the world's greatest dramatists.

Soon after 1700 members of the family came to Philadelphia and founded the Garrigues family so well and honorably known in America.

Among the first members of the Reformed Church, of Philadelphia, were *David Montandon* and *Pierre Le Colle*, who were both men of prominence. Le Colle died in 1734. The family Le Colle must have suffered very severely in the Huguenot persecutions as we find refugees of this name in various Protestant countries.

Paul Casser, of Languedoc, and his wife, Margaret Raymond, were members of the Moravian Church. The latter came from a prominent family seated at Berol, near Montpellier.

Christ Church Records.

In the published records of Christ Episcopal Church of Philadelphia (1) occur the following names of parents of presumed Huguenot antecedents—earliest entries only are given : *Boudinot, Elias,* 1738 ; *Boyer, James,* 1734 ; *Bonnett, John,* 1736 ; *Bruno, John,* 1738 ; *Chevalier, Peter,* 1721 ; *Couche, Daniel,* 1756 ; *Durell, Moses,* 1731 ; *Doutell, Michael,* 1737 ; *Dupee, Daniel,* 1747 ; *Doz, Andrew, Duche, Jacob,* 1734 ; *Fleury, Peter,* 1731 ; *Garrigues, Francis,* 1721 ; *Garrigues, Peter,* 1736 ; *Hillegas, Michael,* 1760 ; *Hodnett, John,* 1737 ; *La Rue, John,* 1739 ; *Le Boyteau, William,* 1711 ; *Le Tort, James,* 1709 ; *Le Dru, Noel,* 1732 ; *Le Dieu, Lewis,* 1758 ; *Le Shemile, Peter,* 1741 ; *Le Gay, Jacob,* 1744 ; *Lacellas, James,* 1759 ; *de Prefontain, Peter,* 1754 ; *Paca, John,* 1758 ; *Pinnard, Joseph,* 1733 ; *Purdieu, William,* 1738 ; *Trippeo, Frederick,* 1713 ; *Renandet, James,* 1733 ; *Vidal, Stephen,* 1754 ; *Votaw, Paul Isaac,* 1747 ; *Voyer, Peter,* 1713.

---

(1). Vide Pa. Mag. of Hist. and Biog., Vols. XIV, XV, XVI.

The records of *St. Michaels Lutheran* Church of Philadelphia bear the following names of parents of probable Huguenot extraction—earliest entries only are given : (1) *Remy, Jacob,* 1745 ; *Huyett, Frantz Carl,* 1747 ; *Remley (de) Conrad,* 1747 ; *Ransier, Frederick,* 1748 ; *Suffrance, John,* 1749 ; *Bouton, John, Daniel,* 1752 ; *Bouton, Jacob,* 1752 ; *Reno, Peter* 1752 ; *Losche, Daniel,* 1752 ; *DuBois, Alex.,* 1753 ; *LeBrant, John Conrad,*(" who died on the Rhein") 1754 ; *Piquart, John Gottfried,* 1754 ; *Qzias, Elizabeth* (wid.,) 1755.

Germantown and vicinity.

The settlement of Germantown, near Philadelphia, was the outgrowth of a visit in 1677 by William Penn to Holland, Germany, and other European countries on behalf of the persecuted Quakers and their co-religionists. One result of this visit was the formation of the Frankfort Land Company which secured a grant of nearly twenty-five thousand acres of land for colonization purposes.

The initial settlement was made in 1683 by thirteen families, who were soon followed by many others from Continental Europe, nearly all of whom were religious refugees. In a few years flourishing settlements were made at New Hanover, Providence, Skippack and Goshahoppen. Among this promiscuous influx there was a considerable Huguenot element, some of whom came direct from France, but the greater number of them had sojourned in other Protestant countries. Among the Huguenot settlers of Germantown prior to 1686, were Jean Le Brun, Jean Dedier, Wigard and Gerhart Levering, all of whom were prominent citizens.

The Leverings were sons of Dr. Rosier Levering, a refugee to Gamen, in Germany, where he married Elizabeth Van der Walle, of Wessel, in Westphalia, and where both the sons were born. Wigard Levering was the founder of Roxborough and a man of considerable prominence (2). The Rt. Rev. J. Mortimer Levering, Bishop of the Moravian Church, is a descendant of Gerhart, also Hon. Joshua Levering, the Prohibition candidate for the United States presidency in 1896.

About 1691 *James De la Plaine,* a son of Nicholas De la Plaine, of New York, settled in Germantown. Because of the removal of most of the Emigrant's family to Pennsylvania, a notice of him in this connection seems to be in place. Nicholas De la Plaine, who

---

(1). Vide Pa. German Pub., Vol. VII.
(2). See "Levering Family" by Horatio Gates Jones. Wigard Levering died at the advanced age of 109 years. (Haz. Reg. I, 281).

is said to have been of patrician origin, fled from France to England long before the Revocation. After a brief sojourn there he came to New York, where his name appears as early as 1657. In 1658 he was married to Susanna Cresson, with whom he had a numerous family. The De la Plaine and Cresson families were Quakers.

Besides James as above, four daughters of Nicholas came to Philadelphia, viz: Elizabeth, the eldest daughter who had married in 1686 Casper Hoodt, in New York; Judith married in 1691 Thomas Griffith; Susanna married in 1685 Arnold Cassel, who had lately arrived from Kresheim in the Palatinate; Crejanne married in 1697 Ives Belangee. The three latter daughters were married in Philadelphia, and all of them by Friend's ceremony.

James De la Plaine, son of the emigrant, and who founded the family name in Pennsylvania, was married to Hannah Cock, of Long Island, New York, in 1692. He was a prominent Friend and influential citizen and died in 1750, in Germantown. Their children so far as known were James, born 1695, married Elizabeth Shoemaker, and later Ann Jones; Nicholas, born 1697, married to Sarah Ong; Hannah, married to John Simpson; Mary, married to Edward Ridgeway; John, married to Sarah Johnson; Sarah married to ———? Holland; and Joshua, married to Maria ———? The latter settled in Colebrookdale, Berks county, where he died in 1788, leaving sons Joshua, John, Joseph and James.

John, the son of Joshua De la Plaine was married to Sophia Miller, and prior to the Revolution removed to Rocky Hill, in Frederick county, Maryland. Joseph, another son, who was an officer in the Revolution, married Catharine Miller, daughter of the emigrant John William Miller, of Oley, Berks county, and also removed to Frederick county, Maryland, sometime after the Revolution. John died in 1804 aged 63 years, and James died in 1818 aged about 74 years. Both left families, and their descendants are very numerous and include many eminent names.

Reference has been made to the Cresson family, the ancestor of which was *Pierre Cresson*, a prominent refugee of Picardy, France, who in 1640 fled to Holland, where he is said to have been gardner to the Prince of Orange. After a seventeen year sojourn in Holland he emigrated to New York. The widow of his son Jacques, with a number of children, came to Philadelphia at an early day. Solomon Cresson, son of the widow, who in 1702 was married to Anna Watson, founded the family name in Philadelphia. Conrad Cresson, whose antecedents are not known, was a resident of Colebrookdale, in Berks county, prior to 1728.

CHAPTER VII.

The Perkiomen and Lower Schuylkill Region.

SKIPPACK—GOSHAHOPPEN—FALKNER SWAMP—EARLY SETTLERS—MANY FRENCH AND ALSATIANS — HILLEGAS — BOYER — DE FRAIN—PECHIN—DUBOIS—BALDY—LESHER.

"Truth forever on the scaffold—
Wrong forever on the throne!
Yet that scaffold sways the future,
And behind the dim unknown—
Standeth GOD within the shadow
Keeping watch above his own."

FIRST TREASURER OF THE UNITED STATES.

RISING in the hill country over the Lehigh county line, and flowing southward through Montgomery county into the Schuylkill river, is the Perkiomen creek. The beautiful valley through which it flows also bears its name. Near the head waters of this stream is a locality known as "Skippack" and "Goshahoppen," with its famous church dating back to about 1730.

Extending westward from this region toward the ancient Cole-brookdale, and the Oley Hills of Berks county, is the *Falkner Swamp*, drained by the Swamp creek, which empties into the Perkiomen.

This region was settled at an early day principally by Palatines and Alsatians, and also some French, a number of whom had previously lived in the Huguenot settlements of New York.

In the Reformed society of Goshahoppen were a considerable number of members with Huguenot antecedents, among others the families *Hillegas, Leshire, Lingel, Griesemere, Transue, Desmond, Labar, Reboteau, de Bleama,* (1) *Somaine.*

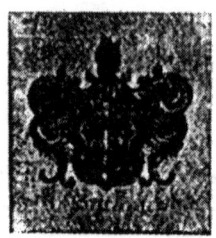
ARMS OF HILLEGAS.

About the time of the Revocation (1685), the *Hillegas* family fled from Alsace to the Palatinate for safety. A number of the younger members later came to Pennsylvania. *John Frederick Hillegas* (2) arrived in 1727 and located in Goshenhoppen, Montgomery county. Two of his sons, who had remained in Europe, arrived—*Leopold* in 1730 and *John Adam* in 1734. *Michael Hillegas* (B. 1696 D. 1749), a brother to John Frederick, also arrived at an early day. He was the father of *Michael Hillegas*, the first Treasurer of the United States (3). *George Peter Hillegas*, who died in Philadelphia county in 1745, is supposed to have been a brother to the senior emigrants. *George Albrecht Hillegas*, who arrived in 1746, and whose relationship to the others is not known, located near Lancaster where he died not many years afterwards. His widow died there in 1780 aged 76 years. The Hillegas name has ever been an honorable one in the history of the Commonwealth, and a very large number of descendents became men of eminence, of whom may be mentioned the Hon. John Richards, a descendent of John Frederick Hillegas (4).

Boyer.—This family is one of the most extensive and honorable in France. Several branches belong to the nobility. Many have been distinguished as ministers, writers, soldiers and statesmen. A notable representative was the late Cardinal Jean Pierre Boyer (1829-1896), Archbishop of Bourges. Prince Lucien Bonaparte, a brother of the great Napoleon, incurred the latter's displeasure by marrying a beautiful girl named Boyer. Many of this name were Huguenots and were scattered to many lands by the persecutions. Mention is elsewhere made of a distinguished officer of this name in the Swedish Colony on the Delaware, and the set-

---

(1). In 1759 Lemiatta de Blema was married at Goshahoppen.

(2). John Frederick Hillegas was born in Alsace in 1685 and died 1764. His family consisted of Leopold, John Adam, Frederick, George, Peter, Conrad, Elisabeth, Ann Margaret, married to Matthias Richard, Ann Regina and Elis. Barbara.

(3). Michael Hillegas, Jr. (1728-1804), a resident of Philadelphia, was a man of sterling worth and one of the foremost men of his times, and a tower of strength in the dark days of the Revolution. In 1776 he was made the first Treasurer of the United States and was retained in that responsible position until 1789.

(4). Hon. John Richards, son of Matthias and Margaret Hillegas Richards, was b. in New Hanover, Pa., 1753, made a Justice 1777, Judge of the Courts 1784, in Congress 1796-1797, State Senate 1801-1807, died November 13, 1822.

tlement of another family in Lancaster county in 1710, while still another—John Boyer—was one of the first settlers in York county. In the counties of Montgomery and Berks we find several ancestral heads of this name and from which a great posterity has came.

The genealogist is met with insuperable difficulty in tracing out the various lines of Boyers in the Schuylkill Valley. It is a remarkable fact that the name was written *Beyer* and *Bayer* upon arrival. From the subjoined note (1) the reader will see how interchangeable the name was in Colonial days. A large number of immigrants of the name Beyer and Bayer arrived in Pennsylvania, of which we only notice such as are now known as Boyer, and which, in our opinion, was the original name of these families. The pioneers of the Boyers in this region were the following:

In 1728 arrived from Alsace, France, *Jacob Bayer*, with wife and sons *Valentine*, *Philip* and *Jacob*, and located in the present vicinity of Boyertown. Hon. Henry Boyer (1778-1857), a prominent member of the Legislature, was of this line (2). In 1731 arrived *Christop. Beyer* and sons *Andreas* and *Martin*. This family we know settled in Montgomery county and the family record is partly in the Archives of the old Goshahoppen Church. This family is said to have been from Grunstadt in the Palatinate. In this same vessel and at the same date arrived *John Philip Bayer*, *Philip Beyer*, *Philip Beyer*, *Jr.*, *John Jacob Beyer*, *Henry Beyer* and *George Beyer*. The two latter were under sixteen years of age. This family likewise located in Montgomery and Berks counties in close proximity. Soon after arrival we find all the foregoing names written *Boyer*. John Philip Bayer, *Sen.* located in Frederick township, (now) Montgomery county, where he died May 7, 1753, and was buried in Oley, Berks county. His son Henry (1714-1814) lived near Boyertown. A great many of the John Philip Boyer line are buried in the old church yard at Amityville, Berks county. *Gabriel Boyer* was a resident of Oley as early as 1732. In the foregoing arrivals we have at least four separate lines. We are inclined to the belief that there was some connection between them.

---

(1). Naturalized in 1743 in Philadelphia (now Montgomery county), Gabriel Bowyer, Philip Beyer, Abraham Beyer, Jr., 1755, Andrew Boyer, Philadelphia City, 1762, Philip Boyer, Berks county, 1759, Nich. Boyer, 1761, *Jacob Boyer*, 1761, Christopher Boyer, Northampton county, 1761, Andrew Boyer, Land Warrants granted, Gabriel Boyer, 1733-1737, Christian Boyer, 1737, Christopher Boyer, Bucks county, 1738, Johannis Beyer, 1738, Johannis Boyer, 1741, Hans (John) Boyer, 1733, John Boyer, York county, 1754, Andrew Bayer, 1734-1735, Andrew Boyer, 1744, Andrew Boyer, Berks county, 1744, Christopher Poyer, 1737, Philip Boyer, 1761, Jacob Boyer, 1757, do. Berks county, 1751; Elias Boyer, Bucks county, 1738.

(2). Vide Proc. Mont. Co. Hist. Soc., 1895, p. 274; also "Keim and Allied families," p. 556.

Among the descendents of the immigrant, John Philip Boyer, was a grandson, Philip Boyer, *Jr.* (1746-1832), who removed to (now) Snyder county, where he died, leaving an honored posterity. His son, Gen. Philip Boyer, an officer in the war of 1812, remained in Montgomery county. The latter was the father of Hon. Benj. M. Boyer (b. 1823), presiding Judge of the courts of Montgomery county, and a member of Congress 1864-1866. From this family also came Col. Zachur Prall Boyer (1832-1900), who served with distinction in the Civil War, and Hon. Henry K. Boyer (b. 1850), a member of the Legislature in 1887, State Treasurer in 1889, and later Director of the United States Mint at Philadelphia.

Prof. Daniel S. Boyer (1827-1899), a grandson of Philip, Sr., of Snyder county, was prominent as an educator. He was the founder of the Freeburg Academy, and for many years Superintendent of the public schools of Snyder county.

De Frain.—This name, variously written "*De Frain*," *Du Frain, Du Fresne*, etc., occurs in many localities in France and represents an honorable lineage, one branch of which belongs to the nobility of Normandy (1). They were largely Protestant and must have suffered very much from the religious persecutions, as we find refugee families of this name in the Palatinate, Switzerland, England and South Carolina, as well as Pennsylvania. The origin of the earliest family in the latter State is somewhat obscure. Among the passengers of the ship "*Louther,*" which arrived in Philadelphia in 1731, was *Maria Forrain* (2). Circumstances point to her as being the mother of the DeFrain family of Montgomery county. Her husband may have perished at sea. Of this family we have the following: *Martin*, who married prior to 1743; *John*, who married prior to 1746; *Jacob*, born 1730 and confirmed at the trap in 1748; *Peter*, who married in 1753; Elisabeth who, prior to 1747, married Adam Heilman. Also *Christian* and *Frederic*. Muehlenburg, the founder of the Lutheran Church in America, in reporting the confirmation of the above mentioned Elisabeth Du Frain, says her parents were Huguenots, with the inference that she was orphaned in early youth (3).

In 1794 *Louis Fontain De Fresne*, of Paris, took the oath of allegiance at Philadelphia. In 1788 Dr. *Albert Du Fresne*, with his family arrived from Switzerland, whither his people had fled from persecution. He was both a minister and physician. He located at Lancaster and was a prominent citizen (b. 1748; d. 1823).

---

(1). Nobility of Normandy, Vol. II p 103.
(2). Penna Arch, Vol. XVII.
(3). "*Halliche Nachrichten,*" Am. Ed., Vol. I p. 342; also note p. 417.

Pechin.—In 1734 arrived *Pierre Pechin* (1706-1775). The name *Pechin* appears among the Huguenot refugees in Prussia. That Pierre Pechin was of a Huguenot family there is no doubt. He brought with him the old family bible they had preserved through the fires of persecution. This book, several centuries old, is now held by a descendent of the refugee and is sacredly preserved as a memento of the trials through which the family passed. Pierre Pechin was a man of more than ordinary standing and intelligence. He brought with him rare books and furniture and evidently had considerable means. His family consisted of three sons and two daughters, (1) the mother having died at sea during the voyage. He located near Philadelphia where he died in 1775. His remains rest at Ardmore. His son, Jean Christopher, located in Philadelphia and engaged in various enterprises and became one of its foremost and wealthiest citizens.

Purviance.—The *Purviance* family seems to have been terribly scattered at the Revocation as refugee branches are found in England, Ireland and the Palatinate. Four brothers of the Irish branch came to America, namely : *Robert* and *Samuel*, who located in Baltimore ; *John*, who located in Philadelphia, and *William*, who went to North Carolina. *Samuel Purviance*, of the English branch, came to Philadelphia prior to 1693. *David Purviance* came from Lorrain in 1754 and located in Dauphin county.

The Baltimore branch were successful business men and acted as financial agents for the Continental Government during the War of the Revolution. From this branch came Commodore Hugh Purviance, (2) a distinguished naval officer who was born in Baltimore in 1799.

Trego, Tricot, Trico.—Several brothers of this name fled to England prior to the Revocation. In 1683 one of them, *Pierre Trego*, came to Pennsylvania and located in Delaware county, where he died prior to 1735. He was a prominent member of the Society of Friends (3). Pierre and Judith Trego had children— *Jacob*, b. 1687 ; *James*, b. 1690 ; *William*, b. 1693 ; *John*, b. 1696 ; *Ann*, b. 1702 ; *Peter*, married in 1726. The Trego family is very extensive and has produced many distinguished men, of whom may be mentioned *Prof. Charles B. Trego*, a scientist of

---

(1). The family of Pierre Pechin consisted of (1) Jean Nicholas, who died unmarried. (2). Peter, who served in the Revolution and removed to Georgia. (3). Jean Christopher, m. in 1765, Christena Bright, a granddaughter of Jacques Simonett. (5). Margaret, who married George Gyger. (4). Susan, whom. Martin Miller.
(2). Biog. Ency. of Maryland, p. 96.
(3). Vide " History of the Trego Family." by Dr. A. Trego Shertzer.

high repute and author of "A Geographical History of Pennsylvania," published in 1843, and J. K. Trego, a noted artist.

That sturdy old Huguenot, *Louis Dubois*, (1) of Ulster county, N. Y., gave posterity to several of Pennsylvania's best families. A son, *Abraham*, with his daughter, Mrs. Philip Ferree, located in Pequea, as is elsewhere noted. In 1713 his son, *Solomon Dubois* (1670–1759), became joint proprietor of a large tract of land in the Perkiomen Valley and is supposed to have resided there. *Isaac Dubois*, a son of Solomon, became seated on this estate in 1716 and died here in 1729. In this region also located *Daniel Desmond* in 1708, and *John LeFever* in 1718. Both are supposed to have came from Esopus in New York. *Abraham Transue* located here in 1730 and *Philip LaBar* in 1738. In the vicinity of Chestnut Hill, near Germantown, located *Adam Boshong* prior to 1733, also *Carl Val. Nich. Schuette* (Shuey) prior to 1734. In the lower Schuylkill Valley located in 1753 *John* and *Frederick Quay*, probably father and son. The name, also written "*leQuay*," appears among the lists of refugees to England and among the galley slaves. It is evident that many were Protestants and suffered severely in the persecutions. One branch located in Canada and from whence came the ancestor of the Hon. Matthew Stanley Quay, United States Senator, son of a Presbyterian minister, and who was born in York county, Pennsylvania, in 1833.

In 1735 arrived *Christian Bliem* who located north of Pottstown. His ancestors fled from France to the Palatinate prior to the Revocation. (2) Christian was born at New Manheim in 1711 and died in 1811, at the age of a century. His posterity is very numerous.

Delliker.—From 1784 to 1799 *Rev. Frederick Delliker* was pastor of the Reformed congregation in Falkner Swamp. He is said to have been of Huguenot parentage, the family name being *De La Cour*. (3) Many of this name are found among the refugees. Reverend Delliker was a man of great ability and usefulness. He died in 1799 at the Swamp Church in Montgomery county.

In 1749 arrived John Michael Missamer from Alsace, and located in the Falkner Swamp, where he died in 1753. His son, *Cassamir Missamer*, born in Alsace, was a prominent man and founder of an honorable posterity.

(1.) Louis Dubois, one of the twelve patentees of New Paltz, N. Y., who is regarded as the founder of that Colony, was born at Wicres, Prov. of Artois, France, in 1626, fled to Manheim, in the Palatinate, and from thence with the Huguenot Colony to the Hudson River in 1660. He was m. in 1655 to Catherine Blanchard, a daughter of a refugee at Manheim. Vide Chap. IV.
(2). Vide Biog. Ency. of Montgomery Co.
(3). Vide Harbaugh's "Fathers of the Reformed Church."

The name *Baldy* occurs prominently among the Huguenot refugees. Several branches fled to Switzerland and England. In the latter country, Rev. David Baldy was pastor of the Huguenot Church at Norwich from 1693 until his death in 1710. (1)

A family, the head of which has not been identified, located in the Schuylkill Valley at an early day. Of this stock, Conrad Baldy had children baptized at the Falkner Swamp Lutheran Church in 1744. A considerable number of the name from this region appear on the lists of Revolutionary soldiers, some as officers. Of the latter was *Christopher Baldy* of Berks county, who located in the West Branch Valley. He was a captain in the Continental army, and later became a brigadier general in the State service. Late in life he removed to Seneca county, N. Y., where he died in 1809. It is probable that this family is identical with that of *Baldus*, which in France is evidently the same. A number of this name appear in our list of immigrants. (2)

Bigony, (*Bigonet*, *Pichonet*).—The seat of this family is in Languedoc, France. The first of the name here was *Jean Bigonet*, a native of the city of Nisms, who came in 1752. May 27th, 1753, he was married in Germantown, Pa., to Cath. Elizabeth, the widow of Henry Ozias. In 1773 arrived *Francois P. Bigonet*, who located in the Falkner Swamp where he married Maria Brant in 1779.

Lorah.—This name, variously written *Lora*, *Lorey* and *Loreaux*, represents a large and influential Huguenot family scattered during the persecutions, while others less fortunate appear on the list of galley slaves. Refugees of this name appear in England, the Palatinate and Switzerland, while one branch of noble rank has long been seated in Austria. (3) Several branches came to Pennsylvania. There was a *Lorcaux* family located in Philadelphia prior to 1715. *John Conrad Lorah* came to Philadelphia in 1754. He was a man of prominence as also was his son *Casper*. Another son named *Conrad* located at Warwick, Lancaster county, soon after their arrival.

John Lorah located in Oley, Berks county, in 1737, and was one of the founders of the Reformed Church of that place. He died in 1768, leaving an honored posterity. *John Henry Lorah* arrived in 1753 and located in York county, where he died in 1763, leaving posterity.

Lesher, originally written "Le Shar," "Le Char" and "Le Shair." This extensive family was scattered to various Protestant

---

(1). Vide Proc. London Hug. Soc., Vol. II p. 138.
(2). In France the name is also written "Baldus." Several of this name came to Pennsylvania and are probably the ancestors of the Baldy family.
(3). See American Geneologist, Vol. I p. 186.

countries at the Revocation. *Jean Le Shair* was a refugee to Ulster, New York, prior to 1700. Of those who came to Pennsylvania *John Nicholas Lesher* located in Skippack, and *Jacob* in Providence, both in 1732. From one of these came *John Lesher* (2) who located in Oley in Berks county and erected extensive iron works in 1760. Several families of this name also located in Lancaster county.

Votaw–Vautie. Several branches of this family came to America. There was a Vautie fumily in the Huguenot Church in New York prior to 1750. *Pierre Vautie* arrived in 1754 and located in Eastern Pennsylvania. There was a Votaw family said to have located near Philadelphia prior to 1740 from which came *Paul, Isaac and John Votaw*, who emigrated to Loudon county, Virginia (2). We suspect that Pierre Votaw, as above, was the head of this family.

Retteau (Rettew).—This name appears among the refugees to England. *William Rettew*, the head of the family in America, arrived prior to 1725. In 1726 he purchased a warrant for a tract of land in Delaware county on which he located. This land he sold to his son Thomas in 1731, who died without issue, and the plantation fell to John Rettew, brother of Thomas, "his heir-at law," and who obtained a patent for the same in 1752. From this recital we infer that the Rettew posterity descend from John, son of the immigrant.

Some time prior to 1735, *Jean Perdeau* (variously written Barto, Bardo, etc.,) located in Colebrookdale, where he died at an advanced age in 1770, leaving a numerous posterity.

The Somaine (3) (now Sumney) family in the Perkiomen region probably came from *Isaac Somaine*, who in 1758 had six children baptized at the Goshahoppen Reformed Church. A little later, *Samuel Somaine*, probably a brother, was married at the same place.

---

(1). John Lesher, Esq., 1711–1794, was a man of prominence. He was a member of the Constitutional Convention, 1776, a member of the General Assembly from 1776 to 1784, and one of the Commissioners to purchase supplies for the Continental army.

(2). Pa. Mag. of Hist., XIII, 254.

(3). Jean Somaine was a Huguenot galley slave. See Dodderer's Historical Notes p. 46.

CHAPTER VIII.

The Oley Valley.

THE EARLY HUGUENOT SETTLERS—THE PIONEER JOHN KEIM—ARRIVAL OF DETURK AND LEDEE—THE BERTOLETS—THE COUNT DEBENNEVILLE, FOUNDER OF UNIVERSALISM IN AMERICA—THE LE VANS AND DE LA PLANCH—MORAVIAN SYNOD.

> "*O, spirit of that early day*
> *So pure, and strong, and true!*
> *Be with us in the narrow way*
> *Our faithful fathers knew.*"
> —*Whittier.*

ABOUT fifty miles northwest of Philadelphia, and in the eastern part of Berks county in Pennsylvania, is situated a small but exceedingly fertile and beautiful valley called Oley by the first settlers. By the Indians it was called "*Wahlink*" (hill-encircled). The whites were early attracted to this charming vale, and it is said on good authority that the Swedes were familiar with it long before the arrival of William Penn.

Among the first settlers were a number of Huguenot families who, after passing through the fires of persecution in the Old World, were permitted by a beneficent Providence to pass their last days in peace in this garden spot.

Keim.—So far as known the first settler of this region was *John Keim*, whose parental home was near Lindau, in Bavaria. His family was of distinguished ancestry and connected with the eminent Huguenot family of De Harcourt, who were of noble rank.

He first came to the Province in 1698 and seated some land on the head waters of the Manatawny creek. After a stay of several years he returned to his home in Europe where he married in 1706, and took his final departure for Oley the following year. He died on his plantation in 1753, leaving a large family. His posterity is both great and honorable.

Being connected with a number of families who soon thereafter followed him to Oley, it is quite probable that he acted in the capacity of a promoter and pioneer for the rest. (1)

De Turk.—In Northern France there was seated a wealthy and highly honorable family named *De Turk*. Their estates embraced extensive vineyards, and peace and happiness, joined with wealth, justify the family tradition that the home of the De Turks was an ideal one.

Over this bright picture, however, the dark shadows of adversity suddenly fell. The family was Protestant, and when the ominous knell of the Revocation of the Edict of Nantes sounded throughout France in 1685 it fell heavily on the hearts of the family. The heartless dragonades ravished their home while the Government confiscated their property. (2)

Among those who escaped was Isaac De Turk who, with many others, fled to Frankenthal in the Palatinate. Seeing no hope of returning in safety to his native home, he resolved to take advantage of the gracious invitation of Queen Ann, of England, to the Huguenots and Palatines to come to her dominions. Coming to London he joined the party of Reverend Joshua Kocherthal and came with them to New York in the autumn of 1709. In this party was an accomplished young widow named *Marie Wemar* and her little daughter Catharine, nearly three years of age. This lady was connected with a prominent family (De Harcourt), as will be seen presently.

Isaac De Turk, who was a bachelor in middle life, was married to Madame Wemar soon after their arrival in New York. Af-

---

(1). See "Keim and Allied Families," by De B. Randolph Keim, 1899.

(2). In the Proceedings of the London Huguenot Society occur a number of refugees of this name from various parts of France to London, Norwich and the Channel Isles.

Note—John De Turk in 1740 married Deborah High and had children as follows: Isaac, b. 1741, died young; Daniel, b. 1742, m. Catharine Le Van. He served as Captain in the Revolution War; Susanna, b. 1745, m. — Shaffer; John, b. 1747, m. Elisabeth Bertolet; Maria, b. 1748, m. Daniel Weiser; Samuel, b. 1750, m. Cath. Crest; Abraham, b. 1752, m. Ann Weiser; Philip, b. 1757, m. (1) Esther Shenkel, (2) Maria High; Joseph, d. young; Deborah, b. 1761, m. Peter Knabb.

Catharine Wemar, the emigrant's step-daughter (born in France 1706), was married to Abraham Le Van, of Oley.

Esther, the only daughter of the emigrant in 1736, married Abraham Bertolet, died in 1798 leaving a large family.

The immigrant just prior to coming to Pennsylvania sojourned in New York city where his daughter Esther was baptized in the French Church, as is recorded in the church records. "Bateme, Amourdhuy dimanche 29c. d'Avril 1712. Monsieur Louis Rou, ministere, Batise Esther le Turque, nee le 30c. d'Aoust dernier fille de Isaac le Turque et Maria sa femme, presente au St. Bateme par Francois Lucas et la mere du dit enfan parein et Marienne. L. Rou, Pasteur."

(Vide Proc. Hug. Soc. of Am., Vol. I p. 122.)

ter a brief stay at Esopus he came to Oley in 1712 and purchased a tract of land, most of which has remained in the family to the present day. In 1721 he purchased another tract adjoining his own which he presented to his only daughter Esther (Bertolet), whose descendants still occupy the homestead. Isaac De Turk had but two children, namely—*John*, born in 1710, and *Esther*, born in 1712. He did not live long to enjoy his peaceful retreat, but died in 1721 and was buried on his plantation. His widow survived him many years. John De Turk, his son, was a prominent Moravian. The visit of Count Zinzendorf and the holding of the third Moravian Synod at his place was an important event.

Bertolet.—The *Bertolet* family of France has been for centuries one of the highest and most honorable of that country, and many of that name have been among the most distingished in her history. The family, which was originally seated in Picardy, is of noble rank (1). During the reformation the Bertolets seem to have been strongly Protestant and many took refuge in foreign lands owing to the persecutions by the Papists. The name occurs among the refugees to Switzerland, London and the Channel Isles.

BISHOP N. B. GRUBB.
(*A Bertolet Descendant*).

Some time during the Revocation period a family of this name fled from Picardy to Chateau deOex, in the canton of Vaud in Switzerland, and of whom *Peter* and *Jean* came to Pennsylvania. The first to arrive was *Peter*, but the date of his coming is uncertain. In 1720 he signed the petition for the erection of Oley township and died about 1727,

(1). See "Dictionary of the French Nobility," Vol. II p. 386. The name is variously written, "Bertholet" being perhaps the most familiar. Auguste Berthelot, a titled and distinguished officer of the French army, gave his life as a sacrifice to the cause of American freedom at the seige of Yorktown, Va., in 1781. Count Louis de Bertholet, who was born in Savoy in 1748 and died in Paris in 1822, was one of the greatest chemists of the age. Another of this name, Pierre Eugene Marcellain Berthelot, born in Paris, 1827, and likewise a great chemist, and also a great publicist, entered the cabinet of President Fauer in 1895, as minister of Foreign Affairs.

as is recited in an application for a patent for his land in 1734. His wife Elizabeth and several children survived him.

In 1711 *Jean Bertolet* was married to Susanna de Harcourt, of Muhlhausen, near Lindau in Bavaria, to which her parents had fled at the Revocation. (1) On account of political unrest and religious persecution, Jean Bertolet removed to Seltz, in Alsace, about twenty-seven miles north-east of Strasburg. Here he engaged in farming about fourteen years, during which time five children were born to them.

Owing to continued persecutions he determined to emigrate to America. This he did in 1726 after securing a certificate of emigration of which the following is a translation :

"We, the undersigned, High Bailiff, the highest officer of the County Palatine, in the community of Guttenberg, do hereby certify, by virtue of this letter—

That the bearer hereof, the highly honored and unpretending Jean Bertolet, a native of *Chartien Duise*, in the Jurisdiction of Berne, Switzerland, together with his wife, was a tenant of the farm belonging to the Convent Selt—which is here located and highly regarded—and behaved himself in a Christian, honorable, upright and faithful manner as it becomes an honest and praiseworthy man, so that we can say nothing otherwise about him than what is commendable and good, and that they both honestly intend and have finally determined to emigrate to the New Country of Pennsylvania, together with their five children, whom they have with them.

Therefore we, each and every one of us, do kindly request that the above-named Jean Bertolet, and his wife Susanna and five children, may not only pass free, safe and unmolested without exacting from them any duty or respect, obedience or service, but that they may be shown all manner of good will and assistance because of their honorable behavior, and we are willing and do kindly offer to return the same favor.

---

(1). *Note*—Both Mrs. Isaac De Turk and Mrs. Jean Bertolet were daughters of Jean De Harcourt, a prominent citizen of Muehlhausen in Lower Alsace and of the French nobility. The De Harcourts were mostly Protestants and seem to have suffered severely through persecution, as the name appears among the refugees to various Protestant countries, notably England.

Among the notable men of this name may be mentioned Henri De Harcourt (1601-1666), who was a famous General. Duke Henri De Harcourt (1653-1703), a General and Marshal of France. Francois Henri De Harcourt (1726-1792) and Francois Harcourt (1786-1865), and also the Hon. Sir William Vernon Harcourt (1827) of England, the successor of Gladstone to the leadership of the Liberal party, who descends from Count Richard De Harcourt, one of the Norman Knights who accompanied William the Conqueror to England in A. D. 1066.

In testimony whereof we have, together with subscribing our own signatures, attached our customary Seal hereunto. So ordered and issued in the Jurisdiction of the High Bailiff of Wimpfeldten, this twenty-ninth day of April, in the year of our Lord one thousand seven hundred and twenty-six.

J. G. WIMPFFEN,
NICHOLAUS SCHOENLAUB,
Attorney.

The Seal of the Court. { L. S. }

ATTEST :—HANS ERHARD BEYER.

Jean Bertolet located in Oley, near the Exeter line, and not far from Mordecai Lincoln, the ancestor of the great President, and George Boon, the ancestor of *Daniel*, the pioneer of Kentucky.

Jean Bertolet was noted for his deep piety and benevolence. He was wont to visit his Indian neighbors and relieve their wants and often gave them religious instruction and prayed with them in their humble cabins. He was one of the first Moravians of Oley and on terms of the closest intimacy with the leading men of the Church, especially Count Zinzendorf, who preached in his house in 1741 and 1742. (1)

Jean Bertolet died in 1754 (2) and was buried on his estate, his wife having preceeded him. It may be here remarked that the references to the Bertolets as being Swiss Germans is incorrect. They were characteristic Huguenots and French was their mother language. The French bible of Jean Bertolet, printed by Francois Perrin in 1567, and which was doubtless carried by earlier generations through the fires of persecution, is still preserved by his descendants and contains his family records and other valuable notes written in French.

Jean Bertolet founded a numerous and honorable posterity, and many of his descendants have been eminent in many walks of

---

(1). "Memorials of the Moravian Church," Vol. I p. 175.
(2). The family of Jean Bertolet consisted of the following: Abraham, b. 1712, d. 1776, married to Esther De Turk with whom he had a large family; Maria, 1715-1802, married to Stephen Barnett; John, 1717-1789, married to a daughter of Peter Pallio; Esther, 1720-1796, married to Dr. George De Bonneville; Susanna, 1722-1800, married to Jacob Fry; Frederick, 1727-1779, b. in America, married to Esther, a daughter of Abraham Le Van.

life, of whom Bishop N. Bertolet Grubb is a notable example. (1)

De Bonneville.—In the year 1741 there arrived in Philadelphia a young Huguenot nobleman, *Dr. George De Bonneville*, whose history calls for more than a passing notice.

The family of De Bonneville is one of the oldest and most honorable of the French nobility, and the reader will find many references to the Lords of Bonneville in the history of France. Their estates were situated near Limoges, the capitol of the Department of Haute-Vienna, and date back to the eleventh century.

Several branches of the De Bonneville family espoused the Protestant cause. Upon the accession of William III. to the throne of England he invited Francis De Bonneville, a prominent Huguenot nobleman, to his Court where he enjoyed great favor.

A son of Francis married into the Granville family in 1697. Of this union was born in 1703 George De Bonneville, the subject of this sketch. The parents dying early, the child was taken under the personal care of Queen Ann, who spared no pains to perfect his education. He was highly educated in theology and medicine, and spoke fluently many European languages. At the early age of seventeen years he went to France to preach the Gospel to the persecuted Huguenots. For two years he was engaged in this work, holding services in secluded places in order to evade the authorities. At last he, with his companion Durant, was arrested, and upon trial were both condemned to death, De Bonneville to be beheaded, and Durant to be hanged. They were then taken to the place of execution. Durant being designated to suffer first, ascended the scaffold joyfully singing the 116th Psalm and died a martyr to the Protestant faith! After this De Bonneville was bound and blindfolded and the executioner made the final preparations to behead him when a reprieve arrived from the King (Louis XV.), obtained through the British ambassador, Queen Ann, of England, having interceded in his behalf. After his release he traveled through Germany, Holland and Flanders, preaching the gospel to the scattered Huguenot refugees for a period of about eighteen years. His health failing entirely he felt constrained to emigrate to the New World. In fact he regarded this inclination as divinely inspired and so took up his journey as a religious duty.

---

(1). Bishop Nathaniel Bertolet Grubb was b. in Montgomery County, Pa., 1850, and is a direct descendant of the Grubb family of Switzerland that suffered martyrdom for their faith. He also descends from Henry Fry, who came from Alsace to Pennsylvania prior to Wm. Penn; also, from the Huguenots of Oley, Isaac De Turk and Jean Bertolet. He entered the ministry of the Mennonite Church in 1872. He was elevated to the episcopacy in 1884. Earnest in spirit, broad-minded in his religious views, he has readily affiliated with the most progressive leaders of Christian work in America, and stands out prominently as a leader in his Church in the field of Christian effort.

The arrival of De Benneville (Americanized form of name), in Philadelphia in 1741 is thus related by a grandson of Christopher Sower, the celebrated German Colonial printer of Germantown: (1)
"Upon a certain occasion Mr. Sower had a dream that a vessel had arrived at Philadelphia having on board a person who was very ill and whispering that he should bring him to his house. He awoke and found it but a dream, and again fell asleep when the dream was repeated. Mentioning the dream to his wife she urged him to do as he was bid. He drove to the city, six miles distant, and upon making inquiry at the wharf, the captain of a vessel informed him that he had a very sick man on board, whom Mr. Sower at once removed to his carriage and took to his home, and where he remained until he was restored to health. After De Benneville's recovery, being skilled in medicine, he assisted in the preparation of prescriptions." (Sower was also proprietor of a drug store).

At the home of Sower he first met Jean Bertolet, of Oley, who was delighted with his many accomplishments and manifest piety. Upon Bertolet's invitation he settled in Oley as a teacher and physician, and in 1745 he married his daughter Susanna. In 1755 he removed to Germantown where he enjoyed a large and lucrative practice in medicine. Here he died in 1793 at the patriarchial age of ninety years, leaving a highly honorable posterity. (2)

De Benneville was not closely allied with any religious denomination in America. He was a Restorationist in belief, and his views on human redemption were too broad and liberal for the narrow sectarianism of his day. He was, nevertheless, an acceptable preacher and traveled far and wide, even in old age preaching the Gospel. About 1745 he erected a large stone edifice near his father-in-law and which is still standing. This building is of peculiar historical interest as being the undoubted birthplace of Universalism in America. In this edifice De Benneville had a large room fitted as a chapel where he was wont to preach the doctrine of universal redemption to his friends and neighbors who gathered to hear him. On June 12, 1890, during a convention of Universalists in Reading, that body of over a hundred in number journeyed to this historic spot and in a befitting manner honored the memory of the founder of American Universalism.

As indicating the high esteem in which the De Benneville family was held by the Court of France, it is a well established fact

---

(1). See "Keim and Allied Families," p. 373.
(2). Family of Dr. George de Benneville and his wife Esther Bertolet: *Daniel* (1753-1827), a noted surgeon of the Revolution ; *George* (1760-1850), a noted physician and on terms of friendship with Washington ; *Esther*, married to Jacob Brown ; *Susanna*, m. to John Keim ; *Marie*, m. to John Linnington ; *Charlotte*, m. to John Bertolet ; *Sarah*, ——.

that during the reactionary period as the result of the Revocation, Louis XVI. sent a commission to America to induce Dr. George De Benneville to return to France and assist in the work of pacification. He wisely refused the overtures of that monarch, and the Kingdom not many years later paid the penalty of her intolerance in the terrors of the French Revolution. (1)

LeVan.—Among the members of the Huguenot Church at Amsterdam, Holland, was *Daniel LeVan* and his wife *Marie Beau*, refugees from Picardy, France. From a baptismal certificate, a fac simile of which is given, it seems that some of their children were born at Amsterdam. About 1715 four sons of the refugee set out for Pennsylvania. They were *Abraham, Isaac, Jacob* and *Joseph*, the latter of whom died at sea. These were followed in 1727 by their brother *Daniel*, and all of whom settled in the limits of Berks County.

In 1748 *Peter LeVan* arrived, whose identity and place of location is not known.

Abraham LeVan, as already noted, married Catharine Weimer, daughter of Mrs. De Turk by a former husband in France. He located near the De Turk's, and his beautiful home is still in the possession of his descendents after a lapse of almost two centuries. (2)

Jacob LeVan located in the Maxatawny Valley, of which he was one of the first settlers. He was an extensive land owner, the present flourishing town of Kutztown being built on part of his estate. He erected the first grist mill in this region, which is still in the possession of his descendents. (3)

There is a family tradition that Count Zinzendorf, the eminent Moravian, preached from the balcony of this mill during his episcopal tour in America in 1742. Jacob LeVan was an important personage in the Province. He was one of the judges of the county court from 1752 to 1762. He bore an important part in the defense of the frontiers during the French and Indian war and was commissioned to provision Fort Allen in 1756. His son, *Sebastian LeVan*, was a man of great prominence. At the outbreak of the

---

(1). See K. and A. Families, p. 670.
(2). Abraham LeVan was b. in Amsterdam 1698 and died in 1771, leaving a wife and children—Daniel, Isaac, Esther Bertolet, Susan Mowry and Catharine. His daughter, Elizabeth Reeser, having preceeded him. His wife, Catharine Weimer, daughter of Mrs. Isaac De Turk, was b. in France, Feb. 22, 1706, and d. Sept. 29, 1768.
(3). Jacob LeVan d. 1768, leaving children—Col. Sebastian LeVan, m. to Susan Snyder; Jacob, Jr., m. 1763 to Susanna Ludwig and d. 1778; Catharine, m. to Valentine Brobst; Elizabeth, m. to Geo. Adam Snyder; Susanna, m. to Charles Neudorf; Eve, m. Peter Yoder, 1762; Maria, m. (1) Jacob Huttenstein, (2) Frederick Hill.

Revolution he represented his district in the Committee of Safety. He was a member of the State Assembly in 1779-1789, and a member of the Supreme Executive Council from 1782 to 1784. He was also a Colonel of militia. He died in 1794.

Daniel LeVan, the emigrant, also settled in Maxatawny. (1) His son, *Daniel Jr.*, was admitted to the bar at Reading in 1768 and became a lawyer of considerable prominence. After filling many important offices he died in 1792.

Isaac LeVan, the emigrant, located in Exeter, near Reading, and where he died in 1758.

Jean LeDee was a neighbor and contemporary settler with Isaac De Turk in 1712. He was one of the petitioners for the erection of the township in 1720.

De la Planch.—One of the first settlers of Oley was *Dr. Jacques De la Planch* (now " Plank "), who has the distinction of having been the first physician of Berks county. His history is an interesting one. Some time after the Revocation his parents made their escape from France by crossing the Alps into Switzerland. While crossing the border the father was arrested by the guards. The mother, however, succeeded in making her escape with Jacques, her only child, and accompanied by a faithful St. Bernard dog. Later her husband having escaped, rejoined her at Basel. James was educated for the medical profession at the university at Basel, and soon after the completion of his studies the family emigrated to America. After a residence of several years in Germantown he removed to Oley and was one of the petitioners for the erection of the township in 1720.

Dr. De la Plank was prominent in religious circles and was a member of the Union Synod held at the house of John De Turk in Oley in 1742 and presided over by Count Zinzendorf.

Dr. De la Plank had but one son, Frederick, who inherited his father's estate in Maxatawny. Peter Plank, grandson of the emigrant (1745-1831), was an eminent minister of the Amish branch

---

(1.) Daniel LeVan died at an advanced age in 1777, leaving a wife Susan and children Peter, Barbara Reeser, Catharine, Mary Siegfried, Susan Kempf, Magdalena, Margaret and Daniel.

NOTE.—It is a significant circumstance that in the same vessel in which Peter Herbine in 1732 came to Philadelphia there also appears in the list of women and children the names of Anna LeVan, 'Christian LeVan, Margaret LeVan, Philip LeVan and Barbara LeVan (Arch. XVII). In 1733 Anna Elizabeth LeVan was married to Sebastian Simmerman in Maxatawny. She was probably a sister to Jacob LeVan, who lived there. In 1731 Sebastian Zimmerman and Anna Elisabeth and Anna Maria LeVan, of Maxatawny, were sponsors at a christening. (Stœver's Records, p. 4 and 54).

of the Mennonite Church, and for upwards of fifty years one of the bishops. Another descendent is the Hon. Joseph C. Bucher. (1)

Dr. De la Plank died in 1760, and his wife, Mary Catharine, in 1773. Their children were *Frederick, Catharine* Shaffer, *Mary* Keim and *Susanna*. The family emanates from the nobility of Picardy (2) and has given many eminent names to the history of France. The Ver Planks and De Planks, early settlers on the Hudson, are said to spring from the same stock.

Udree.—In this connection we may notice the Hon. *Daniel Udree*, a son of Henry Udree, whose ancestors are believed to have been Piedmontese refugees. Daniel Udree was born in Philadelphia in 1751, and when still quite young became connected with the iron industry in Oley. He served throughout the Revolution, first as Captain and later as Colonel of the Second Batallion of Berks County militia, and was in command at the battle of Brandywine and (probably) Germantown. Later he was a Major General of State troops in the war of 1812, served in the Legislature and also in Congress, and died July 15, 1826. His monument may be seen in the Oley Reformed churchyard. General Udree was a man of commanding energy and ability.

Moravian Synod.

Mention has been made of the preaching of Count Zinzendorf at the house of John De Turk in Oley. One of these meetings constitutes an epoch in the history of the Moravian Church, and especially in regard to the conversion to Christianity of the North American Indians, in which work they have been eminently successful.

This meeting, which was held February 21–22, 1742, (3) was the Third Moravian Synod, attended by all the dignitaries of the Church, including Count Zinzendorf. At this Synod Andrew Eschenbach, Christian H. Rauch, Gottlieb Buettner and John Christopher Pyrlæus were ordained as ministers by Count Zinzendorf and Bishop David Nitchman, and the Rev. John Hagan was solemnly set apart as a missionary. At this meeting it was resolved to

---

(1). The Hon. Joseph Casper Bucher, son of Rev. John Casper Bucher, D. D., an eminent Reformed minister, was b. in Middletown, Md., January 26, 1836. He became a lawyer of distinction. In 1871 he was elected presiding Judge of the XXth Judicial District of Pennsylvania. He was re-elected in 1881 and retired in 1891.

(2). *Arms*—D'argent, billete de sable, au lion du meme, lampasse et arme de gueles, et un baton aussi du meme en bande, brochant sur le tout (Science des Armoiries, p. 243).

(3). See "Memorials of the Moravian Church," Vol. I p. 180—"Loskiel's History of Missions," Part II p. 21—Rupp's History of Berks County, p. 237.

abandon the attempt to colonize Georgia, in consequence of which many who had already settled there later came to Pennsylvania. On this occasion three Indians were baptized who are said to have been the first fruits of the Moravians among the Aborigines. The important ceremony is thus described by Loskiel : "The whole Assembly being met the three catecheumens were placed in the midst, and with fervent prayer and supplication devoted to the Lord Jesus Christ as His eternal property, upon which Rauch, with great emotion of heart, baptized these three firstlings of the North American Indians into the death of Jesus, in the name of the Father, Son and Holy Ghost, calling Sabash, *Abrahan*—Seim, *Isaac*—and Kiop, *Jacob*." The meeting was rendered all the more memorable from the fact that a large number of Delaware Indians had gathered there, and to whom the missionaries preached and gave religious instruction, and not until the dawn of the morning did the meeting close.

John De Turk donated several acres of land to the Moravians for church and school purposes. A church was erected here about 1743, and several Mission houses between 1745 and 1748 in which they maintained a flourishing school for a number of years. One of these buildings is still standing in a good state of preservation.

CHAPTER IX.

The Alsatians and Lorraines.

STRASBOURG—SEIZURE OF THE CITY BY THE FRENCH—SURRENDER OF THE PROVINCES—PERSECUTION AND FLIGHT OF THE INHABITANTS—EMIGRATION TO PENNSYLVANIA—ALSACE—MANATAWNY—MEN OF MARK—GOVERNORS RITNER AND BEAVER.

> "*What sought they thus afar ?*
> *Bright jewels of the mine ?*
> *The wealth of seas, the spoils of war ?*
> *They sought at faith's pure shrine.*
> *Aye! call it holy ground,*
> *The soil where first they trod,*
> *The've left unstained what there they found—*
> *Freedom to worship God.*"

IN the northeastern part of France was situated the beautiful Province of Alsace, with its magnificent city of Strasbourg, founded by the Romans near the beginning of the Christian Era. This city during the early Reformation period had a semi-independent character, being what is known as an "*Imperial*" city.

With the great theologian, Dr. Sturm, at its head, it was for many years one of the great bulwarks of religious liberty in Germany, and multitudes of exiled Protestants found a refuge under its protecting walls.

In 1681 the city was treacherously seized by the French King, Louis XIV., the despot who, in 1685, revoked the Edict of Nantes and drenched his dominion with the blood of the Huguenots. The entire Valley of the Rhine, as elsewhere noted, was utterly devastated by the French. Through a lack of unity of the German nation the Sovereigns of the Rhine Provinces were unable to resist the overwhelming foe and they were ceded to France in 1697 by the Peace of Ryswick. The German people, however, could never be reconciled to their loss, and never rested until they were regained as the result of the Franco-Prussian war in 1871.

After gaining possession of Alsace and Lorraine the Protestant religion, while tolerated by the terms of the treaty, was practically interdicted, which led many thousands to emigrate to Switzerland, Holland and America.

Although the great victory of the Allies under the Duke of Marlboro at Blenheim in the Palatinate in 1704 was a crush ng blow to the Papists, nevertheless the subsequent withdrawal of the Duke and his forces rendered the outlook of the Protestants anything but promising. We have therefore, in addition to religious intolerance, the horrors of war as a ground for the Huguenot, Mennonite and Palatine emigration to Pennsylvania.

Thousands of Alsatians and Lorraines came to Pennsylvania, but having so much in common with their Palatine neighbors their identity was almost lost in the general exodus. The Lorraines were mostly French in name and fewer in numbers than the Alsatians. The latter, nevertheless, possessed distinct traits of character which distinguished them from the mass of German emigrants, a distinction so marked as to be traceable at the present day. In common' with the Huguenots their advocacy of liberty, and justice has led an unusual proportion of their descendants into positions of prominence. A very considerable number of them located in Eastern Pennsylvania, especially in the Valley of the Schuylkill.

So numerous were the Alsatians in the present limits of Berks that when the County was erected in 1752 a township immediately north of Reading was named in their honor. "Tradition has it that the Huguenots and German Reformers held religious meetings within a mile or two of Reading, and in conformity with the old custom of their fathers in Europe, conducted their worship in the evening as well as in the day time. They cultivated a spirit of genuine piety and often met after night in each others houses for social prayers. For the purpose of public worship they erected a church of logs. Later the Germans and Swedes worshiped in it until 1751 when the Lutherans erected a church in Reading." (1)

The foregoing, from an author who is recognized as an authority on the Pennsylvania immigrants, makes it probable that the Huguenots made use of their own language and religious forms in their worship. This is not improbable when we consider their numbers in the vicinity of Reading. The slight difference between their worship and that of the Reformed, together with the predominance of the German language, naturally tended to obliterate their identity in the course of a few decades.

The following of undoubted Huguenot antecedents were of the early settlers of this locality and taxables in 1756: Dubree, Jacob, Bolieu, Jacob (now Boiler), Le Mar, John (now Lemmer), Gehret, George and Peter, Gannett, Adam, Noel, William, Le Van, Isaac, Perlett, John, Le Beau, John, Ritner, John Abraham, Lanciscus, George (died 1755), Hoyer, Carl.

In the Maxatawny Valley, northeast of Reading, a considerable number of French people, chiefly Alsatians and Lorraines, located. The name *Horry* (2) and *Pickett* (3) occurs here prior to 1730. These families probably removed south as they disappeared in a short time.

A notable arrival was the Kieffer brothers in 1748. The family name in France was *Tonnellier*. At the Revocation of the Edict of Nantes (1685), the family fled to Deux Ponts (Zweibrucken) for safety, and like many others changed their name for a German equivalent which, in their case, was Kieffer (Cooper). Owing to the devastation of the country by the French armies the sons determined to emigrate. *Abraham* and *Casper* came to Pennsylvania and settled near the present town of Kutztown, while *Martin* and *Michael*, two younger brothers, came to Baltimore in 1765. (4) The Kieffer posterity is both numerous and honorable and has given many names of highest worth to both church and state. One especially, whose name is worthy of honor, is that of Daniel Kieffer, of Oley, Berks county, a plain and unassuming farmer who bequeathed the sum of ten thousand dollars for the endowment of a theological school for the Reformed Church and which was the first gift of that character received by that denomination.

---

(1). Rupp's Hist. of Berks Co., p. 447.
(2). A family of this name was among the Huguenot refugees to South Carolina prior to 1690, ancestors of Gen. Horry, of the Revolution.
(3). See Stoever's Records, p. 53.
(4). Letter of Rev. J. Spangler Kieffer, D. D., to the author.

The *Gobin* family, originally Cobean, comes from an Alsatian refugee, the date of whose arrival is unknown. A son *Charles* was a captain in the Revolution from Berks county. After the war he located at Sunbury. He was the great grandfather of General J. P. S. Gobin, (1) of Lebanon, Pa.

Markle.—One of the earliest Alsatian emigrants to Pennsylvania was *John Christman Merklen* (2) Markley). At the Revocation period his parents retired to Amsterdam, in Holland, from whence John Christman came to the Maxatawny Valley and located at Moslem Springs. *Gaspard Markley*, a son of the emigrant, in 1771 became a trans-Allegheny pioneer and settled at West Newton, in Westmoreland county, where he erected the first mill west of the mountains. He also erected a stockade fort for the protection of the frontier settlers. (3) Some of the descendents of Gaspard Markley became prominent men, notably his son, *General Joseph Markley* (b. 1777, d. 1868), who was for many years prominent in the business and political affairs of Western Pennsylvania. In 1844 he was the Whig candidate for Governor, but was defeated by his opponent, Francis R. Shunk, by a small plurality.

De Long.—The progenitor of the De Long family was *Peter De Long*, (4) originally De Lang, who came to Maxatawny at an early day from New York, where the family had located. The family name will ever be distinguished by the heroic achievements of Lieut. George W. De Long, of the American navy and leader of the ill-fated Jeanette Polar expedition, in which he perished. (5)

Girardin.—The Girardin family (name variously written ''Sheradin,'' ''Cheretin,'' etc.), was established in the Maxatawny Valley, the emigrant ancestor being *Jacob*, who arrived in 1748. Other emigrants of this name and who came to Berks county were doubtless connections.

Ritner.—There is no name that shines with greater lustre on the page of Pennsylvania history than that of Joseph Ritner (1780–

(1.) J. P. S. Gobin was born in 1837. He entered the War for the Union in 1861, retiring from service in 1865 with the rank of Brevet Brigadier General; appointed a Brigadier General in the Spanish-American War by President McKinley; entered the Senate of Pennsylvania 1884: elected Lieutenant Governor 1898.

(2). See Keim and Allied Families, p. 301. The emigrant was born in 1678 and died 1766, leaving children: Peter, George, Christian, Casper, Catharine Stover, Frankina Rough, Mary Hill, Anna Maria Kramer and Anna Lena. Will at Reading.

(3). Frontier Forts of Pennsylvania, Vol. II p. 381.

(4). Peter De Long died at an advanced age in 1760, leaving children: John, Henry, Jacob, Michael, Abraham, Frederick and Barbara. Will at Reading.

(5). Lieut. George W. De Long was born n New York city in 1844. Becoming deeply interested in Arctic explorations, he was sent on detached service to the Polar regions 1879-80, in which he and nearly all his party perished after terrible suffering.

1869). In 1750 his grandfather, *John Abraham Ritner*, bade adieu to his war-scourged home in Alsace and came to Pennsylvania and settled in Berks county. The family was originally seated in Silesia and was of noble origin. One of the sons of the emigrant was *Michael*, who was a soldier in the Revolution and the father of our subject. When still quite young he settled in the Cumberland Valley and at Newville he married Susan Alter, a farmer's daughter. He soon rose to a high degree of public favor and was called to fill many important public offices. He was elected Governor of the Commonwealth in 1835. The acts establishing the public school system had been passed under the administration of his predecessor, Governor Shultz, but did not meet with popular approval and was in imminent danger of repeal when Ritner was inducted into the office.

In his message in 1836 Governor Ritner took such advanced grounds, not only on the subject of popular education but on other great moral and humanitarian questions, especially slavery, as to attract the attention of the entire nation. By his conservation and development of the free school system Governor Ritner conferred a lasting benefit on the Commonwealth while his strong anti-slavery utterances had great weight in shaping national sentiment for its subsequent abolition.

In his advocacy of popular education and other beneficent measures Governor Ritner was fortunate in having the support of Pennsylvania's great Commoner, the Hon. Thaddeus Stevens, who in a great speech in advocacy of the Governor's measures, made the famous expression, "*I shall place myself unhesitatingly in the ranks of him whose banner streams in light.*"

The brave and advanced sentiments of Governor Ritner's message of 1836 was made the subject of a lengthy and stirring lyric by the poet, John Greenleaf Whittier. We herewith give the opening stanza:

> "*Thank God for the token! one lip is still free!*
> *One Spirit untrammeled, unbending one knee,*
> *Like the oak in the mountain, deep rooted and firm,*
> *Erect when the multitude bends to the storm;*
> *When traitors to freedom, and honor, and God,*
> *Are bound to an idol, polluted with blood.*
> *When the recreant North has forgotten her trust,*
> *And the lip of her honor is low in the dust;*
> *Thank God that one arm from the shackle has broken!*
> *Thank God that one man as a freeman has spoken!*"

He was born in 1780 and died in 1869, and was buried at Mount Rock, about eight miles west of Carlisle, Pa., in an obscure graveyard where his grave was neglected. The Pennsylvania Legislature in 1901 made an appropriation to place a suitable monument at his grave which has not yet been done.

Oley Hills.—In the hill country contiguous to the Maxatawny and Oley Valleys were seated a large number of Alsatians and Lorraines at an early day. Among them were the *Reidenours,* (1) *Mosers,* (2) *Gerbers,* (3) *De la Camps,* (4) *Beavers, John Ruhlin, Matthieu Morrett, Nicholas Querin, John George Riehl, Henry Linville, John Mich. Grauel.* The latter arrived in 1733 with a large family and died in 1753.

The Beaver Family.—We learn from the "Hill Church" records that the family of *John George Beaver* came to Pennsylvania in 1732 from Rosenthal, in Alsace. An examination of the archives shows that the ship "Pink" arrived in this year with a very large number of Alsatians, among whom were *Christena, Dorothy* and *Jacob Beaver,* the latter a minor. From a family record we learn that among these was *Anna Sabina Beaver,* b. 1719 and married in 1740 to John Hess, of Oley. It is probable that the father died on the passage to America.

In 1741 arrived from Alsace "*Dieble*" (Dewalt) *Beaver,* aged 43 years, and sons John George, aged 21, John Jacob, aged 19, and "Dieble" Jr. (Dewalt), aged 16 years. They located in the Alsatian Colony in the Oley Hills, a few miles south of Kutztown. It is probable that Dewalt Beaver was a brother of John George, already noticed. This family became very extensive and in Colonial times many of them located on the frontiers. Their early family records may be seen in the archives of the "Mertz" Lutheran Church of that vicinity.

---

(1). John Reidenour, a son of Nicholas and Susanna Reidenour, of Rosenthal, was born in 1690, was married in 1716 and came to America in 1739, died 1755, John and Maria Catharine Reidenour had children as follows: John, b. 1717, d. 1721; George, b. 1718, m. Elisabeth Klippinger and removed to Western Maryland where many of his descendents are found; George Nicholas, b. 1720, did not come to America until 1764; Margaret, b. 1722, m. to John Nicholas Philips; John, b. 1723, m. Elis. Herbine; John Jacob, b. 1725, d. y.; Cath. Barb., b. 1728, m. Peter Kohn; Christina, b. 1729, m. John Adam Forch; Christopher, b. 1731; Maria Ellis, m. 1733 Conrad Smith; Maria Albertina, b. 1735, d. y.; Elisabeth, b. 1737, d. y.; Anna Ursula, b. 1740.

(2). In 1727 arrived the Rosenthal branch of the Moser family, and which was probably connected with others that came from Wurtemberg later. In the above were John Paul, Christian and Jost Moser, probably brothers. John Paul was a son of Nicholas and Maria Elis. Moser, of Rosenthal, and was b. 1697, m. in 1723 Maria Barb. Cassel. They had children: Maria Elis., b. 1724; Francois, b. 1730; Maria Christena, b. 1733; John, b. 1743, d. y.

(3). Gerber.—In 1738 arrived John Christian Gerber, age 46, and George Michael Gerber, age 32 years, from Alsace. They were probably brothers. John Christian settled in the Oley hills.

(4.) De la Camp.—Henry De la Camp settled in the Hills 1753 and where he carried on the manufacture of cutlery for many years.

Of the foregoing John George Beaver had a son, John George, Jr., who served with distinction in the Revolution. The latter had a son, *Peter Beaver* (1782–1849), who became a pioneer minister in the Methodist Episcopal Church and was one of the first ministers of that denomination in America to preach in the German language. He was one of the first ministers of this church in the interior of Pennsylvania and died at New Berlin in (now) Union county, where a granite monument marks his resting place and recounts his labors for humanity.

Rev. Peter Beaver was the grandfather of General James A. Beaver, of Bellefonte, Pa., a gallant soldier of the Civil War, elected Governor of Pennsylvania 1887, made a Judge of the Superior Court of Pennsylvania 1895, of which office he is still an incumbent.

Another eminent descendant of Dewalt Beaver is Prof. George G. Groff, M. A., M. D., professor of organic sciences in Bucknell University, and late U. S. medical inspector of Porto Rico, whose reputation is world-wide as an authority on sanitary and economic science.

In 1768 arrived from Deux Ponts the brothers *Michael*, *Valentine* and *Jacob Biever* (now Beeber), a branch of the same family already noted. They located in the West Branch Valley. From this latter stock comes Judge Dimmer Beeber, of Philadelphia.

In 1817 two brothers, *Melchoir* and *Rudolph Hoch* (High), arrived from Alsace and located in the Schuylkill Valley. In 1725 Rudolph Hoch located in Oley near the De Turks. The Hoch posterity is both numerous and honorable.

The head of the Herbein family fled from France at the Revocation and found asylum in the Palatinate where the name was Germanized. About 1717 a son, *Jonathan Herbein*, arrived and located in Oley. His name appears on the list of petitioners for the erection of the township in 1720. In 1732 *Peter Herbein* arrived. In 1733 we find *Jonathan*, *Peter* and *Abraham Herbein* possessed of extensive plantations in Oley. The supposition is that they were brothers.

In 1730 arrived from Alsace the brothers *John Valentine* and *Casper Griesamer*, both of whom established families. The former located in Goshahoppen in Montgomery, and the latter in Oley, Berks county, where the village of Griesamersville perpetuates the name.

In 1737 *John Jacob Kauffman* arrived from Alsace and also located in Oley, but later removed to Chester county. He received a good education in the city of Strasbourg, his native place, but was compelled to emigrate because of religious persecution. He was for many years a bishop in the Amish branch of the Mennonite Church.

About 1729 *Conrad Reif* arrived from Alsace and located in Oley. His connection with *Jacob Reif*, a prominent citizen of Skippack who came some years earlier, is not known.

In Exeter township, Berks county, bordering along the Schuylkill, a number of Alsatians and Lorraines located. Among others were the *Hugetts*, of whom *George* was a taxable in 1734, and *Peter*, who arrived in 1737. These were heads of families upon arrival. The *Aurands*, from Alsace, were also early arrivals, *Peter* prior to 1737, and *John* prior to 1744. John Aurand, who arrived in 1753, is elsewhere noted. John Willer, who died in 1761, was also an early resident. A Marquett family was early seated in Amity. The Berks county branch derive their ancestry from *Peter* (1763-1810), a son of the immigrant. There was evidently some connection between this family and *John Henry Marquett*, who located in Lebanon county prior to 1743.

CHAPTER X.

The Upper Delaware and Lehigh Region.

HUGUENOT SETTLERS OF BUCKS, NORTHAMPTON AND MONROE COUNTIES—DENORMANDY—BESSONETT—LAVALLEAU—SANTEE—DUCORSON—DETRAY—DEBOLIEU—JOURDAN—LABAR—TOHICKEN—THE REMARKABLE SETTLEMENT OF THE MINISINK—DEPEW FAMILY—MICHELET—BALLIET—GRIMM—THE MORAVIANS—LATROBE—DESCHWEINITZ—CLEVEL—LABAR—LAWALL—LAMAR.

> "*They are slaves who will not choose*
> *Hatred, scoffing and abuse,*
> *Rather than in silence shrink*
> *From the truth they needs must think;*
> *They are slaves who dare not be*
> *In the right with two or three.*"
> —*L. L. Lowell.*

THE settlements in the region embraced in the counties of Bucks, Monroe and Lehigh were greatly augmented by the still earlier settlements on the eastern side of the Delaware. Among the settlers were many Huguenots who came from the Colonies of New Jersey, Long Island, Staten Island and Esopus in New York. Many of them located in Bristol and vicinity.

DeNormandy.—Among the first residents of Bristol was the *DeNormandy* family who descended from the nobility of France. (1) The heads of the house were the Lords De la Mothe. In A. D. 1460 Guillaume DeNormandy was made Governor of Noyon. He was distinguished both for piety and energy, and the Chapel of St. Claire, which he founded, is a fit memorial to his devotion. His wife was a princess in her own right, being a daughter of the Lord De Mialle d'Aisilly and Montiscourt.

Laurent DeNormandy, a descendent of Guilliaume, became prominent in the Reformation. He was on terms of closest intimacy with John Calvin, the leader of the Reformation in France, and was the executor of his will, having with him removed to Geneva, in Switzerland, on account of persecution.

Both Laurent DeNormandy and his sons became prominent in the affairs of the Swiss Republic. Jean DeNormandy was one of the deputies of the Swiss Government to conclude a treaty of peace with the Prince of Savoy in 1603. Joseph, a son of Jean, was also a man of prominence, as was also Michael, son of Joseph.

The American branch came from *Andre*, born in 1651 and a son of Michael. Andre was also a man of note and was in the service of Frederick the Great many years and was his confidential agent at Neufchatel. In 1706 he emigrated to Pennsylvania and located in Bristol where he died in 1724. His son *Abraham* married in 1715 a daughter of Dr. Francis Gandonet, as also his brother John Anthony. Abraham died in 1757 and John Anthony in 1745. Both were men of prominence. Abraham was sheriff of Bucks county in 1719 and chief burgess of Bristol from 1728 to 1731 and from 1742 to 1744.

Bessonett.—The *Bessonetts* were originally seated in the Province of Dauphiny, several of the name being prominent in the Reformation, notably Claude DeBessonett. At the Revocation a branch of the family fled to Ireland and from thence to America. Of this family *Richard Bessonett* was a resident of Burlington, New Jersey, in 1692. The Bessonetts were also seated in Bristol in 1720, of whom was *Charles Bessonett*, (2) Deputy Postmaster General during the Revolution War and a man of great business capacity. He was the first to establish a coach line between New York and Philadelphia.

Santee.—The history of the *Santee* family is somewhat romantic, as the following brief sketch, furnished by Dr. Ellis M. Santee, of Cortland, N. Y., shows: "The story of our ancestor, as

---

(1). Vide Davis' Hist. of Bucks County.
(2). See Davis' Hist. of Bucks County.

handed down to me by my grandfather, is as follows: "In 1685, about the time of the Revocation of the Edict of Nantes, Elias Santee lived in the Province of Bergundy. He was a French nobleman and a favorite of the King. He had a son named *Isaac* who was enamored of a German lady named Hahn, who was one of the Queen's maids. Elias was a Huguenot and the King begged him to renounce his religion and conform to the decree. This he refused to do and was imprisoned. The Queen informed her maid of what was coming to the family and she and Isaac were quietly married and secretly left the country for Holland, there to await the release of Elias. In 1690 Elias died in prison and Isaac and his young wife came to this country, landing at Philadelphia. Soon afterward he went up the Delaware and settled near where Easton now stands."

John Santee, a descendant, was a distinguished officer of the Revolution War.

After the Revocation of the Edict of Nantes *Jean* and *Nicholas Lazelere* came to New York. The former located on Long Island and the latter on Staten Island. *Nicholas, Jr.*, a son of the latter, located in Bucks county in 1741.

DeBoileu.—The *DeBoileu* family is of patrician rank in France and has given many eminent names to history, among them Despereau Boileau (1636–1711), one of the most brilliant of all French writers, and in literature called "The Legislator of Parnassus." A Huguenot branch of this family fled at the Revocation to New York and located on Long Island. *Isaac*, a son of this refugee, came to Bucks county at an early day. He was the father of the distinguished *Nathaniel Boileu*. (1)

The *DuCorson* family were also refugees who located on Long Island, and from whence *Benjamin* came to Bucks county in 1726, and located at the present village of Addersville.

In 1737 *Christian DeTray* located where the town of Telford now stands. In 1762 *Conrad DeTray* was naturalized in Philadelphia. His connection with the foregoing is not known.

Charles LeValleu settled at Bristol prior to 1695. *Abraham LaRue* and sons *Abraham, Isaac* and *David* were also early arrivals. *Ralph Dracot*, of a refugee family in New Jersey, became a resident of the county in 1712.

---

(1). Nathaniel Boileu was born in Bucks county in 1763 and died in 1850. In 1808 he was elected Speaker of the House of Representatives and later was appointed Secretary of the Commonwealth by Governor Snyder. He held the office three terms.

The Minisink.

Near the Delaware Water Gap, in Monroe county, are the Minisink Flats, the settlement of which antedates the founding of the Province by William Penn. The Minisink settlers were mostly Huguenots from Esopus, on the Hudson river. Prior to the English occupancy they had constructed a wagon road through the wilderness from Esopus to the Water Gap on the Delaware, a distance of about one hundred miles, over which they conveyed minerals and other products from the Delaware to the Hudson river.

This Colony is remarkable from the fact that there are no records of its establishment. It had no connection whatever with the Colonies on the Lower Delaware, and of which the Minisink settlers are said to have had no knowledge whatever. (1)

They were left undisturbed on their lands by the Pennsylvania Proprietors until 1730 when the Surveyor General, Nicholas Scull, and his deputy, John Lukens, proceeded to the settlement to investigate its character and titles. The surveyors were not able to ascertain definitely the time of settlement, but they concluded from the appearance of the buildings, orchards, etc., that it had been made a long while ago.

DePew.—Among the settlers was *Samuel DePew*, who located on the New Jersey side of the Delaware in 1697. Later he purchased from the Indians a large body of land on the Pennsylvania side and on which the village of Shawnee is located.

Nicholas DePui (Depew), a son of Samuel, settled above Easton on the Delaware about 1725. He was a man of considerable means and ability and erected the first grist mill in this region. Count Zinzendorf, the eminent founder of the Moravian Church in America, visited him in 1742. Nicholas DePui, *Sr.*, was a member of the Council of Safety which met December 24, 1774, at Easton to consider the threatening relations of the Colonies with the Mother country. During the Revolution Nicholas, *Jr.*, and Benjamin DePui were members of the Committee of Safety and officers in the Continental service. Moses DePui, probably a brother to Nicholas, Sr., was a justice of the peace for Bucks county in 1747 and many years thereafter.

The DePew family is of noble origin and has furnished many names notable in the history of France. Barthelmy Dupuy, born about 1650, was a trusted lieutenant in the household guard of Louis XIV. About 1682 he retired from the service of the King and married the Countess Susanna Lavillon. At the time of the Revocation (1685) he was summoned to recant his Huguenot faith.

---
(1). Hazzard's Register, Vol. I, 439.

At his request to consider over the matter he embraced the opportunity during the night to make his escape to Germany. After remaining there fourteen years he went to England in 1699, and from thence to the Huguenot Colony on the James river in Virginia. Here he died some time after 1714, leaving to America the example of a truly noble life. Many of his posterity have been among our most distinguished citizens. Chauncy F. Depew, a descendant of the emigrant to New York, has shed lustre on the family name.

In this Colony also was the Decha (now Desha) family from Esopus. After the Revolution a branch of them emigrated to Kentucky. Several of this name have became eminent, of whom Joseph Desha, born in Pennsylvania in 1768 and Governor of Kentucky 1824-1828, was perhaps the best known.

Jourdan.—In 1738 arrived *Jean Jourdan*, whose father fled from France to the Palatinate at the Revocation. He established himself at Mt. Pleasant, in Hunterdon county in New Jersey, but his family eventually located in Pennsylvania. Among the sons of the emigrant was *Frederick*, born in 1744, and whose son *John*, born 1770, located in Philadelphia. *John Jordan, Jr.* (1808-1890), a son of the latter, was an eminent Moravian philanthropist who, among other noble deeds, so munificently supported and endowed the Pennsylvania Historical Society.

Tohickon.—In the Reformed society of Tohickon, which was organized prior to 1733, there is said to have been a considerable number of Huguenot members. The identity of most, however, has been lost by the unfortunate transformation of names elsewhere noted. Among the names preserved is that of the *Laux* family, the head of which was *Peter Laux*, who arrived in 1737—then also the *Sallada* family. Tradition has it that there were five immigrant brothers. A fuller note on this family will be elsewhere found.

The Lehigh Region.

In the romantic Valley of the Lehigh and the region adjacent, a considerable number of Huguenots, principally Alsatians, settled at an early day. Among the first arrivals in Whitehall township, in Lehigh county, was *John Jacob Mickley*, who came to America in 1733 and was the founder of a prominent family. *Jean Jacques Michelet* (this was his French name) was descended from a noble and distinguished Protestant family of the city of Metz. (1.) His father, Louis Michelet 1675-1750), was a young merchant in that city when he was married in 1697 to Suzanne Mangeot,

---

(1). In 1546 Michael Michelet was given the choice of recanting his faith or burning at the stake. He chose the latter, declaring: "Inasmuch as God has given me grace to confess the truth He will not deny me strength to suffer for it."

a pious and accomplished young lady of that place. No marriage of Protestants being legal in France they proceeded to the free city of Zweibrucken where they were married, and where they also remained until after the birth of Jean Jacques the same year.

Louis Michelet was an earnest and devoted man and soon after his marriage began to exercise the office of the ministry. In course of time he became the pastor of the Huguenot congregation in Zweibrucken where he continued to reside until his death. One of his sons, *Louis*, born in 1705, in 1720 went to Berlin where he established an influential family. The late distinguished Professor Charles Louis Michelet, of Berlin, was a grandson. (1)

Upon his arrival in America John Jacob Mickley proceeded to Berks county where he made his home with his kinsman, Jacob LeVan. A few years later he came to the Lehigh Valley where he married Elizabeth Barbara, a daughter of Ulrich Burkhalter, and established himself on a large estate on which the village of Mickleys is situated. Here he died in 1769. (2) Many of his descendents have shed additional lustre on the honored family name. His three sons served with distinction in the war of the Revolution, viz.: *John Jacob*, *John Martin* and *John Henry*. The first is noted as having brought the Liberty Bell from Philadelphia to Bethlehem in September, 1777, in order to save it from capture by the British. The late Joseph J. Mickley (1799-1878), a great grandson of the emigrant, was a world-renowned antiquarian and numismatist. He was the first President of the Numismatic and Antiquarian Society of Philadelphia, besides being a member of various foreign societies.

Balliet.—Paul *Balliet* arrived in the Lehigh Valley in 1738, and his brother *Joseph* in 1749. This family was of patrician origin and has been traced back to A. D. 500, when one of this name was commander of the army of King Clodowic.

In the days of William the Conqueror (A. D. 1066), an officer of this name and connected with that expedition, remained in England and settled in Sussex.

The Balliet family is traced in many important relations which we cannot here detail until the XVth century, when a reformer of this name was one of the first to suffer death for the cause of the Reformation in the Province of Languedoc.

---

(1). Professor Michelet (1801-1893), was one of the profoundest scholars of the last century and founder of a distinct school of thought. In his biographies mention is made of his Huguenot ancestry.

(2). John Jacob Mickley had children: John Jacob, 1737-1808; John Martin, 1745-1830, settled in Adams county; John Peter, 1752-1828, settled in Bucks county; Henry, b. 1754, killed by the Indians in 1763; Barbara, born 1756, killed by the Indians 1763; Magdalena, 1745-1827; Susanna, b.—

At a later period, when the horrors of the Revocation (1685) burst upon this Province, Jacques Balliet fled for refuge to Salm, a small District between Alsace and Lorraine. The family, however, soon found that there was no safety for Protestants in the French Kingdom and sought refuge in foreign lands. Of this family were *Paul* and *Joseph*, grandsons of Jacques. Paul Balliet was married prior to his emigration to Pennsylvania to Magdalena Voturin, of Lorraine. (1) The name is known in this country in its Germanized form of "Woodring." Several of Mrs. Balliet's relatives, among them Abraham Voturin and John Voturin (Woodring), also came to Pennsylvania. The former settled in Lehigh and the latter in York county. The Balliet family has been an honor to this State. *Stephen*, the third son of Paul, was a prominent man in his day and filled many important positions. He was a Colonel in the Revolution, in which capacity he rendered distinguished service to his country. (2)

LaRose.—In the vicinity of Macungie *Jean Louis LaRose* (Laros), settled prior to 1740. He is said to have been of noble parentage and was compelled to flee from his native country because of his religion. His son, John Jacob LaRose (1755–1845), was a distinguished minister of the German Reformed Church in America.

Vesqueau.—In this same region also settled *Jean Vesqueau* (Wesco) and his son *Francois*, who fled from Alsace, their native land, to Holland, where they resided for some time and from thence came to Pennsylvania. The thriving town of Wescosville, in Lehigh county, perpetuates their honored name.

Grimm.—In Weisenburg, Lehigh county, located in 1728 *Egidius Grimm*, who came to Pennsylvania in the same vessel with the noted pioneer minister of the Lutheran Church, John Casper Stœver. The Grimm family is of patrician origin and long seated in Normandy. One branch established itself in Alsace from whence Egidius Grimm emigrated to America as the result of religious persecution. An interesting circumstance attaches to this family from the fact that an ancient pedigree, tracing the family back to a Norman Baron who lived in the days of William the

---

(1). Paul Balliet, b. 1717, d. 1777. Children : Jacob, Nicholas, Col. Stephen, 1753–1821 ; John, 1761–1837 ; Paul, 1766–1845 ; Catharine, 1752–1823 ; Susan——; Eva, 1763–1797 ; Magdalena——.

(2). Col. Stephen Balliet was born 1753. He was a man of great energy and capability, as is evinced by the fact that he was given the command of a battalion at the opening of the Revolution. At the head of his command he participated in the battle of Brandywine in 1777, member of the Supreme Executive Council 1783–1786, member of the Convention to ratify the Federal Constitution 1787, member of the General Assembly 1788–1790, member of House of Representatives (Congress) 1794–1797, Revenue Collector 1797. He died August 4, 1821.

Conqueror, was brought by the emigrant to America. The first Grimm family reunion was held at Hancock, Pa., in 1897, at which time the connection numbered over one thousand souls.

LaBar.—In Mt. Bethel township, Northampton county, were located the *LaBars* as early as 1730. Of this family were the brothers *Peter*, *Charles* and *Abraham*. The latter became a distinguished officer in the Revolution. He first served as Major of the First, and afterwards as Colonel of the Fifth Battalion of Northampton County Associators, and rendered important service as Commandant of the Guard at Easton Ferry. A number of the family became men of mark, notably the late Judge DePew LaBar, a descendant of Colonel LaBar.

About midway between Bethlehem and Easton located *Daniel LaWall*, father of Captain *Henry LaWall*, of the Revolution. Other immigrants of this name are supposed to have been connections. In this county also located a *LaMar* family from which came the famous *Major Marien LaMar*, who fell at the massacre of Paoli September 20, 1777.

Moravian Huguenots.

The Moravian Church (Unitas Fratrum) owes its existence in America to the devotion of Count Zinzendorf, a godly nobleman of Saxony, who in 1722 began to gather the terribly persecuted followers of the great Reformer, John Huss, on his estates at Berthelsdorf. Espousing their cause he became their patron and Bishop. Through his fostering care a considerable town called Herrnhut was established on his estate by them, and from which place as a center they sent out many missionaries and small Colonies to distant parts of the world in their work of evangelization and in which they have excelled all other churches in liberality and self-sacrifice. Among the refugees thus gathered from all parts of Europe and united in the bonds of the ancient Faith were a considerable number of Huguenots.

In 1735 a Colony of Moravians was established in Georgia which, on account of difficulties with Spain in 1741, was disturbed, many of the Colonists coming to Pennsylvania. In 1741, under the leadership of their Bishop, David Nitchman, they founded Bethlehem, and later Nazareth and other places. In 1741 Count Zinzendorf, with his devoted wife, came to America on a tour of inspection and evangelization. On this visit he seems to have been on terms of warmest friendship with some of the most prominent Huguenot refugees in the Province, preaching in their houses, etc. Among them may be mentioned Jean Bertolet and John DeTurk, of

Oley, Jacob LeVan, of Maxatawny, Nicholas DePew, above Easton, and John Stephen Benezet, of Philadelphia.

These facts may serve to indicate the intimate connection between the Moravians and Huguenots in the early days of their dispersion. In later times there have not been wanting interesting links connecting the history of the past with present associations. When Count Zinzendorf returned to Europe in 1743 he took with him to London Miss Anna Margaretha Antes, whose father, Henry Antes, of the Falkner Swamp, near Philadelphia, was one of the prominent lights of the Moravian faith. The object of the young woman's journey to the Old World was to complete her education in the Moravian schools. In England she met and married the Rev. Benjamin Latrobe, a young Huguenot Moravian minister. Three sons born of this union became men of eminence, and of whom Benjamin came to Philadelphia in 1796. (1)

Another interesting link is the eminent Moravian family of DeSchweinitz. After the Revocation of the Edict of Nantes a Huguenot family named *LeDoux* fled to Stettin in Prussia. The LeDoux family suffered terribly as the result of their faith. Soon after 1565 Philip LeDoux suffered a martyr's death. A family of this name was among the Huguenot refugees to New York. A descendant of the refugee to Stettin, Amalie LeDoux, born in 1791, married the Rev. David DeSchweinitz (2) in 1812, with whom she came to America, and from them the present American family descends. It is also worthy of record that Rev. J. Mortimer Levering, a distinguished Bishop of the Moravians, also descends from the Huguenots through his ancestor, Wigard Levering.

Clevel.—One of the most prominent French Moravian families in Northampton county is the *Clevel* (now Clewell) family. Their history, like that of their coreligionists, is a story of suffering for the sake of "the Faith once delivered to the Saints." (Jude, v. 3). The name appears among the exiles to various lands as well as among the galley slaves. One branch retired to Switzerland, from which came Rev. David Clevel (b. 1754), a distinguished minister. At the Revocation period one family fled from Dauphiny, France, to Auerbach, in Baden. The names of the parents and children

---

(1). Benjamin Latrobe, Jr. (1767–1820), was unquestionably one of the greatest architects of his age. He was in the service of the United States many years and designed many public buildings, among which the American Capitol is his most conspicuous monument. He was also a famous engineer and planned many of the first river and harbor improvements of America.

(2). Lewis David De Schweinitz, Ph. D., born in Bethlehem, Pa., 1780, educated in Europe where he married in 1812. Returned to America and labored as a Moravian minister, locating finally at Bethlehem in 1821, and where he died in 1834. He was Senior Civilis Unitis Fratrum. He is known to scientists as one of the most accomplished botanists of America.

are unknown with the exception of Francois, who was married to Louisa Frache, of Geneva, Switzerland, with whom he had two sons, *Francis* and *George*. Becoming for the second time a widow, she and her sons in 1737 set out to find a home in the New World, coming to Philadelphia poor in worldly goods but brave in heart. The boys became Redemptioners and sold their services to a farmer for a period of several years in return for the payment of their passage. Francis, the eldest of the sons, married Salome Kichlein in 1746. Soon after his marriage he removed to Bucks county, locating on the Bushkill Creek, about two miles north of Nazareth, where he died in 1798 in the 78th year of his age. He was the father of three sons and nine daughters. (1) He was a pillar in the Moravian Church and his house was a preaching place from 1755 to 1762.

George Clevel, his brother, was also a Moravian and settled at Shœneck, a short distance north of Nazareth, where he died in 1793. His family consisted of nine sons and three daughters. (2) The emigrant mother, Louisa Frache Clevel, also lived at Shœneck, where she died. (3)

Several Moravian ministers of prominence were Alsatian refugees. They were *John Philip Meurer* and *John Reinhart Ronner*. The former arrived in 1742 and the same year was ordained as a minister and labored extensively in various congregations until his death at Bethlehem in 1760.

John Reinhart Ronner was born near Strasburg, in Alsace, in 1698, and came to Bethlehem in 1743, where he was ordained to the ministry the same year. After a brief but very active ministry, five years of which were spent in mission work among the aborigines in St. Thomas, West Indies, he died at Bethlehem in 1756.

In the Bethlehem congregation were a number of members of Huguenot extraction. *Judith Brashier* (nee Gasherie) was born at Esopus, whither her parents had fled at the Revocation. *Mary Appolonia*, the wife of John Bechtel, was born in Heidelberg in 1691, whither her parents, named *Marrett*, had fled. *Martha Hussey* was born in Paris in 1719. Her parents, named *Wilkes*, fled to England, from whence she came to Bethlehem, and where she died in 1790.

(1). His children were: Francis, Nathaniel, John, Magdalena, Rosena, Juliana, Catharine, Salome, Veronica, Maria and three others.

(2). Children: Jacob, John, Daniel, George, Joseph, Abraham, Francis, Christian, Elisabeth, Catharine and Salome.

(3). The inscription on her tombstone is: "Louise Kuechley, geborne Frache, geboren Dec., 1695; Zu Geneve in der, Schweiz, mutter von Franz und George Clewell, Sie war die Stam, mutter, Von der Zalreichen, Clewell Familie, Gestorben October, 1767.

Translation—Louise Kuechley, a born Frache, born December, 1695, in Geneva, Switzerland, mother of Franz and George Clewell, and ancestress of the numerous Clewell family, died October, 1767.

CHAPTER XI.

The Huguenots of Lancaster County.

THE VALLEY OF THE CONESTOGA—THE FRENCH TRADERS—THE LANCASTER CHURCH RECORDS—MANY DISTINGUISHED DESCENDANTS OF THE HUGUENOTS—THE MASSACRE OF THE LE ROYS.

> "*Be this my home till some fair star*
> *Stoops earthward and shall beckon me;*
> *For surely Godland lies not far*
> *From these green heights and this great sea.*
> *My friend, my lover, trend this way—*
> *Not far along lies Arcady.*"

THE remarkably beautiful and fertile Valley of the Conestoga, in Lancaster county, derives its name from a tribe of Indians originally seated there. William Penn visited the valley and was much impressed with it. For many years the whites and Indians lived together here on terms of amity and a number of important treaties were consummated here between the Proprietors and the Indians.

Among the first settlers were a number of French traders who had lived on the Schuylkill as early as 1690, and soon after 1700 removed to this valley. Chief among them were *Peter Bezillion, Martin Chartier, Joseph Jessup* and *Captain James Letort*. They were shrewd business men, well acquainted with the various Indian languages, and were frequently employed as agents and interpreters for the Provincial authorities. The many references to them in the Colonial records are generally in important and honorable connections. Bezillion came to the Province prior to 1687 and was a very extensive land owner. He was a member of the Protestant Episcopal Church, and at his death (1) in 1742 left a legacy for St. John's parish. Chartier came to the Province prior to 1690 and

---
(1). Bazillion's grave may be seen in St. John's churchyard, on the Lancaster turnpike, near the Lancaster and Chester line. He died July 18, 1742, aged 80 years. Near him also reposes his brother-in-law, John Coombe, who died September 12, 1736, aged 78 years.

is sometimes referred to as "the French glover of Philadelphia." His trading post was on the Susquehanna, near the present city of Columbia, and where he died in 1718. His son Peter, also a trader, removed to the Ohio Valley where he later associated himself with the French and Indians in hostility to Pennsylvania.

The Letort family were members of the Episcopal Church and came to the Province prior to 1689. Captain James Letort was a resident of Philadelphia for many years. Both he and his sons were engaged in traffic on the frontiers and were frequently in the service of the Government. There is considerable confusion in the Colonial Records regarding the personality of the Letorts arising from the failure of the writers to distinguish between father and son. (1) There are references to the traders as Papists, (2) but there were other traders besides those mentioned and who became involved in difficulties with the authorities to whom the reference doubtless applies. (3) It is worthy of note that *Lewis Mitchelle*, the advance agent and prospector of the Bernese Mennonites, spent a number of years with these traders (1703–1707) on terms of intimacy, and was accused by the authorities on the occasion of a misunderstanding of having led the Frenchmen here. (4) It is hardly probable that he would make Papists his boon companions while seeking a home for his people where they might be free from religious persecution.

The chief interest of the French Protestant emigration to this region centers around the arrival of the *Ferree* and *Lefever* families in 1712 and the advance refugees of the Mennonites who arrived near the same time, an account of which the reader will find elsewhere in this work.

Among the first arrivals was *Samuel Boyer* (1710) with a large family. A notice of the Boyers in Pennsylvania is elsewhere given in this work.

---

(1). The dual Letort personality may be seen in the first two references following. He is referred to as "Captain" in 1689 (Col. Records, Vol. I p. 557), speaks of having been "bred to the service of this Government from infancy" (Col. Rec., Vol. II p. 100). He had a trading post at Conestoga prior to 1703 (Col. Rec., Vol. II p. 123). Had a trading post at Letort Springs, near Carlisle, in 1731, and lived there in 1735 (Hazzard's Register, Vol. XV p. 82). James, son of James and Mary Letort, buried at Christ Episcopal Church, Philadelphia, 1709 (Penna. Mag. of Hist., Vol. V). Judith Letort, same parents, buried 1711. Elisabeth Letort, wife of James, died 1732. Francis Letort, son of Captain Letort, was killed by the Indians while hunting on the Potomac river.

(2). Proud's Hist. of Penna., Vol. I p. 482.

(3). Col. Rec., Vol. II p. 405, 406. Col. Rec., Vol. II p. 420. Conyngham, an early historian of Conestoga, says Letort was a Huguenot. Rupp's Lanc. Co., p. 515.

(4). Col. Rec., Vol. II p. 420.

Thomas Perrine (died 1747), of Huguenot ancestry, was one of the first settlers and was probably a son of Matthew Perrine, of England, who died in 1695 leaving lands in Pennsylvania. (Penna. Archives, XIV., 384). Also *Peter Lemont*, (1) *Jonas Larue, Jacob Barree*, (2) and *Hubert Hubertson*, a friend and fellow-emigrant of the Ferrees. The initial settlement made and the pioneers favorably situated the news spread with surprising rapidity among the exiles in Holland, Switzerland and the Palatinate, and Lancaster county soon became an objective point for many in a few years.

There was no distinctive religious organization maintained by them for the reason that they had already affiliated themselves with various branches of the Protestant Church in the land of their exile. The baptismal record of the First Reformed Church of Lancaster city, which was founded in 1731, contains the names of a large number of Huguenot parents, and it is known that Rev. Charles Lewis Boehm, who was pastor of the church from 1771 to 1775, sometimes preached in the French language, which presupposes a considerable number of French speaking parishoners. (3) From the church records we extract the following names of Huguenot fathers and the earliest entry of children for baptism :

John Casper Viller, 1733; Abr. DeGaston, 1736; Melchoir Boyer, 1741 ; Jacob Rudisill, 1742 ; Jacob Velschang, 1742 ; Andrew Beauchamp, 1745 ; Melchoir Fortune and David Mich. Fortuney, 1749 ; Jacob Fortuney, 1753 (Forteneaux) ; John Ferree, 1745 ; Cornelius Ferree, 1745 ; Abraham Ferree, 1758 ; David Fortunet, 1747 ; Peter LaRou, 1749; John Messakop, 1750 ; Henry Racque, 1752 ; Peter Bonnett, Lorenz·Marquet and DeBeau Rosier; Martin Boyer, 1753 ; Abraham DeDieu, 1755 ; Jean De-Dieu, 1773 ; John Jacob Allemand, 1755 ; John Jacob Huttier, 1753 ; Jacques Calvin Berott, John LeFever, Justice Trebert, 1756 ; Jacob LeCrone, Abraham Caupat (Gobat), 1759; Francois Delancy, 1760 ; John Peter Roller, 1761 ; Adam LeRoy, Henry DuKeyness, 1762 ; Peter Mumma, 1764; John Henry Vissard, 1765 ; Henry Maquinnett, 1765 ; Samuel Gurier, 1766 ; Jean Pierre Vosin, 1767 ; Conrad Hillegas, 1768 ; Conrad DuBois, 1770 ; Joseph LeBrant, 1771 ; Nicholas Dello, 1773. Besides the foregoing the Doute, Raiguel, Jacques, (4) DuFresne, Dundore, Armeson and Lorah families were members.

---
(1). Rupp's Hist. Lanc. Co., p. 516.
(2). Ibid.
(3). " Brand, Elisabeth, daughter of Joseph and Magdalena, born July 28 and baptized August 25, 1771. N. B.—This child was baptized in the French language previous to the sermon which was preached in the same language." Extract from Record.
(4). Jean Jacques, b. 1694 in France and died 1778. He was the ancestor of the Jacobs family.

The Trinity Lutheran Church of Lancaster, which was also founded very early, had likewise a large Huguenot membership. The following is a list of fathers with the earliest baptismal entry of children:

Bernhart Hubele, 1748; Michael Hubele, 1749; Mich. Morett, 1754; Peter Bonnett, 1751; Francois Moreau, 1755; Jean Mathiot, 1757; George Mathiot, 1764; John Peter Moreau, 1765; Jacques Santeau, 1766; Jean DeMars.

Besides the foregoing were the families Marquette, Dillier, Rudesill, Cossart, (1) Bertle and Sponselier. (2)

Mathiot.—The *Mathiot* family claims ancestry from Jean Mathiot, who was an officer in the French army at the time of the massacre of St. Bartholomew. Being a Huguenot he retired to the mountainous region of the Jura for safety and where the family became established. The emigrants to Pennsylvania were sons of *Marcus Mathiot* and his wife, Jane Bautonet, of Dasle, in the Department of Doubs. In June, 1753, their son Jean married Margaret Catharine, (3) a daughter of Hon. Jacques Bernard, the mayor of Dampierre, and his wife, Anna Maria Cuenot. Both the Mathiot and Bernard families, the latter of whom were of patrician rank, were of the Huguenot faith.

In 1754 *Jean Mathiot* and his brother *George* came to America and located near Lancaster. Both were members of Trinity Lutheran Church of that place. (4) The Mathiot family in America has ever maintained an honorable character. *John*, a son of Jean, was sheriff of the county. He resided near Columbia where he was accidentally killed by a companion while hunting.

George, another son, in 1776, when a mere youth, entered the war for Independence and served to its close. He was a non-commissioned officer and served as interpreter. In 1787 he was married to Ruth Davis, whose father, Joshua Davis, was a prominent Friend of Elicott Mills in Maryland. Here George Mathiot

---

(1). Theopholis Cassart, a printer and publisher,. was a prominent citizen about the Revolutionary period.

(2). Philip Sponselier was b. in Lorraine in 1676, m. 1711 his wife Barbara. He came to Lancaster county 1732, died 1752, leaving widow, three sons and three daughters.

(3). The baptismal certificate of Margaret Catharine Bernard and the contract between Marcus Mathiot and Hon. Jacques Bernard for the marriage of their children is still in the possession of the American descendants.

(4). In Trinity Lutheran Church are recorded the baptisms of children of Jean and Margaret Catharine Mathiot as follows : (1)—Christian, 1757 ; (2)—George, 1759 ; (3)—John, 1761 ; (4)—Anna Barbara, 1763, died 1768 ; (5)—Catharine, 1769 ; (6)—Martin, 1771.

Of the children of George and Lucia Mathiot are recorded : (1)—John, b. 1764 ; (2)—John Jacob, 1765 ; (3)—Mary and Sarah, twins, 1770. It is said that Christian son of Jean Mathiot, was the father of nineteen children.

resided till 1796, when he removed to Fayette county, Pennsylvania, where he died in 1840. He too was a Friend of proverbial integrity and the founder of an honored posterity. His son, Dr. Henry Bernard Mathiot, was a widely-known physician and father of the noted specialist, Dr. Henry B. Mathiot, *Jr.*, of Pittsburg.

Another son of George Mathiot was *Joshua* (1800–1849), an eminent lawyer of Newark, Ohio. He was a recognized leader of the Whig party and was elected to Congress in 1841, where he at once took high rank as an eloquent and safe counsellor on the momentous issues of his day. He was a worthy compeer of such notable men as Daniel Webster and Henry Clay. His brilliant career was suddenly terminated by death of cholera.

Forney.—This name, so honorably known in America, emanates from several emigrant heads, all undoubtedly traceable to the ancestral family seat at Ferney, a town in the Department of Ain, on the borders of France, and near to the city of Geneva. The name occurs prominently in French history. Some of this name of the Huguenot faith forsook their native land because of the religious persecutions and located in Switzerland and the Palatinate immediately adjacent, and from whence they came to America. It is a significant fact that nearly all the immigrants of this name came in the company of Huguenots. While we are not prepared to say that all of the Forney immigrants were of Huguenot antecedents, it is established beyond a doubt that *Peter Forney, Sr.*, who came to Lancaster county prior to 1733, must be designated as one. He is known to have came from the borders of France, near Geneva, which would incline to the belief that his home was at or near the town from which the family took its name. The date of his arrival is not certainly known. In 1733 he obtained a warrant for land on the Cocalico, and where he died intestate in 1749, leaving five children (1) and a considerable estate.

It is a significant fact that his minor daughter, Anna, choose as her guardian "*Christian Farnoy,*" who was probably an uncle, and arrived in 1734. The descendents of Peter Forney preserve many traditions of their Huguenot antecedents. The late Colonel John W. Forney, during a visit to France in 1875, had the pleasure of meeting several distinguished personages of his name who claimed kinship. Among the descendants of Peter Forney were

---

(1). He left children: Abraham, Peter, Jr., Ann, Mary and Susan.

Col. John W. Forney (1) and Col. Wien Forney, (2) both of whom were born in Lancaster county.

The father of *Jacob Forney* (1721-1806), fled from France to the Palatinate, from whence the son came to Pennsylvania. In Lancaster county he married Maria Bergner, and in 1754 removed to Lincoln county, North Carolina, where he and his sons *Jacob, Peter* and *Abraham* became very prominent. The son, *Gen. Peter Forney* (1756-1834), served in the Revolution and was one of the foremost men of the State. He was a member of Congress 1813-1815. His brother Abraham (1758-1849) also served in the Revolution and greatly distinguished himself at the battle of King's Mountain.

Hubele.—Among the families dispersed by the Revocation was the *Hubele* or *Oublier* family. *Augustine Hubele* was a member of the Huguenot Church in New York prior to 1690, (3) while a number who had sojourned in the Palatinate came to Pennsylvania. In regard to the immigrants there is some confusion. One family historian holds (4) that the progenitor was *Bernard Hubele*, a member of the refugee family and who, after residing in Germany many years, came to Philadelphia with his sons *Bernard* (b. 1719), and *Michael* (b. 1722, d. 1804). The father is said to have died soon after arrival. Another well-informed writer maintains that *Joseph Hubele*, who arrived in 1732, was the progenitor, (5) which is more probable. Be this as it may we know that all the immigrants of this name to Pennsylvania were closely related and all located in Lancaster county.

Barnard Hubele, one of the younger immigrants, became prominent and wealthy. He served as county treasurer from 1756 to 1762. During the Revolution War he was a staunch patriot and commandant of the Lancaster Barracks and had charge of the British and Hessian prisoners. His sons *Adam* (1743-1793), and *Barnard, Jr.* (1754-1810), became prominent. Adam removed to Philadelphia where he became a merchant. At the outbreak of the

---

(1). Col. John Weiss Forney was b. 1817, entered the profession of journalism, became editor of "Lancaster Intelligencer" 1837, removed to Philadelphia and took charge of the "Pennsylvanian" 1841, elected to Congress and was Clerk of the Lower House 1851, re-elected 1853, became editor of the "Union" at Washington, Clerk of U. S. Senate 1861, editor "Philadelphia Press," later editor of "Progress," author of several interesting books. During the Civil War he was a trusted and confidential officer of the Government.

(2). Col. Wein Forney (1826-1898), a cousin to Col. John W. Forney, entered the profession of journalism and was the founder and editor of several newspapers. He was a brilliant writer, ripe scholar, and for twelve years State Librarian of Pennsylvania.

(3). Proc. Hug. Soc. of America. Vol. I p. 12.
(4). "Notes and Queries," by Dr. Egle, 1897.
(5). Ibid., 1898.

Revolution he warmly espoused the cause of the Colonists. He was a member of the Provincial Assembly in 1775 and later became a Colonel in the Provincial forces.

Barnard, Jr., who served with distinction as an officer in the German regiment, located at Northumberland at the close of the Revolution where he lived on terms of intimacy with the famous scientist and discoverer of oxygen, Dr. Joseph Priestly. Turning his attention to literary pursuits he wrote a number of books, the most important being a history of the Revolution War, published in 1807, and which is said to have been the first book written on that subject.

Michael Hubele, the emigrant, also located at Lancaster and was a man of influence. His sons *Adam* (1759–1798), and *John* (1747–1821), became men of distinction. Adam became a resident of Philadelphia and took a prominent part in the Revolutionary struggle. He served throughout the war and retired at the close as Colonel of the Eleventh Regiment Pennsylvania Line. John Hubele was an eminent lawyer and member of the Constitutional Convention 1776, member of Committee of Safety 1776-1777, appointed Major and put in charge of commissary stores in 1777, made a Justice in 1777 and a member of the Convention to frame the Federal Constitution in 1787. *Frederick Hubely*, also an emigrant, died in 1769.

At the Revocation the *LeRoy* family took refuge in Switzerland, and from whence *Abraham* (1) and *Jean Jacques LeRoy*, brothers and both heads of families, came to America. The family of Abraham became well established, the name being Germanized to "Kœnig" or "King." His daughter *Susan* in 1762 became the wife of Rev. Philip W. Otterbine, (2) the founder of the Church of the United Brethren in Christ. Elizabeth became the wife of the celebrated Rev. William Hendel, D. D.

Jean Jacques LeRoy in 1754 removed to the frontiers where he located by the side of a fine spring about two miles south of the present town of Mifflinburg, in Union county. Upon the outbreak of the French and Indian War in 1755 the savages of the Ohio region made a hostile incursion on the frontiers, and on October 16, 1755, devastated this entire region, murdering upwards of twenty-

---

(1). He settled in Heidelberg township, now Lebanon county, where he died 1764, leaving children: Abraham, John Peter, Susan, Ann Maria, Salome and Elisabeth.

(2). Philip William Otterbine (1726-1813), a learned young minister of the Reformed Church, was sent in 1752 by the Synod of Holland as a missionary to Pennsylvania. He located in Lancaster. In 1774 he removed to Baltimore where he founded a society differing in polity from the Reformed Church, and from which sprang the United Brethren in Christ, of which Otterbein is regarded as the founder.

five persons. LeRoy and his entire family, with the exception of two children, met a horrible fate. They were cruelly butchered and their cabin was burned over their heads. Among those taken into captivity were Annie and Jacob LeRoy, Barbara and Rachael Lininger and Annie Willard, the Liningers and Miss Willard being visiting relatives from Lancaster. After a captivity of almost four years Anna LeRoy and Barbara Lininger made their escape from the savages, A narrative of their remarkable experiences was published. (1)

Roller.—The Roller family of France is both ancient and honorable and early espoused the cause of the Reformation, and in consequence of persecution several branches fled to adjacent countries. It is interesting to know that the family in France still adheres to the Huguenot faith notwithstanding the terrible ordeals through which it has passed. Many of this name have achieved honorable distinction, notably *Dr. Jean Louis Theophile Roller* (1829–1895), one of the leading ministers of the French Reformed Church. Dr. Roller first served a congregation at Balbec in Normandy, after which he removed to Naples in Italy where he was pastor of the French-German Protestant Church for six years. From thence he removed to Rome, where he was pastor of the French Church ten years. During his pastorate at Rome he thoroughly explored the catacombs and remains of the ancient Christian Church in that city. The results of his immense labors were published in two folio volumes, justly regarded as the greatest work of its kind in existence. Failing health compelled him to return to France, where he soon afterward died at Tocqueville en Caux. (2).

Among the refugees to Erlangen in Bavaria in 1685 was a branch of this family and from which came *Dr. Conrad Roller*, a distinguished Lutheran minister in America. He was educated at the University at Erlangen and came to Pennsylvania when still young. He was a close friend of Muhlenberg, the founder of the Lutheran Church in America, and his name appears as a member of the first Synod in 1748.

John Peter Roller, supposed to have been a brother to Dr. Conrad Roller, arrived in 1752 and located at Lancaster, and in 1767 removed to the Shenandoah Valley, Va. A distinguished descendant is Gen. John E. Roller, of Harrisonburg. The connection of this family with other immigrants of this name is not known.

---

(1). Penna. Archives, Vol. III p. 633. Ibid., VIII., p. 403.
(2). It is worthy of note that upon the death of Dr. Roller his immediate family sent a mortuary notice to the representatives of the various branches throughout the world in accordance with the old Huguenot custom. That received by Gen. J. E. Roller, of Virginia, is interesting.

The *Bonnett* family belongs to the nobility of Lorraine (1) and was of high standing during the Reformation period. The name is often met with in Huguenot literature. Being mostly Protestants they were greatly scattered during the persecutions, some going to England, Switzerland and the Palatinate. It was from Switzerland (2) that the several branches in America came. One of the earliest of this name in Pennsylvania was Jean Jacques Bonnett and wife Marie who arrived in 1733 with a considerable family.

The *Marchand* family has given many distinguished names to France, a distinction well maintained in America, as among the descendants of the emigrant David Marchand, who located at Lancaster, a number became noted, and of whom was Hon. David Marchand, Jr., who was elected to Congress in 1817, serving two terms, Hon. Albert G. Marchand, who was elected to Congress in 1839, and also served two terms, then also Commodore John Bonnett Marchand who so greatly distinguished himself in the battle of Mobile Bay in 1864. (3)

Francois Mentjes and his wife *Elisabeth Bouvier* were among the early Lancaster Huguenots of whom we know little except that they were refugees and that the father probably died soon after their arrival.

Two children only of the emigrant are known. They were *Francis*, an officer in the Revolution, (4) and *Elisabeth*, who became the wife of Casper Egle, the ancestor of the noted historian, Dr. W. H. Egle, of Harrisburg.

Among the refugees to Holland at the Revocation was a descendant of the Huguenot author and minister *Jean Dillier*. A son of the refugee named *Casper* went to England where he married. From thence he removed to Hidleberg, in the Palatinate, where his children were born. In 1738 he emigrated to Pennsylvania. He located near New Holland, where he died in 1773 at the advanced age of one hundred years. (5) In 1752 Francis Dillier, whose connection with the foregoing is not known, located in Brecknock, where he died in 1784.

---

(1). "Science des Armoiries."—P. 254, *Arms.* "D'azur a un bouf d' or, surmounte de trois etoiles du meme rangies en chef."

(2). The noted scientist, Dr. Charles Bonnett, was born at Geneva in 1720.

(3). Commodore Marchand was born in Pennsylvania in 1808, entered the navy in 1828, and served with distinction in the Seminole, Mexican and Civil war. In the battle of Mobile Bay he commanded the "Lackawanna"; Was made a Commodore in 1866, and died in Carlisle, Pennsylvania, 1875.

(4). Colonel Francis Mentjes served throughout the Revolution. He commanded for a time the Fifth Pennsylvania Line; served with Wayne in the West; died at Cincinnatti about 1812.

(5). He had sons—Philip Adam, who died in 1781; John Martin and Casper Elias, besides seven daughters.

DeBow (DeBus).—This name, originally *DeBeau*, often met with on the lists of Huguenot refugees, was well represented among the arrivals in Pennsylvania. The first to appear were *Abraham* and *Philip* DeBos, also Anna, all in the same vessel in 1732. These were doubtless relatives. In 1734 Philip was married in Coventry, Chester county, by Rev. John Casper Stoever, and in 1750 his will was filed at Lancaster. In 1743 arrived *Ludwig DeBos*, aged 36, *Daniel*, aged 28, and *Jacob*, aged 26 years. They came in the same vessel and were doubtless brothers. In 1745 Daniel died at Lititz, in Lancaster county. In 1750 arrived *Christian DeBos*, aged 23 years.

The family were early pioneers in the South and West. *Solomon DeBow*, from Bucks county, Pa., was a resident of Orange county, North Carolina, in 1755. Rev. *John DeBow* was sent as a missionary by the Presbytery of New Brunswick, New Jersey, to the Huguenot settlement in Duplin county, North Carolina, at an early day, and died there about 1778.

DuTay, Douty, Doute.—Many branches of this family were exiles, and the name appears among the refugees to various Protestant countries, and also on the lists of galley slaves. A refugee family of this name, the head of which has not been ascertained, located in Lancaster county at an early day. Two sons are definitely known, namely *Nicholas* and *Henry Baldy Douty*, both of whom were born in France. The former removed to the mouth of Seneca lake, in New York, and the latter, who was an accomplished scholar and schoolmaster, was one of the first residents of Milton, Pennsylvania. He suddenly disappeared in 1790, and was supposed to have been murdered.

Sumois.—In 1733 arrived *Pierre Sumois* with a number of adult sons, all of whom took up land in Lancaster county. The name appears on the land and court house records in its Germanized form of *Sumey*. Peter, Jr., one of the sons, located in Tulpehocken prior to 1755, where his name appears on the records of the Reformed Church in its French form of *Sumois*.

Fortineaux.—Several branches of the *Fortineaux* (Fordny) family were dispersed from France by the persecutions. The name is met with among the refugees in various lands. *Jean Henri Fortineaux* came to Pennsylvania about 1720, and was naturalized in 1727. He was one of the first settlers in Frederick county, Maryland. In 1737 arrived the brothers *Francis*, aged 26, *Michael*, aged 22, and *Melchoir*, aged 19 years, all of whom located in Lancaster and became prominent citizens. Melchoir died in 1754, and Michael in 1778. Other arrivals of this name have not been located.

Beauchamp.—In 1731 arrived *Jean Beauchamp*, (1) and wife Barbara, the head of the *"Bushong"* family, now so numorous in America. He located in East Lampeter, near the Heller Church. He was born in France in 1692. His son *Jacob* located in Berks county and was the head of the Bushong family of Berks county, while another son, *Peter*, emigrated to the Shenandoah Valley in Virginia, and founded the Southern branch. There was also a Jacob Bouchon in York county prior to 1755.

Pons.—Several Protestant branches of the *DePons* family lo-located in Lancaster county at an early day. In France the family is of noble rank and has given many illustrious names to history. *Jacques Pons* was an eminent Huguenot divine. Another notable personage was *Mareshal DePons* who was the French minister to the court of Prussia in 1772. At the Revocation of the Edict of Nantes one branch of the family fled for safety to Offenbach, in the Palatinate, and from whence several members came to Pennsylvania. *Jacque* in 1727, *Augustus* in 1738, and *Abraham* in 1751.

Ranc (Ranck).—This family was prominent in the French Protestant Church, and one of this name sealed his faith with his life. This was Rev. Louis Ranc, pastor of the church at Die, who suffered death in 1745. The ancestors of the American branch were the brothers *John Michael Ranc*, who arrived in 1728, and *John Philip Ranc* who arrived a year later. They came from Alsace, and both located in Lancaster county. During the war of Independence the Ranc family was especially noted for its patriotism, and nearly all its members capable of bearing arms were in the war.

Litiz.—In 1742 Count Zinzendorf founded the Moravian Society of Litiz, in Lancaster county. Connected with this community were a number of members who were of Huguenot origin, of whom were the following: *Rev. Philip Meurer*, who was born in Alsace, and came to Pennsylvania in 1742. He died in Donegal in 1759. *Henry Haller*, born in Alsace in 1719, arrived in 1733, and was the father of the distinguished *Colonel Henry Haller* of the Revolution. *Daniel Heckendorn* from Alsace, 1736, father of an honorable posterity, and who died in 1782, and *Daniel Lecrone* prior to 1750.

In *Warwick* township, in the vicinity of Brickerville, were located the following: *Jacques Simonett*, who arrived in 1727. He was then well advanced in years. His warrantee for land is dated 1733, in which year the name of Isaac also appears, who was doubtless a son. *Nicholas Parrett*, 1730, *Jacques* and *Herman*

---

(1). Jean Beauchamp's family consisted of John, Philip, Peter, Henry, Jacob, David, Mary, Barbara and Elisabeth.

La Tour, 1749. The latter died in 1774. *Martin Oberlin* in 1730, with sons, *John Michael* and *John Adam*. The Oberlins are distinguished in the history of France, notably the Reformer of Ban-de-la- Roche, (1) who was a relative of the Pennsylvania Oberlins.

In *Cocalico* appears the name of *Sebastian Coquelin*, who arrived in 1739 with his family, of whom *Jean* and *Dietrich* were adults. The name has been perverted to "Cockly" and "Cocklin." *John* and *George Achey*, *Francis Dutill, Leonard, John* and *Jacob Mumma* and the *Guilliaume* family, (Williams), all of whom appear about the middle of the century.

Among others of Huguenot antecedents who located within the bounds of Lancaster county were the following : *Henry Bleim* who died in 1739; *Pierre Delone, John Detar, Casperius Viellard, Jean Jacques Lapierre*. This name was early Germanized to "Stein," (Stone), with the result that most of the descendants are unaware of their Huguenot ancestry. *Jacques Duey* (Dewy), *Jean* and *Paul LeCene*, the former was born in 1686, and the latter in 1688, and died 1766 ; *Jacques LeJune*, changed soon after arrival to its English equivalent "Young," several of the *Martine* family, *John Michael Motter* (originally Motteur), *Jean Hotel, Francis Peter Laurans*, who died in 1758, *Laurans Pierson, Pierre Armeson* came in 1753 and died in 1774, *James Picquart*, who died in 1749, *Pierre Fleury*, who came in 1732, *Jean Chateau* (now Shadow), *John Jacob Laschet* (Lawshe). Then also the families *Mercier, Roque* (Rockey), *Deshong, Rosher* and *Raquet*.

---

(1). Jean Frederick Oberlin (1740-1826), a distinguished minister of Alsace, who in 1766 became pastor of the Stein-thal or Ban-de-la-Roche, a wild mountainous region. The manner in which he effected the moral and industrial revolution of the valley was wonderful indeed.

CHAPTER XII.

The Pequea Colony.

THE FERREES—THE FAMILY FLEE TO GERMANY—THEY ARE JOINED BY ISAAC LEFEVER—THEY RESOLVE TO EMIGRATE TO AMERICA—THEY GO TO LONDON—THE MADAME IS INTRODUCED TO QUEEN ANN BY WILLIAM PENN—THEY JOIN REV. JOSHUA KOCHERTHAL'S PARTY AND GO TO ESOPUS IN NEW YORK—FROM THENCE JOURNEY TO PENNSYLVANIA—ARE RECEIVED BY THE INDIAN CHIEF TAWANA—MADAME FERREE DIES IN PEACE—HER FAMILY AND DISTINGUISHED DESCENDANTS.

"While here we stand with planted feet
Steadfast where loyal souls have stood,
Upon us let the tempest beat
Around us swell and surge the flood,
We fall or triumph on the spot—
God helping us we falter not."

DURING the dark and troubled period of the Revocation of the Edict of Nantes (1685) there lived in France a family named Ferree. (1) The parents, Daniel and Mary Ferree, were married in 1669. The fruit of this union were six children, viz: Daniel, John, Philip, Catharine, Mary and Jane. The Ferrees descend from the nobility (1) and were people of the highest respectability and staunch and fearless in their adherence to the Reformed faith. Daniel Ferree was a silk manufacturer, and from what can be gathered he was a man of wealth and high position in his native place. In order to carry out the provisions of the Edict to wholly extirpate the Reformed religion from the Realm the cruel Dragonades were sent to

---

(1). The Ferree, Ferrie, LaFerree, family are of the nobility of France and was originally seated at Forchamps, in Lower Normandy. The founder of the family was Robert Ferree, who in A. D. 1265 was confirmed to an extensive estate. M. Ferry, a great statesman of France, was of this stock. For Ferree history see "Nobility of Normandy," Vol. II p. 357.

Ferree Arms—De gueules, a trois annelets d'or Couronne; De Compte—supports, Deux lions.

the town in which Ferree lived and were quartered upon the Protestant citizens of the place. We may well imagine the misery and wretchedness caused by their coming to the unfortunate Protestants. Amid all this confusion the Ferrees escaped in the darkness of the night and fled to Strasbourg. How long the Ferree family remained at Strasbourg is not known. From here they went to Lindau in Bavaria, which was also an Imperial city, and hence afforded them security. Here Daniel Ferree died, and after his death his widow assumed her maiden name of Warembur as an additional means of safety, and it is a remarkable fact that she thereafter preferred to be known by that name. Family tradition has it that they also sojourned in Holland, but from a number of circumstancs we deem this improbable except, perhaps, for a brief period while on their way to London.

During the sojourn of the Ferrees in Germany they were joined by Isaac LeFever, whose parental home had been broken up and some of the family had perished at the hands of the Papists. This young man, of whom more will be said presently, married Catharine Ferree, eldest daughter of the Madame, several years prior to their emigration to America. The situation of the French Protestants who had fled to the Palatinate, while infinitely better than in their native land was, nevertheless, unsatisfactory. Besides being overcrowded with refugees, the Rhine Provinces were again and again ravaged by the Papal troops to such an extent that thousands of the inhabitants determined to seek peace and quietude in the wilds of the New World.

It is therefore no wonder that the Huguenots should follow the example of their German brethren to seek a home where they might serve the Lord unmolested by the cruel Inquisitor and brutal Dragoon.

The Ferree family also decided upon emigration. The head of the family now was Daniel, the eldest son, and who was a man of family, the rest, with the exception of Mrs. LeFever, being still single.

Madame Ferree's Passport.

The first step necessary in taking their departure was to secure from the civil authorities a certificate of standing and passport. This was done by Madame Ferree on behalf of the family. The original document, of which the following is a translation, is said to be still in the possession of her descendants:

"WHEREAS, Maria, Daniel Fuehre's widow, and her son, Daniel Ferie, with his wife and six single children, in view of improving their condition and in furtherance of their prosperity, purpose to emigrate from Steinweiler, in the Mayorality of Bittingheim, High Bailiwick Germersheim, via Holland and England, to the Island of Pennsylvania, to reside there. They have requested an accredited certificate that they have left the town of Steinweiler with the knowledge of the proper authorities, and have deported themselves, and without cause for censure, and are indebted to no one, and not subject to vassalage, being duly solicited it has been thought proper to grant their petition, declaring that the above-named persons are not moving away clandestinely.

"That during the time their father, the widow and children resided in this place they behaved themselves piously and honestly that it would have been highly gratifying to us to see them remain among us; that they are not subject to bodily bondage, the Mayorality not being subject to vassalage. They have also paid for their permission to emigrate. Mr. Fisher, the Mayor of Steinweiler, being expressly interrogated, it has been ascertained that they are not liable for any debts. In witness whereof I have, in the absence of the Counsellor of the Palatinate, etc., signed these presents, gave the same to the persons who intend to emigrate.

"Dated Bittingheim, March 10, 1708.

{ L. S. }   "J. P. DIETRICH, Court Clerk."

The civil passport having been obtained the next step was to obtain a certificate of standing and dismissal from the French Reformed Church at Pelican, of which they were members. That given to Daniel Ferree is given in the following translation:

"Certificate for Daniel Firre and his family.

"WE, the Pastors, Elders and Deacons of the Reformed Walloon Church of Pelican, in the Lower Palatinate, having been requested by the Honorable Daniel Firre, his wife, Anne Maria Leininger, and their children, Andrew and John Firre, to grant them a testimonial of their life and religion, do certify and attest that they have always made profession of the pure Reformed religion, frequented our sacred assemblies, and have partaken of the supper of the Lord with the other members of the faith, in addition to which they have always conducted themselves uprightly without having given cause for scandal that has come to our knowledge. Being now on their departure to settle elsewhere we commend them to the protection of God and to the kindness of all our brethren in the Lord Christ. In witness whereof we have signed this present testimonial with our signature and usual marks. Done at Pelican, in our Consistory, the 10th day of May, 1708.

MICHAEL MESSAKOP,
J. ROMAN, Pastor,
PETER SCHARLET,
JAMES BAILLEAUX, Deacon.
JOHN BAPTISTE LAPLACE, Deacon."

"THE undersigned children, to wit:—Andrew and John Firre—were baptized, the first in the church at Steinweiler in the year 1701, on the 28th of September. His sponsors were Andrew Leininger and his wife Margaret Leininger. The other, to wit:—John—was baptized in the Church of Rhorbac in the year 1703, on the 8th of February. The sponsors were Abraham Ptillon and Judith Miller, both of Steinweiler."

The Start For London.

With these documents in hand the party set out for England in order to make further arrangements regarding their settlement in America. Upon their arrival in London Madame Ferree visited William Penn in person, and to whom she made known her situation. Penn became deeply interested in the sad story of her misfortunes and the next day he introduced her to Queen Ann, the Sovereign of England. The good Queen, whose great kindness of heart had already been shown in her open hand of charity to thousands of French and German refugees, was likewise deeply moved with pity at her misfortune and promised her substantial aid, which she in due time rendered. William Penn covenanted to give her a tract of land and which she obtained upon her settlement in Pennsylvania.

Embark For America.

The party remained in London about six months during which time the Colony of Rev. Joshua Kocherthal was organized, composed of French and Palatine refugees from Lindau in Bavaria. This party, which the Ferrees and LeFevre joined, obtained from the Queen a patent of naturalization and permission to colonize in America. The instrument, which is dated August 27, 1708, contains the names of fifty-four persons, most of whom came to Pennsylvania some years later. The party arrived safely in New York, from whence they proceeded to Esopus, nearly a hundred miles up the Hudson river, and where they remained several years with their Huguenot friends. (1)

---

(1). Michael Ferree was one of the early Huguenot settlers of Esopus. At the destruction of Wiltwyck by the savages June 7, 1663, his house was burned, a child taken captive and himself wounded so severely that he later died from the effects. The Lefever family was also established at Esopus quite early. Andreas Lefevre was one of the 12 Patentees, 1677. (Doc. Hist. N. Y., XIII p. 245–506). They were all, without doubt, relatives to the Pennsylvania immigrants.

The Ferree family had no intention of settling permanently in New York, since the interviews of the Madame with Penn and his liberal grant to her of a great body of land presupposes arrangements for a settlement on them. Circumstances at length became favorable for their departure to Pennsylvania to take possession of their estates. This land, consisting of two thousand acres, was a part of the 10,000 acres granted by William Penn to Martin Kindig and others, agents of the Mennonite Colony. The lands were selected by the agents in 1709. The warrant is dated October 10, 1710. The land was surveyed on the 23d of the same month and subdivided April 27, 1711, by the Surveyor General. (1)

From the pen of an unknown writer we give an account of the arrival of the Ferree's in Lancaster county in 1712. (2) " It was on the evening of a summer day when the Huguenots reached the verge of a hill commanding a view of the Valley of the Pequea. It was a woodland scene, a forest inhabited by wild beasts, for no indication of civilized life was very near. Scattered along the Pequea, among the dark green hazel, could be discovered the Indian wigwams—the smoke issuing therefrom in its spiral form. No sound was heard but the songs of the birds. In silence they contemplated the beautiful prospect which Nature presented to their view. Suddenly a number of Indians darted from the woods. The females shrieked, when an Indian advanced and in broken English said to Madame Ferree : ' Indian no harm White ; White good to Indian ; go to our Chief ; come to Beaver.' Few were the words of the Indian. They went with him to Beaver's cabin, and Beaver, with the humanity that distinguished the Indian of that period, gave to the emigrants his wigwam. The next day he introduced them to

---

(1). The following is the allotment of Madame Ferree's estate by the Proprietors (see Penna. Archives, Vol. XIX p. 529) :

" Sept. 10, 1712.
"The late commissioners having granted ten thousand acres of land to the Palatines by their warrant dated October 10, 1710, in pursuance thereof there was laid out to Martin Kindig (besides the two thousand acres already confirmed to him and paid for) the like quantity of two thousand acres towards the Susquehanna, of which the Surveyor General has made a return. The said Martin now appearing desires that the said land may be granted and confirmed by patent to Maria Warenbur, widow, for whom the same was taken up or intended, and who is to pay the consideration for it. But, upon further consideration of the matter, it is agreed among themselves that the said lands shall be confirmed to Daniel Fierre and Isaac Lefever, two of the said widow's sons, and the consideration money, viz : 140 pounds at 7 pounds per hundred, by agreement having been for some time due but is now to be paid down in one sum, tis agreed that they shall pay only 10 pounds for interest—that is 150 pounds in the whole."

The Archives show many subsequent grants to various members of the family indicating a degree of prosperity in marked contrast with their former impoverished condition.

(2). See Rupp's History of Dauphin Co., p. 37.

Tawana, (1) who lived on the great flats of Pequea and was a Chief of a branch of the Conestoga Indians who at that time occupied this region.

The friendship formed between the Red Men of the forest with the Huguenots upon their arrival was maintained for many years, each race giving the other assistance in time of need."

Death of Madame Ferree.

Not long after her arrival in Pequea Madame Ferree vested in the care of trustees a plot of ground as a burial place for the settlement. This place, now known as Carpenter's Graveyard, is situated near Paradise. Here this noble woman, who had drank so deeply from the cup of misfortune, found a peaceful grave in 1716. She had accomplished her purpose to establish a new home for her posterity, many of whom are slumbering by her side. Her influence still lives in the great multitude of her descendants who belong to the aristocracy of personal worth. Her descendants, including of course, the LeFevers, are thousands in number and are to be found in many States of the Union.

The Family.

Daniel Ferree (1677–1750), eldest son of the Madame, had, besides his sons *Andrew* (1701–1739), and *John* (1703–1773), who were born in Europe, a son named *Daniel, Jr.* (d. 1762), who was married in 1739 to Mary Carpenter, whose father, Henry Carpenter, was one of the earliest and most prominent Swiss emigrants in the Province. *John Ferree*, the second son of the Madame, became a Quaker, as also most of his descendants after him.

Philip Ferree (1687–1753), the third son of the Madame, was married during their sojourn at Esopus to Leah Dubois, the daughter of Abraham Dubois, whose father *Louis* was the founder of New Platz in 1660. Soon after his marriage, which was about 1711, he came to Pequea and settled on a part of the Ferree grant. Upon his arrival he constructed a temporary habitation of forked poles, bark roof, etc. In this queer house their first child was born. Philip and Leah Ferree had eight children as follows: *Abraham* (d. 1775), *Isaac* (d. 1782), *Jacob, Philip, Joel,* and daughters *Lena*, married to William Buffington, *Leah*, married to Peter Baker, and *Elisabeth*, married to Isaac Ferree, her cousin. *Abraham*, the eldest son of Philip Ferree, the emigrant, was married about 1736 to a Miss Eltinge, of Esopus, N. Y. Their children were *Cornelius*, who settled in Virginia, *Israel*, and a daughter *Rebecca*, who married David Shreiver and removed to Frederick county, Maryland.

(1). Tawana is said to have been one of the signatories to the famous Penn Treaty with the Indians at Philadelphia.

Eminent Descendants.

A very large number of Madame Ferree's decendants have attained distinction in the various walks of life. The mere mention of them would fill pages. Among them are great scholars, jurists, ministers, statesmen, capitalists and soldiers. No other family in America can show a grander record of service for the public good. Prominent among the men of distinction was Colonel John Ferree, who commanded the Tenth Pennsylvania Rifles in the New Jersey campaign of the Revolution. Then also Colonel Joel Ferree, (1) Commander of the First Battalion of Lancaster Associators, and Major Michael Ferree and Lieutenant George Lefever. All these served with distinction in the Revolution, besides a host of others as non-commissioned officers and privates. Joseph Ferree, also a grandson of the Madame, was prominent in Colonial affairs. He was a member of the Assembly for Lancaster county 1771–1773, and a member of the County Committee in 1774 to consider the general dissatisfaction against the British Government.

In the War of 1812 the family was again prominent. Among others was Colonel Joel Ferree (1771–1813), of Allegheny county, who died at Zanesville, Ohio, while in active service. Also Colonel Daniel Lefever (1788–1855), son of Lieutenant George Lefever, of Newville, Pa.

In the Civil War a very large number of descendants were conspicuous, but we pass them all by but *one*, whose high military talents and glorious achievements has not only shed a lustre on his Huguenot ancestry but covered his memory with an undying glory. This was *Major General John F. Reynolds*, (2) Commander of the First Army Corps, and who commanded the left wing of the Union army. His great achievement at Gettysburg, where he held for many hours at bay with his single corps the entire army of the invaders, and the sacrifice of his gallant life in that mighty struggle, constitutes one of the most interesting episodes in our national history.

Another line of Madame Ferree's descendants who have made a most honorable record is the *Schreiver* family of Maryland. As already stated, David and Rebecca Ferree Schreiver removed from Pennsylvania to Frederick, Maryland. Their family was a noted one. Among the sons was *Abraham* (1771–1848), for many years

---

(1). Colonel Joel Ferree, of Lyken's Valley, was killed by the Indians in 1801 in Allegheny county while visiting relatives there.

(2). Major General John F. Reynolds, who fell at Gettysburg July 1, 1863, came from the Ferree-Lefever line. He was born at Lancaster, Pa., 1820, and graduated at West Point 1841, served throughout the Mexican war, and was one of the chief commanders in the Civil War at the time of his death.

the Judge of the Frederick county courts and whose high sense of rectitude is still a cherished memory in Western Maryland.

Another distinguished member of this family is *Admiral Winfield Scott Schley*, (*1*) the hero of Santiago, whose naval achievement in destroying the entire Spanish fleet is without a parallel in modern times. Nothstanding the questionable attempts, prompted by envy, to rob him of this crowning glory of American naval warfare, it is perhaps sufficient to say that the great mass of intelligent readers who have no connection whatever with departmental regulations supposed to govern the case, will never cease to regard him as the true leader and hero of that engagement.

LeFevre.—As already noted, *Isaac LeFevre* married Catharine, the daughter of Madame Ferree. The name LeFevre occurs in many honorable connections in France. Jacques LeFevre, of Meaux, was one of the first Reformers and died a martyr's death. Francois Joseph LeFevre (1755-1820), Duke of Dantzic, one of the great Napoleon's Marshals, was born in Alsace and was one of the greatest soldiers of the past century.

The family (2) to which Isaac LeFevre belonged were scattered at the Revocation and several lost their lives. It is quite probable that he was connected with the LeFevers of Esopus, New York, who emigrated thither long before the Revocation. In fact there is a strong probability that Isaac LeFevre had been in America years before his marriage and immigration with the Ferree family. He was a man of great energy and ability as well as a scholar, as his numerous notes and comments in his French Bible testify. He acquired very rich and extensive estates in the Pequea Valley and at his death owned over fifteen hundred acres of the choicest land.

The descendants of Isaac LeFevre have been an honor to their Huguenot ancestry. Philip LeFevre (1710–1761), the second son of the immigrant, was a noted manufacturer of tools and firearms. One of the sons of Philip LeFevre was George LeFevre (1739–

---

(1). Admiral Schley derives his paternal ancestry from John Thomas Schley, b. in the Palatinate 1712, leader of a Colony to Maryland 1735, founded Frederick 1745, died 1790. His grandson, John Schley (1771–1830), m. Mary Schreiver, b. 1773, daughter of David and Rebecca (Ferree) Schreiver. John and Mary (Schreiver) Schley were the grandparents of the Admiral. It will thus be seen that his descent from Madame Ferree and of Louis DuBois, the founder of New Paltz, N. Y., is easily traced.

(2). In one of his bibles is a record of his brothers and sisters, but unfortunately for posterity he failed to record the names of his parents. The record is as follows: Judith, b. October 20, 1660; Philip, b. May 1, 1664; Jacob, b. December 20, 1666; Isaac, b. March 26, 1669; Mary, born June 15, 1671; Susanna, b. September 12, 1672; Charles, b. October 24, 1680.

The children of Isaac and Catharine Ferree LeFevre were: Abraham, b. April 9, 1706; Philip, b. March 16, 1710; Daniel, b. March 29, 1713; Mary, b. August 24, 1715; Esther, b. May 3, 1717; Samuel, b. May 3, 1719.

1820), who married Anna B., a daughter of Lawrence and granddaughter of the noted immigrant, Matthias Schliermacher (Slaymaker). After serving as an officer in the Revolution George LeFevre in 1780 removed to Newville, in Cumberland county, where he established an honored posterity.

Daniel LeFevre (1788–1855), the youngest son of George LeFevre, early in life removed to Crawford county, but died near Detroit, in Michigan. He was a man of prominence and served as a Colonel in the War of 1812.

Among other notable descendants of the immigrant, Isaac LeFevre, may be mentioned in this connection Major General John F. Reynolds, of the Civil War, and Judge O. E. Lefever, of Denver, Colorado.

CHAPTER XIII.

The Non-Resistant Denominations.

THE MENNONITES AND DUNKARDS—THEIR PEACEFUL CHARACTER—PERSECUTIONS AND MARTYRDOMS—THEIR DISPERSION—SOME TAKE REFUGE IN ALSACE—THE PALATINATE DEVASTATED—THEY SEEK A HOME IN THE NEW WORLD.

> "*Faith of our Fathers—living faith,*
> *In spite of dungeon, fire and sword,*
> *Oh! how our hearts beat high with joy*
> *When'er we hear that glorious word.*
> *Faith of our Fathers—Holy faith,*
> *We will be true to thee till death.*"

OF all the branches of the Christian Church having their origin in the Reformation, there is none that has passed through a more fiery ordeal than the Mennonites. (1) This body of Christians was scattered over Central Europe, and through their rigid faith and austere mode of life came in sharp conflict not only

---

(1). The Mennonites were not Huguenots in the proper sense of that term. Their settlement in Alsace, however, which was annexed to France during their sojourn there, made them French citizens, and in which relation many of them came to Pennsylvania. This, we think, entitles them a place in these Memorials.

The Mennonite Church was founded by Menno Simon, a distinguished reformer, who was born at Witmarsum, Friesland, in 1505. About 1538 he began to organize his adherents into societies. After many years of truly apostolic labors in many lands he died in 1561. In many respects he was far in advance of his age. His views on war and non-resistance, religious toleration, education, and many kindred subjects, are being absorbed by advanced reformers of all Christian persuasions as never before and mark the lines of highest civil and religious effort at the present day.

with Papists but in many instances with the Protestants. Their opposition to war, physical resistance, civil courts and oath-taking marked a wide divergence from the civil and political laws and usages of the day, while their advocacy of complete religious toleration and education brought them in conflict with the narrow bigotry of nearly all the established Churches. Their ministers and teachers took no stated salary but, like the Apostles of old, traveled about to preach and indoctrinate the people in the faith. There never was a more devoted class of ministers in any other Protestant denomination, and we have never read or heard of any of them abjuring their faith under the most dreadful torture ever inflicted on man.

We will give, in this connection, a brief account of the sufferings of a number whose descendants and kindred found a refuge in Pennsylvania. Many hundred, perhaps thousands bearing the names of the martyrs given are found in America still adhering to the faith of their fathers.

The persecution of the Mennonites was especially severe in Switzerland, the storm center being the city of Zurich. Here in the cloister tower of the *Othenbach* great numbers were confined, many of whom were starved to death or died of neglect, besides those who suffered at the stake, block or gibbet. In 1528 *John Sechler*, and in 1529 *Conrad Eicher*, of Staffsburg, suffered death. In 1535 *Peter Kuster*, (1) and in 1537 *Peter Stucke* and *Ulrich Huber*, of the north of Holland, were beheaded. At Amsterdam in 1529 *George Bowman*, of Wurtemberg, suffered. In 1538 *Offrus Grissinger*, an eminent minister, was burned in the Tyrol. In 1536 *Peter Lydecker* and *Peter Gerhart*, teachers of Zurich, were beheaded. In 1538 *Michael Wideman* was burned. In 1539 *Lorentz Eberly* and *Lorentz Rudolph Eisley*, of Gronau, were cast into prison and subsequently suffered death.

In 1543 *Christian Oberlin* suffered. In 1557 *Martin DeWall*, of Antwerp, was beheaded. In 1576 *Matthew Binder*, an eminent minister of Wurtemburg, was arrested and taken to Stuttgart where he defended himself before the civil and ecclesiastical courts with great vigor and ability. He was thrown into the "Hohenwiltingschloss" with many other coreligionists. During their imprisonment the schloss (Castle) took fire. Binder and his fellow-prisoners labored hard to extinguish the flames and did not take advantage of the opportunity to escape, which was purposely afforded them. The prisoners then petitioned the civil authorities for their release inas-

---

(1). The supposed ancestor of Major General George A. Custer (1840–1876), a gallant officer of the Civil War, and who, with his entire command, was killed by the Sioux Indians in Montana.

much as they had done no wrong to the State and were not indicted as criminals. Upon this the prison officials quickly presented their petition to the Prince who generously liberated them ere the ecclesiastical authorities could interfere in the matter.

In 1614 *John Landis*, (*1*) an eminent minister who lived on the Rhine, was arrested and dragged before a tribunal, and after a mock trial was beheaded at Zurich. When he was about to suffer martyrdom his wife and children came into his presence weeping bitterly. This so touched his heart that he bade them withdraw in order that he might show no sign of weakness when suffering for "the faith once delivered to the saints." Landis was a great light in the Church and had traveled extensively in Alsace, Switzerland and the Palatinate. Notwithstanding this calamity the family remained true to the faith and in 1642 *Felix Landis*, a son of the martyr, and also a minister, died of starvation in the Othenbach. At the same time *Varena Landis* was terribly persecuted. Being given her choice of the Othenbach or remaining a prisoner in her own house because of her advanced age and enfeebled condition, she choose the latter, and in 1643 died of starvation and neglect.

In this same year *Mrs. Barbara Neff* was imprisoned and shamefully maltreated. A remarkable instance of courage was shown in the case of a youth named *Rudolph Sehner*, of Gronningen, who was confined in the Othenbach over two years. He was given his liberty on condition that he attend the Established Church. This agreement he immediately regretted as being equivalent to an abjuration of his faith. He was thereupon recommitted to prison and perished of hunger in 1643.

The *Bachman* and *Meylin* families, so well and favorably known in Pennsylvania, were dreadfully persecuted between 1638 and 1643. *Rudolph Bachman* and *John Meylin*, with his two sons and daughters *Barbara* and *Elisabeth*, were all thrown into the Othenbach from which the women finally made their escape, but the men suffered death. *Martin Meylin*, one of the sons of John, was an able mininster and had traveled extensively in Alsace and the Palatinate.

In 1640–'41 *John Rudolph Bowman*, with many others whose names are lost, was cast into the Othenbach where he was confined for sixty weeks, living mostly on bread and water. Finally he embraced an opportunity to escape only to find his family scattered and his property confiscated.

Among the Othenbach prisoners at this time was aged *Warner Phiester*, with his wife and daughter-in-law. The wife managed to escape but the others perished with hunger.

---

(1). Ancestor of the Landis immigrants to Lancaster county.

Jacob Egly, of Gronningen, a prominent minister and teacher, suffered all the horrors of the Othenbach for seventy weeks before he succumbed to hunger in 1639. In 1659 the following ministers were imprisoned in Bern: *Ulrich Baumgardner, Anthony Himmelberg, Iegley Schelbach, Ulrich Baumgardner* (2d), *Christian Christianas, Rhoda Peters* and *John Zug.* (*1*) After being under arrest for a period of twelve years they were liberated on the condition that they leave the country and not return without special permission, they having rejected all former overtures as compromising their faith.

The reader will have observed that the years from 1638 to 1643 were fruitful in Mennonite martyrdoms, and it is humiliating to confess that Protestants as well as Catholics must be held responsible for the sacrifice of many inoffensive lives. In 1626 the Mennonites were recognized as a Protestant denomination in Holland which ended their active persecution in that country. The authorities even went so far as to champion their cause, and in 1642 the Council of Amsterdam addressed a vigorous protest to the Council of Zurich in Switzerland against their continued persecution there. The protest, however, seems to have been unavailing, as in 1650 a special edict was issued against them at Schauffhausen which was followed by another in 1653. (2)

It was during this period that the Mennonites determined to migrate to America, their first intention being to form a settlement in New York. In 1662 they addressed a petition to the authorities of Amsterdam setting forth their purpose, but the disturbed relations between Holland and England at that time, and the surrender of New York city to the English in 1664, made their plans in that direction futile. (3)

About 1671 (4) their situation becoming intolerable by persecution a large number of them emigrated to Alsace, in the vicinity

---

(1). In 1727 Ulrich Zug, a grandson of the sufferer, came to Pennsylvania and settled in Lancaster county where he died in 1758. In 1742 three brothers—Moritz, John and Christian Zug, also grandsons—arrived. In 1738 Christian and Jacob Zug arrived. Their connection with the foregoing is not known. The connection in America now numbers thousands of the best citizens to be found and most of whom still cling to the faith of their fathers. Some became eminent Mennonite and Dunkard ministers. Among those distinguished in the public service may be mentioned Brigadier General Samuel K. Zook, who was born in Pennsylvania in 1823. In 1848 he removed to New York city and became a noted electrician and made many valuable discoveries in electrical science. He organized and commanded the Fifty-seventh Regiment of New York Volunteers of the Civil War. He was promoted for bravery in action in 1862 and fell mortally wounded at the head of his brigade at Gettysburg July 2, 1863.

(2). Bracht's Hist. of the Mennonites, p. 1019-1023.
(3). Doc. Hist. of N. Y., Vol. II p. 176.
(4). Bracht, p. 1022.

of Strasbourg which, at that time, was an Imperial city and enjoyed a full measure of religious liberty. Their repose in Alsace, however, was of brief duration as the Valley of the Rhine soon thereafter became the battlefield of the Orleans succession to the Palatinate (1686-'97). During these years of turmoil the Rhine Valley run red with the blood of the Huguenots, Mennonites and Palatines. Death and destruction marked the advance of Count Turenne's army. (1) During these years of dire calamity both Alsace and Lorraine fell a prey to French aggression and were annexed to that realm. Scarcely had the Peace of Ryswick (1697) cleared away the smoke of battle when the long and bloody war of the Spanish Succession broke out (1700-1713) and the Palatinate again became the arena of conflict for the great armies of Continental Europe.

It was amid such dark and bloody days as these that our Huguenot, Mennonite and Palatine ancestors, while witnessing the destruction of their homes, the slaughter of their kindred and the subversion of their faith, looked with longing vision across the Atlantic to the fertile valleys of Pennsylvania as a possible place of refuge. The hands on the dial of Providence indicated that the hour of their deliverance had arrived.

In 1683 a large number of Mennonites, under encouragement from William Penn, emigrated from Creyfels, in the Duchy of Cleves, to Pennsylvania and founded Germantown, which place soon became the objective point of hundreds of refugees.

The withdrawal of the Allied army under the Duke of Marlborough from the Palatinate after the battle of Blenheim in 1704 seems to have precipitated a crisis for the Protestants of this region.

In 1703 the Mennonites of Bern, in Switzerland, sent Louis Mitchelle, an expert in mining and agriculture, to America with a view of locating suitable lands for them. (2). After some years of exploration he returned to Europe to render a report of his work. In 1708, in company with the eminent Swiss nobleman, Christopher DeGraffenreid, he again came to America to consummate final arrangements, which resulted in the founding of the Swiss Colony at Newburn, in North Carolina, in 1709. (3)

About 1707 (4) a number of Mennonites proceeded to London to confer with Penn in regard to locating a Colony in his Province. The result of the visit was so satisfactory that a number of them set out as soon as possible for Pennsylvania. A selection of lands

---

(1). About 2000 towns and villages were sacked and mostly destroyed. Nearly all the large cities, such as Heidelberg, Manheim and Speir, were left in ruins.
(2). Col. Records, Vol. II p. 420. Rupp's Lanc. County, pp. 55-58.
(3). Rupp's Lanc. County, pp. 70-71.
(4). Rupp's Lanc. County, p. 74.

was made and a settlement effected in the Pequea Valley in Lancaster county in 1709. (1) They received a warrant for the survey of their lands, which embraced ten thousand acres, on August 10, 1710. (2) Of this tract two thousand acres were expressly reserved for Madame Ferree and her family. (3) The leaders of this movement were *Martin Kendig, John Meylen* and *John Herr,* the latter an aged and highly respected minister. These men, with the following, were the pioneers: *John Rudolf Bundley, Jacob Miller, John Funk, Wendell Bowman, Martin* and *Ulrich Oberholtzer.* After they were comfortably located a council was held to select one of their number to return to Europe and superintend the removal of many to the new settlement. In conformity with their custom they cast lots, with the result that their minister, John Herr, was selected for the arduous task. Owing to his advanced age and the reluctance of the Colony to part with their pastor for such an uncertain undertaking, Martin Kindig volunteered to take his place. (4). Kindig set out for Europe at once with the result that he returned with a considerable number of Colonists in 1712. He evidently brought over another party in 1727. (5)

The Colony continued to develop in numbers and in material prosperity so that long before the close of the Provincial period they had established a great number of societies in many parts of the Province. They have now, through a beneficent Providence, multiplied into a mighty host. America has no more pious, law-abiding and thrifty citizens than the Mennonites, and they have by their consummate skill as tillers of the soil made Lancaster county their first asylum in the New World the richest agricultural county in America. (6) The township in which they located was called Strasburg, in honor of the city from which many of the Colony had come.

The Baptist Brethren.

Like the Mennonites the Baptist Brethren, or Dunkards, as they are most familiarly known, are also a non-resistant people and, like them, passed through the fires of persecution ere they established themselves in Pennsylvania. Among the refugees were a number of leading families with Huguenot antecedents.

In 1682 *Ulrich Urner* fled from Canton Uri in Switzerland to Alsace, France, for greater security. In 1708 he came to Penn-

---

(1). Colonial Records, Vol. III p. 397.
(2). Warrant Book, p. 229.
(3). Penna. Archives, Vol. XIX p. 529.
(4). Rupp's Lanc. County, p. 81.
(5). Penna. Arch., Vol. XVII p. 10.
(6). See U. S. statistics for 1890.

sylvania and settled in Coventry, Lancaster county. His son *Martin*, born in Alsace 1695, and died in Pennsylvania 1755, became one of the early and prominent ministers of the Brethren Church in America. He was ordained as an elder by Alexander Mack, the founder, immediately after the latter's arrival in 1729, and succeeded him as the senior of that denomination upon his death.

Abraham DuBois (1679-1748) was born of Huguenot parentage at Epstein. He identified himself with the Brethren in 1712, and in 1715 became a minister and assistant of Alexander Mack, the founder, and with him suffered great persecution in Europe. In 1732 he came to Pennsylvania where he entered upon ministerial labors, which continued until his death. He was a delegate to the Union Synod of 1742.

Royer.—The *Royer* family (also written Reyer and Rier) has ever been a prominent one in France and many noted men of this name occur. The family was mostly seated in the northern part, especially in the vicinity of Metz, from whence a number retired to the Palatinate in consequence of the Revocation. One branch was numbered with the nobility. A nobleman named *Jacques Royer*, a prominent Protestant, suffered the loss of his estates in the persecutions prior to the Revocation. An association in America by the descendants of the early Royer emigrants to Pennsylvania was formed in 1897 for the recovery of the confiscated estates of that nobleman, whom they claim as their ancestor. Several families of this name fled from Tours at the Revocation and came with the Huguenot Colony to South Carolina.

Sebastian Royer, who was born near the city of Metz, retired to the Palatinate about the Revocation period, and in 1718 came to Pennsylvania and settled in Lancaster county. He was a prominent member of the Baptist Brethren and his numerous descendants have mostly adhered to that faith. Many have been eminent as ministers and teachers.

In 1729 *John Jacob Royer*, another prominent member of the Brethren Church, arrived and located near Lititz in the same county. Another branch emanate from *John Michael Royer*, (1) who arrived in 1732 and located in Upper Salford, Montgomery county.

The family Lasche (Laschett) was scattered by the persecutions of the Revocation period. One branch found shelter in a secluded place in Italy, and from thence they removed to Saxony, Prussia and Switzerland. A branch of this family came to America

---

(1). He was the son of John Michael and Catharine Royer, and was born 1686 in Swabach in the Palatinate. He was thrice married and the father of twenty-four children and the progenitor of a great posterity. See "The Perkiomen Region," Vol. I.

in 1854 and located in Wisconsin. In 1736 arrived John Jacob (Van) Laschet, who was then 50 years of age, and his sons John Peter and Christian, aged 25 and 18 years respectively. This branch had located at Crefels, in the Duchy of Cleves, where it became identified with the Brethren, and of which society they became prominent members, several being ministers. The immigrant located in Earl township, Lancaster county, where he died prior to 1754. (1) He was a delegate to the famous Union Sỳnod held at Germantown in 1742. The family was established at Germantown and on the Conewago in York county, and also at Amwell, N. J., at an early day.

In 1738 arrived *John Wendel Laschet*, whose relation to the foregoing family is not known.

Ephrata.

The famous Seventh Day Baptist Community, founded in 1725 at Ephrata by Conrad Beissel and composed of Sabbatarian and Pietistic refugees of various nationalities, had also among its members some of Huguenot antecedents. (2) Among the number was *Conrad Dubois*, who arrived in 1728 and whose wife died at the Cloister in 1737. The name does not subsequently occur on the records of the Community. In 1757 the will of Conrad Dubois, presumably the same individual, was probated at Reading.

In the diary of the Community reference is made to another French member under the church name of "*Jonadab*," whose wife and daughter died in 1740. No clew is given as to their identity although it is expressly stated that the family were Huguenots.

For many years the dominant spirits of the Ephrata Community were the *Eckerline* brothers, under whose skillful management the society was brought up to a high state of material prosperity, and their expulsion in 1745 because of their progressiveness marks the beginning of the Community's decline.

These men, so celebrated in the history of the Community, were the sons of *Michael Eckerline*, a substantial citizen of Strasbourg, in Alsace, then a part of France. About 1700 he became identified with a Pietist movement in his city and which was immediately interdicted by the authorities. Because of this persecution he withdrew to Schwartzenau where he identified himself with the movement which resulted in the organization of the German Baptist

---

(1). In a patent granted to his son Christian in 1754 for land taken up by his father, John Jacob Lasche, it is stated that the father had died before he received a patent for said land.

(2). For a full account of the Ephrata and kindred societies see "The German Sectarians of Pennsylvania," 2 vols., by Julius F. Sachse.

Society (Dunkard) under Alexander Mack, and which subsequently came to Pennsylvania. Michael Eckerline died at Schwartzenau at a time when the adherents of his faith were preparing to seek freedom from persecution by a general exodus to the Western World.

In 1725 the widow, then quite aged, and her sons Israel, Samuel, Emanuel and Gabriel, emigrated to Pennsylvania and located in the vicinity of Germantown among the members of their faith. In 1727 Israel, the oldest of the brothers, joined the Ephrata Community, which was then in its infancy. He was soon joined by his mother and brothers, and the family contributed the major share of the talent, energy and business tact which made the Ephrata Colony one of the wonders of America. Israel, under the spiritual name of *Onesimus*, became the Prior of the institution, while his brothers also held important positions and wielded a great influence. Samuel was a physician of no mean ability. It would seem that their great talents and business qualities which they freely exercised to the great enrichment of the Community provoked the jealousy of the Founder and his friends with the result that they were excluded, as already stated. The brothers, upon their exclusion, in company with several associates, journeyed to the wilds of Virginia where they once more established themselves on the Community plan. Their enterprise, however, failed. Some time after 1750 the three brothers—Israel, Samuel and Gabriel—located on the Monongahala river, in now West Virginia, where their settlement was destroyed by the French in 1757 and Israel and Gabriel were carried captives to Canada and from thence to France, where they died. Samuel fortunately was absent at the time of the incursion and escaped the fate of his brothers. He died in 1781.

Early Mennonite and Huguenot Settlers.

The following list, nearly all heads of families, embraces only such as arrived prior to 1718 in Lancaster county: *Bare* (1) Jacob, Sr. (died 1736), Jacob, Jr., Henry and John; *Baumgardner*, Peter; *Boyer*, Samuel; *Brand*, Adam; *Brubaker*. John; *Bæhm*, Jacob; *Brenneman*, Melchoir, Adam, Christopher and Christian; *Biere*, Jacob; *Bowman*, Michael and John Wendell; *Burkholder*, John, Sr., John, Jr. and Abraham; *Christopher*, Carl; *Dondore*, Michael; *Erisman*, Melchoir; *Eby*, Theodorus, Peter and John; *Eshelman*, Daniel; *Faber*, John; *Frederick*, John; *Ferree*, (2) John, Daniel and Philip; *Funk*, John Jacob, and Henry; *Francis-*

---

(1). Originally "*Barree*" Huguenots.
(2). Sons of Madame Ferree, which see.

cus, (*1*) Christopher ; *Groff*, Hans (2) and Martin ; *Guth* (Good), John and Jacob ; *Harnish*, Martin ; *Hershey*, Christian ; *Herr*, Hans and Abraham ; *Hess*, John ; *Hermau*, Christian ; *Hoover*, Ulrich ; *Hostetter*, Jacob ; *Houser*, Christian and Ulrich ; *Hufford*, Melchoir ; *Hubert*, Hubertson (1709) ; *Kaigy*, Hans ; *Kauffman*, John, Andrew and Jacob ; *Kœnig* (King), Simon ; *Krider*, John Jacob ; *Kindig*, Martin, George ; *Kreitser*, Jacob ; *Larue*, Jonas, (*3*) ; *Lefever*, (*4*) Isaac ; *Leamon*, (*5*) Peter ; *Landis*, Felix ; *Le-Bo*, John ; *Landert*, Sigismund ; *Line*, John ; *Lochman*, Casper ; *Lighte* (Light), John and John Jacob ; *Meylin*, Martin and John ; *Mire* (Mier, Moyer), Michael, Jacob, Rudy, Abraham and John ; *Miller*, Jacob, Sr., Jacob, Jr. and Martin ; *Musselman*, Henry ; *Neff*, (*6*) Francis, Sr., Francis, Jr., John Henry, Sr., John Henry, Jr., and Henry ; *Nissley*, Jacob ; *Newcomer*, Peter ; *Oberholtzer*, Martin and Ulrich ; *Peelman*, Christian ; *Ream*, Eberhart ; *Royer*, Sebastian ; *Rudy*, Ulrich ; *Shank*, John and Michael ; *Sower* (7) Christopher ; *Steinman*, Christian and Joseph ; *Shultz*, Andrew ; *Schliermacher* (*8*) (Slaymaker), Mathias ; *Steiner*, Christian ;

---

(1). A noted Swiss patriot who had taken refuge in Alsace. He came to Pequea in 1710.

(2). Born of distinguished parentage in Switzerland 1661. Fled as a Mennonite to Alsace where he bore the title of Baron Von Weldon. About 1695-'96, accompanied by his brother, he came to Germantown. He was one of the first settlers of Lancaster county, locating at "Graff's Thal" (Rupp's Lanc. County, p. 133). He was a wealthy and important personage, Earl township being named in his honor (Col. Rec., Vol. III. pp. 420, 673). He founded a great posterity. He was the grandfather of Sebastian and Andrew Groff, noted Revolutionary patriots.

Sebastian Groff (3d), born in Earl township, Lancaster county, about 1750 ; delegate to the Provincial Convention 1775 ; delegate to the Federal Constitution Ratification Convention 1787 ; State Constitutional Convention 1787 ; State Senator 1790 ; died 1792. His brother Andrew was also a man of prominence and member of the Provincial Assembly 1776 and treasurer of Lancaster county many years.

(3). A Huguenot and associate of the Ferrees.

(4). Son-in-law to Madame Ferree.

(5). Originally "*Lemont*" (Rupp's Lanc. County, p. 516).

(6). Francis and Dr. John Henry Neff belonged to an eminent Swiss Mennonite family, some of whom perished for their faith. They fled to Alsace where they resided before coming to America. Dr. Neff was the first regular physician in Lancaster county (Rupp, p. 125).

(7). The famous German printer who located in Germantown and where in 1743 he printed the first Bible in America in a European language.

(8). Emanated from a notable family and for some time seated at Strasbourg, in Alsace, owing to persecution. He came to Pennsylvania in 1716. Henry Slaymaker, son of Mathias, was born in Strasburg, Lancaster county, 1730 ; a Captain in active service 1776 ; member of Constitutional Convention 1776 ; a Justice ; succeeded Judge Hubley as Judge of the Courts 1784 ; died 1785. His son Amos, b. 1755, was a Captain in the Revolution, member of Congress 1811-1814, and later a member of Penna. Senate. He held many important offices and died in 1840.

Schnebly, John Jacob, Sr. and John Jacob, Jr. ; *Stoy*, Frederick ; *Swope*, John ; *Stompher*, John ; *Weaver* (Webber), Jacob, Henry, John and George ; *Wenerick*, Benedictus ; *Witmer*, Benedictus ; *Woolslegel*, John ; *Zimmerman* (1) (Carpenter), Henry, Emanuel and Gabriel.

CHAPTER XIV.

The Tulpehocken—Swatara—Lebanon.

THE OVERLAND JOURNEY FROM SCHOHARIE—SETTLEMENT OF THE TULPEHOCKEN VALLEY—LEBANON—DAUPHIN—DISTINGUISHED FAMILIES OF HUGUENOT DESCENT.

> " *They were men of present valor,*
> *Stalwart old iconoclasts,*
> *Unconvinced by axe or gibbet*
> *That all virtue was the past.*
> *But we make their truth our falsehood*
> *Thinking that has made us free,*
> *Hoarding it in mouldy parchments,*
> *While our tender spirits flee,*
> *The rude grasp of that impulse*
> *Which drew them across the sea."*
> — *Lowell.*

THE beautiful and fertile Valley of the Tulpehocken is ten or more miles north of Reading, in Berks county, Pennsylvania. It is watered by the Swatara and Tulpehocken Creek, and anciently embraced far more than the present township of that name. Its first settlers were Palatines, who came overland from Schoharie, in New York, in 1723 and 1727, and among whom was the celebrated Conrad Weiser. These Palatines had emigrated to England at the invitation of Queen Ann owing to the devastation of the Palatinate by the French. Many thousands of them arrived in London prior to 1709 in a deplorable condition. In 1709 about three thousand of them were sent to New York at the expense of the Government. They wintered at Livingston Manor in 1710 (2) and eventually a large number of them came to Pennsylvania (Chap. V). Among these refugees were many Huguenots whose names reappear in this work.

---

(1). Henry Zimmerman, a Swiss, first came in 1698. Returned to Europe and brought over his family in 1706 (Rupp, p. 126). Many of his descendants became prominent men.

(2). For list see "Rupp's 30,000 names of Emigrants"—Appendix.

Sellaire.—Among the Huguenot exiles were several branches of the ancient *Sellaire* or Cellier family of France. The name is met with among the refugees to England and America prior to the Revocation, and even in far away Cape Colony where a descendant, General Cellier, became famous as a Boer leader in the Transvaal war. One branch retired to the Palatinate about the period of the Revocation. Of this family was *Jean Henri Sellaire* who, with his family, followed the great exodus of Palatines to London in 1708. In 1709 he came to New York with the Palatines, where his name and that of his son *John* as "*Zeller*" appears among the settlers of Livingston Manor in 1710. About 1727 he came overland through the trackless wilderness to Tulpehocken, locating near the present town of Sheridan, where he established a considerable estate and where he died at a very advanced age in 1756. (1) His house, a massive stone edifice, erected with a view to protect the family and neighbors in case of attack by the Indians, is still standing.

Pontius.—In 1738 *John Pontius* arrived and located in Tulpehocken. He was born in Alsace in 1718. In 1743 he married Anna Catharine, a daughter of John Zellers, already referred to. He had a considerable family and his sons were great pioneers. (2) Several were among the first settlers in Buffalo Valley in (now) Union county, and many of the next generation were of the first in Ohio and Illinois.

Aurand.—Among the Huguenot refugees to the Palatinate was a branch of the *Aurand* family, and of which was Henry Aurand and his wife Anna Catharine. After a sojourn of some years in Holland they settled near Heidelberg where most of their children were born. In 1753 John Aurand (1725–1807), a son of the foregoing, came to America and located in Berks county where he married Mary, a daughter of John Pontius. In 1772 he removed to (now) Union county. His son *Dietrich* (1760–1841) was a soldier of the Revolution and for many years a noted minister of the Reformed Church. (3)

Bashore (Le Baiseur).—This family, so numerous and so widely scattered throughout America, is of eminent Huguenot origin. The name, according to Prof. I. D. Rupp (himself a descendant), is a corruption of *Le Baiseur.* Several of this name are found

---

(1). He was survived by his wife, Anna Maria, and children John George, his chief heir, John Henry, John David, Martin, John, Anna Mary Saltzgiver, Barbaralis Lerew, Catharine Pontius and Ann Elisabeth Battorf.

(2). The sons were John Henry, b. 1744; John Peter, b. 1747.; John, b. 1751; Andrew Michael, George and Frederick.

(3). See "Fathers of the Reformed Church." The children of the emigrant were Henry, Peter, Jacob, Daniel, Dietrich, George, Elisabeth Zeller and Mary Reem, all of whom became heads of families.

among the refugees to foreign lands. Jacques Le Baiseur fled to England in 1614. Another of this name was a member of the Huguenot Church of New York prior to 1700. John Le Baiseur was married in Philadelphia in 1789 (Pa. Arch. Vol. IX).

Several heads of families of this name located in Pennsylvania. They were in all probability brothers. In 1735 we find *Jacob Bashore* with a family in Earl, Lancaster county. He died in 1779. *Baltzer Bashore*, who died in 1791, was a resident in the same locality in 1739. *George Bashore* located in Bethel township, in Berks county, prior to 1738. From the latter immigrant sprang many men of eminence, among them the late Prof. I. D. Rupp (1) and Hon. Charles S. Wolf, of Lewisburg, an able statesman and a leader in the Pennsylvania Legislature.

Bennech, (Bennage).—In northern Berks county also located the *Bennech* family, a name noted in Huguenot history. Many of this name were scattered by the persecutions to Switzerland, the Palatinate and England. Of the immigrants to America *Simon Bennech* located in Heidelberg township in Berks county, where he died in 1757, leaving posterity. The family arrived in 1732, at which time Simon was thirteen years of age. Inasmuch as the father's name does not appear on the list with the family upon arrival it is probable that he died on the voyage to America.

Achey.—The *Achey* (Augey) family of America emanate from the nobility of Normandy and the name occurs in many honorable connections in French history. (2) A Knight of this name accompanied William the Conqueror in his expedition to England (A. D. 1066), while the noted Admiral, the Count DeAchey (1717–1775), shed lustre on the family name in more recent years. The name has suffered many variations, and it is worthy of note that the great naturalist, Prof. Louis Agassiz (1807–1873), in a letter to Prof. S. Aughey (of the Pennsylvania branch,) in 1872, claimed kinship with the family under consideration. Several branches emigrated to other countries in the early stages of the Huguenot persecutions.

Prof. I. Daniel Rupp.

(1). This distinguished scholar was born in Cumberland county, Pa., July 10, 1803, and died in Philadelphia May 31, 1878. Mr. Rupp had but very few scholastic advantages, but by close and constant application he gained an immense fund of knowledge, as is shown in the wide range of his productions. His published works are over thirty in number, mostly of a historical character, and constitute a vast mine of historical lore respecting the settlement of Pennsylvania and from which later historians have freely drawn. His chief works are his various county histories, seven volumes, 1844–'47 : "The Bloody Theatre, or Martyr's Mirror," 1048 pages, translated from the German ; "He Pasa Eklesia," 1844 ; "A History of Religious Denominations in America," and "A Collection of Thirty Thousand Names of German, Swiss, Dutch and French Immigrants."

(2). For the several conferments of nobility on the Achey family see DeMaigney's French Heraldry, pages 24 and 344.

In 1558 Jacques DeAuchy, a merchant of Leuwaarden in Holland who had embraced the doctrines of the Mennonites, was apprehended by the authorities. His able defense of his life and doctrine shows him to have been an extraordinary man. After a year's imprisonment he suffered a martyr's death in 1559.

The immediate antecedents of the American branch is enshrouded in the gloom that followed the Revocation period, during which time a Huguenot father suffered death for conscience sake. The widow with her children and a brother effected their escape to Switzerland, and from whence the sons removed to the Palatinate. Upon the mother's death the sons came to Pennsylvania in 1752. They were *John Ludwig*, *John Jacob*, and *Herman*. Soon after their arrival we find the brothers in the Tulpehocken region. John Ludwig Achey acquired a considerable estate near Lingelstown, where he died in 1792. His son Henry, b. 1759, was married to Elisabeth Shuey, also of Huguenot ancestry. They were the ancestors of Prof. S. Aughey, the noted scientist of the State University of Nebraska.

The emigrant was proud of his noble ancestry and had his coaches and furniture decorated with the Achey coat of arms.

LeBeau, (Lebo.—This family, now so numerous throughout the Union, was scattered at the Revocation, several branches retiring to the Palatinate and Switzerland, from whence the younger members emigrated to America. All the following herewith given were heads of families : *John Lebo* was naturalized in Lancaster county in 1718. Another *John Lebo* was located in the present limits of Montgomery county as early as 1734. *Peter Lebo* was located in Tulpehocken prior to 1738, and died advanced in age in 1783. *John Abraham Lebo* lived on the Swatara, prior to 1742. *John Lebo*, in Alsace township, Berks county, prior to 1740, and where he died in 1759 at an advanced age, leaving a large family.

De Avier.—In 1732 arrived *Jean De Avier* who located in the Tulpehocken. It is probable that he was a son of *Lambertus De Avier*, whose father. a Huguenot minister, with his family suffered death in 1680. Albertus, then a mere youth, made his escape to Geneva, where he became a prominent member of the French colony, and was noted for his remarkable visions of the final Judgment, while in a trance. The narration of what De Avier seen and heard as given by contemporary writers is truly wonderful. (1)

De Laux, (Laux).—This family is one of the most ancient and honorable of France, and for many centuries seated in Angoumois

---

(1). Vide " Der Historie der Wiedergebohren."

and Bearn. The family was mainly Protestant and ranged itself under the standard of the House of Navarre in the civil and religious struggles of the Huguenots.

At the Revocation several branches were compelled to flee to the adjoining Protestant countries from whence a number came to Pennsylvania. Of these *John Jacob Laux* was a member of the old Tohicken church in Bucks county. *Peter Laux* located in Lancaster county, 1738, both were ancestors to an honorable posterity. From the latter comes the Hon. James B. Laux, of New York, a noted historian and writer.

Dundore.—The Dundore family is seated in Alsace, from whence several heads came to Pennsylvania. *Nicholas Dundore* located in Lancaster county prior to 1718. In 1741 arrived *John* and *Jacob Dundore*. They are said to have been father and son. (1) The former located at Atolhoe, at the base of the Blue mountains, (2) and the latter in Bern. (3)

In Tulpehocken also located *Gotfried Reidenour* and *Englehart Flory*, who came from Alsace. Also *Nicholas Riehl*, all prior to 1732. *Jacob De Grenoble*, who died in 1777 at an advanced age, was located here later. In the vicinity of Lebanon located *Isaac Cushwa* and *Jacob Mumma* in 1731. *Jacob Bonnett*, *John DeFrance*, *John Henry Marquett*, *Christian Dupee*, and *Jacob Loresh*, (now "Larrish").

Shuey, Shuett.—This family fled to Switzerland at the Revocation, and from whence the younger members came to Pennsylvania. *Carl Valentine Nicholas Shuett* located prior to 1734, in Montgomery county. *Daniel* (4) and *John Ludwig Shuey* about this time located in the Swatara valley. From these a great and honorable posterity has come.

Albert.—An Albert family fled to Deux Ponts at the Revocation, of these came *John Michael Albert* to the Swatara prior to 1750, when well advanced in years. His sons, *John Michael Jr.*, *Peter*, and *Francis*, were then also heads of families. The latter who was born in 1719, at Deux Pont, was cruelly murdered by the savages, June 26th, 1756, leaving a family.

---

(1). Notes and Queries, Vol. I p. 2.

(2). Stover's Record, p. 34.

(3). Jacob Dundore was married to Anna Maria Brecht, a daughter of Wendell Brecht, and had children: John Christian, b. 1746; Maria Catharine, b. 1749; Susanna, b. 1747; John, 1751–1853; John Jacob, 1756–1821; Michael, 1754; David, 1758; Catharine and Elisabeth.

(4). Daniel Shuey died 1777, leaving children: Ludwig, Peter, Elisabeth, Daniel, John, Martin, Ann Margaret, Catharine and Barbara.

The *Kieffer* family of Lebanon county descended from *Jacob* Kieffer, (1717-1804), who came from Gersdorf, in Alsace, and located near the Bindnagel Church, where he is buried.

The *De Hass* family are said to have been of patrician rank in France, and from whence a branch fled to Holland in the earlier stages of the Protestant persecutions. We have already noticed the arrival of Captain John De Hass on the Delaware during the Dutch occupation. In 1749 *George Philip De Hass* arrived and settled near Lebanon. He was the father of General Philip De Hass. (1)

Cochet, (Couche).—Several branches of this family came to Pennsylvania, among them *Isaac Couchet*, born in 1721 at Gros Villers, in France, and who came to America in 1768 and located in Lebanon. *John Isaac, George Dietrich*, and *Francis Couchet* who accompanied him were presumably his sons.

Leroux, (Lerew).—The name of this family is met with very early and in many honorable connections. Probably the first arrival was *Francis Laroux* who fled from La Rochelle to the Huguenot colony on the Hudson, where he died in 1689. He was probably the ancestor of *Abraham Laroux, Sr.*, who was one of the early settlers of Bucks county, Pennsylvania, and perhaps also of *Abraham Laroux* who died in York county in 1757, and likewise of the pioneers of this name to the South, of whom the reader will learn in another connection. *Jonas Laroux*, an associate of the Ferrees, located near them prior to 1719. He died in 1761, and was the founder of the Lancaster county branch.

About 1741 *George Laroux* located in (now) Lebanon county, where he died very aged about 1764. (2) He was the ancestor of a very large posterity scattered over the United States.

---

(1). General John Philip DeHass was born in Holland in 1735 and came with his father to America and located in Lebanon. He entered the military service of the Province as an ensign under General Armstrong in the Kittanning expedition, serving also under Colonels Burd and Bouquet in their expeditions against the hostile Indians. He was promoted to the rank of Major in 1764. At the outbreak of the Revolution he at once tendered his services to the Colonial Government and was commissioned in 1776 Colonel of the First Pennsylvania Battalion and participated in the Long Island campaign. In 1777 he was promoted by Congress to the rank of Brigadier General and remained in the service throughout the war. In 1779 he removed to Philadelphia where he died in 1786. His son, John Philip DeHass, Jr., a Lieutenant in the Revolution, located on the military lands of his father at Beech Creek, in Clinton county, and where he died in 1821. It is said that General DeHass prided himself in his noble ancestry and used a seal which may enable Heraldists to connect his family. " Between two wings displayed a stag springing and at the bottom of the shield a stag courant." (See Penna. Mag. of Hist., Vol. II p. 347. See also list of Norman nobility in Appendix of this work).

(2). His family consisted of *Jonas*, b. 1709, d. 1776, leaving a family; *George*, who d. 1770, leaving a family; *Isaac*, d. prior to 1770, leaving a family; *Henry*; *Peter*, who died prior to 1762, leaving a family.

Sallada.—The head of the *Sallade* family fled at the Revocation to Basil, in Switzerland, from whence five brothers, sons of the Refugee, came to Pennsylvania. *Jacob*, located at Tohickon, in Bucks county, another in Lancaster county. *Nicholas Sallade* located in Bern township, Berks county, while *Fredcrick* located in Wiconisco, Dauphin county, where he died in 1770. His son *John* (1739–1827), was an officer in the Revolution, and a man of great prominence in the state. His wife, a daughter of George Eberhart, of Berks county, had a remarkable experience. In 1755, when but eight years of age, she was carried into captivity by the savages to the Miami Country in Ohio. After many years of captivity she was rescued by the expedition under Col. Henry Bouquet. Colonel Simon Sallada, (1785–1854) a son of the foregoing, was likewise a man of prominence and a member of the Legislature several terms.

Lingel.—The present thriving town of Lingelstown, at the base of the Blue Mountain, was named in honor of *Paul Lingel* (1709-1786). At the Revocation the head of the family retired to Switzerland. Of this family several came to Pennsylvania. *Jacob*, who located in Montgomery county, and *Paul* as above.

Leasure.—The *Leasure* family is both ancient and honorable, and was originally seated in the province of Navarre. At the Revocation a branch of this family was compelled to flee to Switzerland for safety, and from whence came *Abraham Leasure*, who arrived in 1754, and located in upper Dauphin county, where the family name is still extant. A son of the immigrant located in Westmoreland county where his descendants became prominent, notably General *Daniel Leasure*, a distinguished officer of the Civil war.

Raiguel.—In 1754 *Abraham Raiguel*, of "Erquel Terre de Ranaltes," arrived and located in Lebanon county. He was a man of prominence and social distinction, and at his death, in 1795, devised his estates mostly to his brothers Jean and Pierre, and nephews *Frederick* and *Abraham Raiguel*, all of whom were still in France. The nephews, however, came to America and took possession of their estates soon afterwards.

Beau Jacques.—An important immigrant to Lykens Valley was *Francis Charles Beau Jacques*. The name is now known in its English form of "Jacobs." He located in 1768 at the present site of Millersburg, and became a very extensive land owner, and erected the first mill in the valley.

Joray.—The *Juray* (Jury) family fled from France to Switzerland at the Revocation, where their son *Abraham* was born, and who came to the Lykens Valley in 1754. Although well advanced in years he with his son Samuel served in the war of the Revolution. (1)

In West Hanover, Dauphin county, died in 1748 *James De Armand*, (2) a name rendered famous in American history by the distinguished services of the Marquis De Armand, the noted French general, commander of "De Armand's Legion" during the Revolution.

Among other immigrants with Huguanot antecedents who located in the bounds of Dauphin county were *Frederick Showa, John Paul Seal, John Seyzer, Valentine* and *Peter Delabach, Henry Lorang*, originally *"L'Orange," Jacob Fontain, David Sausser*, (De Saussier), *Jean Pierre Monin*, from Lorraine. The name is now written "Money," *David Purviance*, and *Jean Jacques Grosjean* (Groshong).

CHAPTER XV.

Trans-Susquehanna.

HUGUENOT SETTLERS WEST OF THE SUSQUEHANNA RIVER—THE CONEWAGO COLONY—PITTSBURG—THE GENEVAN COLONY ON THE MONONGAHALA RIVER—WESTERN MARYLAND—THE SHENANDOAH VALLEY.

> " *Ever the Truth comes uppermost*
> *And ever is Justice done,*
> *For humanity sweeps onward*
> *Where to-day the martyr stands.*
> *For in front the cross stands ready*
> *And the crackling faggots burn ;*
> *While the hooting mob of yesterday*
> *In silent awe returns,*
> *To glean up the scattered ashes*
> *Into History's golden urn.*"

IN the present limits of York county a considerable number of people with Huguenot antecedents located, and it is a noteworthy fact that the first mayor of York, the late Hon. D. K. Noel, was a descendant of a Huguenot who fled from France to Deux Ponts (Zweibrucken). His father, *Jacob Noel*, emigrated from

---

(1). He died in 1785 leaving children: Samuel, Abraham, Mary, Magdalene, Margaret, Catharine, Susanna and Salome.

(2). James DeArmand left a widow, Mary, and children John, Richard, Margaret and Sarah.

Deux Ponts to Baltimore in 1795, and later located in York county, Pennsylvania. He served in the war of 1812, and was wounded in the battle of North Point, from the effects of which he died.

Berrot.—At the Revocation a family named *Berrot,* (also Perrot), fled from France to Alsheim, in the Palatinate. Among their children was *Frantz Ludwig,* born at Alsheim, in 1699, who came to America in 1738. He was a prominent citizen and one of the founders of the Moravian church in York. He died in 1778, leaving several sons, who removed to North Carolina. His connection with *Hellbarth Berrot,* who located in Berks, and *Jacques Berrot,* of Lancaster county, has not been established.

About 1750 *John Daniel Dinkle* (died 1755) and wife *Ursula* arrived from the city of Strasburg, in Alsace, both of whom are said to have been of patrician origin. Their descendants are numerous and of the highest respectability.

John Hay, of Alsace, and father of Colonel John Hay, of the Revolution, (1) was also one of the first citizens of York.

Dutill.—The *Dutill* family (also written Doutel), was greatly scattered by the persecutions, as the name is met with in various Huguenot colonies. Some younger members, perhaps brothers, came to Pennsylvania in 1738. *John Dutill* was married by Rev. George Michael Weis, in Montgomery county, prior to 1755. *Francis Dutill* was long a resident in Lancaster county, but the records of his estate is at Reading, dated 1766.

In 1737 Michael Doutel had a child baptized at Christ Church, Philadelphia. In 1751, *Michael Doutell,* of Robinson, now in Berks county, died, leaving a family.

Jacob Dutill was one of the first residents of York, and a man of prominence. He died in 1777. He was the father of *Daniel Doutel,* (1727-1828), and of Captain *Michael Doutel,* (1732-1805), an officer of the Revolution who had the honor of leading the first company of Pennsylvania soldiers into the War of Independence. (2) They left York for Washington's camp near Boston, July 1st, 1775. Captain Doutel's grave may be seen in the rear of Christ Lutheran church, in York.

In 1739 arrived *Jean Voturin,* (now Woodring), who was born at Helleringen, Loraine, in 1711. He was one of the first Moravians of York. At his death he was survived by six daughters and

---

(1). John Hay, Jr., b. in Alsace, France, 1733, died in York, Pa., 1810, was one of the leading men of the State. He was a justice for many years. A member of the Provincial Assembly 1775, a member of the constitutional Convenvention 1776, was a colonel of a York county batallion in active service in the Revolution and a member of Assembly 1779-1784.

(2). Rupp's History of Lancaster and York counties, p. 608-612.

a son, *John Voturin, Jr.*, who removed to Graceham, Md., where he died in 1779.

John Moreau, (now Morrow), and *Peter Gasha*, who died in 1778, were also early residents of York.

Elsewhere in the county of York, besides the Huguenot colony from New Jersey, to be noticed presently, there were the following: *Christian Sangree*, (originally St. Gris), located on Springettsbury Manor prior to 1738. In 1749 arrived *John Ludwig Sengris* (Sangree), whose relation to the former is not known. In 1739 arrived *Abraham Chedron* from Lorraine, and located near York. He was the ancestor of the extensive Shetrone family. *Andres Bailley* and *John Barone* both appear before 1747. *Jean De Grange* prior to 1751. *Abraham De Fleury, John Henry Lorah, Abraham Larew, Nicholas Darone, Croft Billet, Peter Delo, Barthel La Gneau, Leonard Lecrone, Daniel Renolle, Adam De Gomois* (De Goma), *Michael Le Boob*, all appear at an early date. *Dietrich Werley*, who was born in Steinthal, in Alsace, in 1695, came to America in 1736, and located west of York. His posterity is very numerous. *Antoine Bevenour, Thomas Petit, Jean La Mothe*, (La Mott), *David Fournier* and *John Noel*, came prior to 1750. *Nicholas Pierie* arrived in 1727 and located on the Codorus in 1736. *Albert La Bott* came in 1737. *John Joho, Adam Beidinger*, the *Bernitz and Boyer* families arrived in York county in 1738. The *Rutisilia* (now Rudisill) family, now so numerous and widely scattered throughout the land, is said to be of Huguenot origin. Several heads of families came to Pennsylvania, as will be seen in the general list. *Philip Rutisilia* was married at Conestoga in 1734. (1) *Weirich Rutisilia*, born in 1697, arrived in 1737, in the same vessel with John Adam Beidinger. He located on the Codorus, east of Hanover, and was the ancestor of the York county branch.

La Mothe, (La Mott).—The Lords *De La Mothe* ranked among the highest of the French nobility. (2) Several branches of the house embraced the Protestant faith and suffered great persecutions in consequence. One member, General De La Mothe Fouquet, a distinguished officer of the French army, took refuge in Prussia at the Revocation. Madame De La Mothe-Guion was a noted devotional writer of the Reformation period, whose works were translated into many languages.

In 1754 *Jean Henry De La Mothe* (1705-1794), who was born in Provence, France, arrived, and located near Hanover. Later he removed to York, where he died. In early life he forsook his

(1). Stoever's Records p. 54, Ibid p. 17.
(2). See the Nobility of Normandy, Vol. I.

native land because of the persecutions, and traveled extensively before coming to Pennsylvania. He was of a reserved disposition and said but little concerning his distinguished ancestry.

During the first visit of the Count De LaFayette to the Continental Congress, then sitting in York, in 1777, a nobleman of his staff, Captain Nicholas De La Mothe, visited him and claimed kinship.

Barnitz.—The history of this family, both in France and America, has been an honorable one. One branch is of noble rank and has given many distinguished names to French history. (1) The date of the arrival of the Bernitz family in Pennsylvania is uncertain, as there is no record of them in the Archives. The earliest appearance of the name is in the record of Rev. John Casper Stoever, of baptisms on the Conewago.

In May, 1738, *John Leonard Bernitz*, whom we take to have been the head of the family, stood as baptismal sponsor, and several times thereafter. In 1749, *John George Carl*, (2) and in 1741 *Elias Daniel Barnitz* appear as sponsors in the same locality. The Barnitz family came from Alsace, and in our opinion arrived in 1737, in company with other Alsatians with whom we find their names associated.

Of the foregoing, *John George Barnitz* was born in 1722, and died in 1796. His monument may be seen in the rear of Christ Lutheran Church, in York. His sons all became men of prominence, and several took a conspicuous part in the Revolution. *Jacob* was an officer in the war, and was severely wounded and taken prisoner by the British at Fort Washington in 1776. He became a man of great prominence and died in 1828. His son *Jacob* was an eminent lawyer and a member of the Twenty-third Congress.

Beidinger, (Bittenger).—In 1736 arrived from Alsace *John Adam Beidinger*, (3) aged 39, and *Peter Beidinger*, aged 34 years. They were probably brothers. The former located near Abbotstown, where he died in 1768. His son *Nicholas* (1743-1804) was a man of prominence in Colonial days. In the Revolution he served on the Committee of Safety, and also as a captain in Colonel Swope's regiment of the famous "Flying Camp," that rendered such valuable service in New York and New Jersey in 1776-'77.

---

(1). "Science des Armoiries," p 346.
(2). The children of John George Carl Barnitz were Jacob, Daniel, John, George associate Judge of York county, Michael, Susan Eichelberger and Barbara Lauman.
(3). The children of the immigrant were Nicholas, Henry Michael, Peter, Marillos, George, Adam, Christian, Frederick and Eve. The Hon. J. W. Bittenger, Judge of the York county courts is a great grandson of Captain Nicholas Bittenger.

De Cessna.—Among the heroes of the Duke De Schomburg at the battle of the Boyne, (1690) was a young Huguenot soldier, *Jean De Cessna*, who remained in Ireland after the forces of William, Prince of Orange, were withdrawn. In 1718 he came to Pennsylvania and located in Lancaster county. (1) Later he removed to York county where he died in 1751. (2) Several of his sons located in Shippensburg as early as 1751, and the later removed to Bedford county, where the family became prominent. John De Cessna, (1718–1800) of Bedford county, was one of the leading men of the Province. He was a member of the Provincial Assembly and Constitutional Convention of 1775, and a Colonel in the Revolution war. His brother, Charles De Cessna, was likewise a Colonel in in the war of Independence. The late Hon. John De Cessna, State Senator and member of Congress, was a great grandson of Col. John De Cessna. Another son of the immigrant was Stephen De Cessna, who prior to 1750 was a resident of Cumberland county.

Piatt, Pyatt.—This family seated in Dauphiny, fled to Holland at the Revocation period, and later came to New Jersey. The name of the father is not known. Of the sons, *John Piatt* was a prominent citizen of Somerset county, New Jersey, of which he was sheriff in 1732. He died in 1760, while on a visit to the Island of St. Thomas, where he owned a sugar plantation. All his sons, five in number, were soldiers in the Revolution, under the following grades: *John*, b. 1739, a private; *Abraham*, b. 1741, a quartermaster; *William*, b. 1745, a captain; *Daniel*, b. 1745, a major, and *Jacob*, b. 1747, a captain. The Piatt family were great pioneers. John, at the close of the Revolution removed to (now) Lycoming county, in Pennsylvania, where a township is named in his honor. *Abraham* removed to (now) Centre county, and was Judge of the Courts of Northumberland county in 1786. (3) He died in 1791, and his family all removed to Ohio. *Jacob Piatt*, youngest son of John the immigrant son, removed to Kentucky.

Jacob Piatt, evidently a second son of the immigrant, appears in Lancaster county, Pennsylvania, as an Indian trader at an early day. *Jacob Piatt, Jr.* was a pioneer on the frontiers, and was dispossessed of his lands in Path Valley as an intruder in 1750.

Lischey's lists.—In 1742 arrived Rev. Jacob Lischey, a Moravian minister, and who soon afterwards was married to a daughter of John Stephen Benezette, of Philadelphia. Soon after his arrival he became disaffected and assumed charge of several Reformed congregations in York county. His baptismal record, lately recovered,

---

(1). See Pa. Mag. of Hist. Vol. III.
(2). Will at York, Pa.
(3). Pa. Arch. 2nd ser. III, p. 760.

beautifully written, and most valuable in character, discloses a number of Huguenot names. In some instances the entries of French people are made in the French language. The following are names of parents with earliest entry of baptisms of children : (1)

Pierre Gerot and w. *Catharine*, 1755, (sponsor, *Jacques Verdieux*). The foregoing was probably Pierre Gerra, who is recorded in the Archives as having arrived in 1746. *Daniel Renolle*, 1755 ; *John* and *Jacob Rudesilly*, 1755 ; *Jacob Bouchon*, 1756 ; *John Chamblin*, 1756 ; *David Fournier*, 1756.

("Dulommum et sa femme," sponsors).

The Conewago Colony.

On the head waters of the Conewago creek, in the eastern limits of Adams county, a considerable number of Huguenots located at an early day. Among these were *James Pettit*, who had a large plantation here soon after 1740, and died at a very advanced age in 1770, leaving sons *Thomas* and *James*. *Abraham Larue*, who died in 1757, leaving a family. *Adam De Gomis*, (previously noted), and who died here in 1772. *John Noel* prior to 1750, and who died in 1766, very aged, and leaving a large posterity. Also *Daniel Renolle* prior to 1751. None of the foregoing appear on the lists as foreign emigrants, and it is therefore a fair presumption that they came hither from an older colony. That this inference is correct is born out by the fact that the Pettit and other families named are found among the Huguenots who came to New York and New Jersey. Soon after 1760 a large number of French and a few Dutch families removed hither from Shrallenburg, in Bergen county, New Jersey. Their settlement was confined to a locality now in the townships of Straban and Berwick in Adams county. They were rigid adherents of the Dutch Reformed faith, and built a church on the Conewago about two miles east of the present village of Hunterstown. About 1781 many of them concluded to attempt another colonial experiment by securing a large body of land in Shelby county, Kentucky. To this new centre over a hundred, of all ages removed, before the close of the century. In 1793 another colony of nine families left the Conewago settlement and located at Owasco lake, in Cayuga county, in New York. To such an extent was the Conewago colony reduced by removals and defections that the maintenance of a distinctive congregation of their faith, (the Dutch Reformed), became impractical and in 1817 they petitioned the Legislature for permission to sell their church, which was granted.

---

(1). For the recovery of these names the author is indebted to Luther R. Kelker, Esq., of Harrisburg, Pa.

In the absence of any records concerning this colony we must rely on the land and mortuary records at York and elsewhere. Among the colonists of French extraction not already noted were the following: *John Bodine*, will probated in 1786. *George Brocaw*, who died in 1794, at an advanced age leaving sons, *Peter, George* and *John*. *Peter Cosine*, who died aged in 1779, leaving sons *Cornelius, Markimus* and *Peter-Cornelius Cosine* who died in 1786 leaving a number of married children. *Andri Ridett*, who died in 1776, and in his will mentions his brother, *John Ridett. Michæl Le Boob*, who died in 1781. *Peter Montfort*, who died in 1769, quite aged, leaving sons *Peter, Anay* and *John*. *John Montfort*, who died in 1777, leaving sons *Francis, Peter, John* and *Laurence. Francis Cassart*, (1) *George Laschelles, Gerrett Demarest, Samuel Durye* and *Abraham Lovine*.

The Dutch colonists were Joris Brinkerhoff, (1717–1810), father of a large family, and whose son George (1761–1813) was for a time pastor of the church. Henry Banta, who had an unusually large family, nearly all of whom removed to Kentucky. Martin Nevius, who died in 1790, John Vanarsdalen, died 1772, William Vanderbilt, died 1772, David Vandine, died 1795, Iosta Shamp, and probably others who have not been identified.

Western Pennsylvania.

In the Western part of Pennsylvania a considerable number of the early settlers were of Huguenot origin, many of whom, such as the Bonnetts, Marchands, Leisures, De Cessnas and others, were the descendants of emmigrants already noticed in previous chapters. Among those not hitherto noticed, and who were identified with the region under consideration were the following:

---

(1). Cassart, Cassatt.—Francis Cassart was born about 1713 in Bergen county, New Jersey. His grandfather Jacques Cassart arrived in America as a refugee about 1657 with his family, (Baird's Hug. Em. to America, Vol. I, p. 183). Among others, he had a son *David*, bap. June 18, 1671, d. 1740, m. 1696, Styntie Van Horn. Of this union Francis was the seventh child. In 1760 he located at the Indian Springs, six m. east of (now) Gettysburg, in Adams county, Pa., where he died near 1795, and was buried in the graveyard of the "Jersey" colony. He was a man of great prominence; and took a notable part in the stirring events of the Revolution period. In 1775 he was a member of the Committee of Correspondence for York county. A member of the Provincial Assembly in 1776, and a member of the convention that framed the first state constitution 1776. He had three sons, Peter, who before the Revolution removed to Kentucky where he was killed by the Indians. David b. 1743, and d. 1824. Jacob b. 1751, d. 1813. The two latter are buried in the "Jersey" colonists graveyard where their tombstones may be seen. Many of the descedants became prominent in various walks of life. David (1768–1824) son of David, was an eminent lawyer of York, while Jacob, 1778–1838), also a son of the latter died while a member of the legislature. Another son of David Cassart was Dennis, the grandfather of Hon. A. J. Cassatt, of Philadelphia, the noted financier and president of the Pennsylvania Railroad Company.

In 1749 arrived *Frederick Pershing*, (1724-1792), of Alsace, and located in Westmoreland county. He was the ancestor of the distinguished jurist, Hon. Cyrus L. Pershing, of Pottsville, Pa. (1)

On the Monongahala river, in Fayette county, is situated the town of New Geneva, founded by *Albert Gallatin*, and named by him in honor of his native city, Geneva in Switzerland.

Induced by Albert Gallatin, several Genevan families, of Huguenot antecedents, took up their residence in this region. Among these was *Charles Andre Mestrezat*, who descended from the Huguenot divine, Jean Mestrezat, (2) of Paris, and was a relative of Albert Gallatin.

The emigrant was a son of *Rev. Jacob Mestrezat*, who was also a minister of note. He was born in 1766, and came to Pennsylvania in 1795, and was accidentally drowned in the Monongahela river in 1815. He was the grandfather of the noted jurist, Hon. S. L. Mestrezat, of Uniontown, Pa.

Brunot, Bruno.—Ever since the days of Saint Bruno, (3) the founder of the Carthusian order of monks, at Grenoble, in A. D. 1086, the name Bruno and Brunot has been an honorable one. Several branches belong to the nobility, and the name is met with in many high and important relations. The name was early introduced into Pennsylvania. *Felix Brunot* arrived in 1732 and located in Eastern Pennsylvania. *John Brunot* was a resident of Philadelphia prior to 1738.

The name became most honorably associated with Pittsburg through a younger branch in the person of *Dr. Felix Brunot*, who eminated from the nobility. Dr. Brunot was born at Morey, in France, 1752. He is said to have been a foster brother to the Count De Lafayette, and accompanied him to America as a member of his medical staff.

---

(1). Hon. C. L. Pershing was born in Westmoreland county. Entered the legal profession and rose to eminent distinction. In 1772 he was elected a judge of Schuylkill county, in which capacity he served with marked ability until 1898 when he was compelled to retire because of ill health. In 1875 he was the Democratic candidate for the governorship of Pennsylvania.

(2). This eminent divine was born in Geneva, 1591, and was educated at the Huguenot College of St. Samur. He became the pastor of the famous Charenton Temple at Paris, where he died in 1657. He was famous as a writer and as an eloquent orator. Rev. Jacob Mestrezat was b. at Marseilles, France, in 1713. He was ordained to the ministry in 1740, was chaplain of the Dutch Embassy at Paris, 1748-1750. Pastor at Amsterdam 1751-1752, and several other places until 1777, when he retired because of failing health. He had one daughter and three sons of whom the youngest, Charles Alexander came to Pennsylvania. The latter had ten children, of whom Jean Louis Guillaume Mestrezat, was the father of Judge S. Leslie Mestrezat of the Supreme Court of Pennsylvania.

(3). St. Bruno was born at Cologne, A. D. 1051, and died at Calabria, A. D., 1101. In 1089 Pope Urban who had been one of his pupils summoned him to Rome. He was canonized in A. D., 1628.

After the Revolution he became a Protestant and located in Philadelphia, and in 1797 removed to Pittsburg, where he died in 1838. He had two sons, *Hilary*, born in 1795, and *Felix, Jr.*, born in 1815. Both father and sons were intimately connected with the public interests of the city. The latter especially will ever be held in grateful remembrance for his philanthropic deeds.

Doctor Brunot was married in 1789 to Elisabeth Kreider, whose mother, Susanna Pons Breton, was a daughter of Jacques Pons, a Huguenot refugee to Offenbach, in the Palatinate, and from whence the family emigrated to Pennsylvania.

There lived with the Brunot family in Pittsburg for many years, *Jean Marie*, (b. in France, 1727, and still living in 1808), who came as a young man to Pennsylvania because of persecution.

Dravo.—In 1789 there came to Western Pennsylvania with the *Marquis De Lusiere*, a young man of distinguished family, named Antoine Dreyvault, a name now changed to *Dravo*. He was born in Paris, August 16th, 1767, and died in Pittsburg, Pa., October 16, 1851. Anthony Dravo was a Protestant, and prominent as a Methodist. He erected a brick house, which was one of the first and finest in Pittsburg, and where he dispensed a generous hospitality. He entertained the Marquis De Lafayette during his visit to America in 1725, and also *Louis Phillippi*, then an exile, but later the King of France. Anthony Dravo was the founder of a highly honorable posterity. (1)

Maryland.

Following the Palatines in their migration to Western Maryland and the Shenandoah Valley, of Virginia, we find a considerable number of early settlers of Huguenot ancestry among them. The descendants of these people are among the most progressive and intelligent citizens in the South, and take a just pride in their ancestry. The initial settlements in Frederick county were made on the Monocacy, east of Frederick City.

Among the first settlers was *Jean Henri Fortineaux*, who arrived in Philadelphia in 1727. His posterity now generally write the name "*Fortny.*" The *Dilaplain* brothers, *John, Joseph* and *Joshua*, came from Colebrookdale, in Berks county, Pa. The first named prior to 1771. The family history is elsewhere given. *Joseph Mayhew* came prior to 1735. The Mayhew name appears among the refugees to several Protestant countries. (2) *Peter Cushan* came near 1750.

---

(1). Anthony Dravo had children—Pierre, Michael, William, John, Antoine, François, Harriet and Margaret.

(2). Proc. London Hug. Soc. Vol. I.

Jacob Buckey, who arrived at Philadelphia in 1743, and located at Buckeystown, is an instance of how a name may be disguised under a phonetic form. The original was *Bouquet*, and represents a family despoiled by the persecutions and scattered to England, where they appear among the refugees, and to Switzerland, from whence came General Henry Bouquet, who, as a British officer, rendered such valuable service to our colonies on the frontiers. (1) In 1754 arrived *Nicholas* and *Daniel Hauer*, brothers, who were born at Dildendorf, in Lorraine, and were of the Huguenot faith. They were both among the first residents of Frederick. Daniel was born in 1733, and was the grandfather of the venerable Daniel Hauer, D. D.. (1803–1901), the oldest Lutheran minister in America.

On the Monocacy also located at an early day *David Shreiver*, whose wife was a Ferree, a descendant of Madame Ferree, and whose history is elsewhere given. They were the parents of Judge Abraham Shreiver, (1771–1848), and also the ancestor of the distinguished Admiral Schley. (Chap. XII).

Other Huguenot names in Frederick county prior to 1780 were *Boyer, Brevett, Cavy, Cocke, Delatter, De La Course, Doupe, De Lashmut, De Losier, De Bos, Duckett, De La Vincendiere, Demorest, De Bow, Tillard, La Mar, Le Nashu, De Marcellain, Pearre.*

North of the South Mountain in the present limits of Washington county, the first settlements were made by Pennsylvania Germans prior to 1735, in the vicinity of Clear Spring.

Among the settlers with Huguenot antecedents was *Dewalt Ancony*, who arrived at Philadelphia from Europe in 1746, and died at Clear Spring in 1781, at a very advanced age. He was the founder of a great posterity. *George Reidenour*, who was born in Rosenthal, Alsace, in 1718, and came with his parents to Pennsylvania in 1739, also located at Clear Spring prior to 1754. *Jacob*

---

(1). Henri Bouquet was b. 1719 of Huguenot parentage in Switzerland. He was given an excellent education and at an early age entered the military service of Holland where he soon rose to distinction. In 1756 he entered the British army with the rank of Colonel, and was sent to Pennsylvania and participated in the hostilities against the French and Indians. He was second in command in the expedition of General Forbes against Fort Duquesne at Pittsburg. In 1763 he led the expedition for the relief of Fort Pitt in which he was successful after first defeating the Indians at Bushy Run. The following year he utterly vanquished the confederated tribes in Ohio, and compelled them to deliver to him the hundreds of white captives, mostly women and children, whom they had taken. Those he brought back to Carlisle, Pa., from whence they were restored to their homes. In 1765 he was naturalized by the Supreme Court of Pennsylvania, doubtless as a step to promotion to the rank of general which immediately followed: With his promotion he was placed in charge of the department of the South with headquarters at Pensacola, Florida. Immediately upon his arrival he was smitten with fever and died 1765.

Bushong. who died in 1785, was a son of the immigrant *Jean Beauchamp.* *Jacob Cushwa,* the founder of a notable family, was the son of *Isaac Cushwa,* of Lebanon county, Pennsylvania. He was a teamster in Braddock's army in its march through this region to the crushing defeat at Fort Duquesne in 1755. After quiet was restored on the frontiers he located at Clear Spring.

The notable *Bregunier* family came from a refugee who appears on the arrival list at Philadelphia, in 1740, as *John Nicholas Peckonier,* and who located at Clear Spring. His grandson, *Rev. Daniel Bregunier,* (1807-1867). was a distinguished minister of the Reformed church, and the original of "Old Mr. Huguenot" in "The Young Parson," by Dr. Peter Davis.

In 1749, *John Michæl Mottier,* (now Motter), whose parents were driven from France, landed at Philadelphia, and later located in this locality, where the name is honorably established.

In 1739 *John Perrine* located on a tract of land near the South Mountain. This name stands for a great Huguenot family elsewhere noted, many members of which fled from France and found a refuge in foreign lands.

In the western part of the county located in 1740 *Lanceolot Jacques,* whose parents fled to England after the Revocation. Lancelot Jacques first came to Annapolis as agent for a company of planters. In 1765, in company with others, he acquired a tract of 15,900 acres of land near Clear Spring, where they erected the first furnace in Western Maryland. *Abraham Voturin* (Woodring) came with his parents from Lorraine and located in Eastern Pennsylvania. From thence he removed to Hagerstown, in the Provincial period, and was one of the founders of the Reformed church at that place.

Michæl Horry, (1729-1788), who was born in the Palatinate, of Huguenot parents, was also an early resident here.

The *Mumma, Dupre, Bouvard* and *Millott* (1) families all located in this region in Provincial times.

The Shenandoah Valley.

Most of the early settlers of the Shenandoah Valley, in Virginia, were Pennsylvania Germans, with a few Scotch Irish, and Quakers, from the same Province. With these, was a sprinkling of Huguenots, who although the most insignificant in point of numbers, have nevertheless left many conspicuous marks of their presence. With the exception of a few scattered pioneers, the first distinctive settlements in the Valley was the result of an agreement made between the Governor of Virginia and *John Jost Heydt,* of

---

(1). From the latter came Col. Daniel Millott (1771-1854).

Pennsylvania, and Jacob Van Meeter, whereby the Governor ceded to the aforenamed two, over twenty-five thousand acres of land on the condition that they locate thereon at least two hundred families. This was in 1732, and immediately afterwards Jost Heydt located on the Opequon within five miles of the present city of Winchester. This was the beginning of the great migration of the Pennsylvania Germans to the Valley of Virginia, and which continued southward until great numbers had penetrated the wilderness to the forks of the Yadkin, in North Carolina, where they had a flourishing settlement on Dutchman's creek, prior to 1750.

Jost Heydt was a native of Strasburg, in Alsace. He was a member of an ancient Protestant family, despoiled and ruined by the Papists under *Louis XIV.*, when he treacherously seized the city, as elsewhere narrated in this work. (1) Jost Heydt first located in Montgomery county, in Pennsylvania, in 1717, and was a man of prominence and great business capacity. He was well advanced in years when he and his wife *Anna Maria*, and seven children, four sons and three daughters, removed to the South. His family consisted at this time of sons, *John*, *Jacob*, *Isaac* and *Thomas*, and sons-in-law, *Jacob Christman*, *Ceorge Bowman* and *Paul Froman*. Several sons were also at this time heads of families. The descendents of Jost Heydt are now very numerous, and constitute a very honorable posterity. Among the notable descendants was *James*, who died in 1779, a son of Joseph Heydt. He was a member of the Provincial Assembly for a period of sixteen years.

The *Larue* family of the South mostly came from two branches of this name, who made their escape from France at the Revocation, and came to New Jersey, where they located in Hunterdon county. One of these, had among others, three sons, *Abraham*, *Isaac* and *Jacob*. Of these, Abraham and Jacob were pioneers in Kentuckey, where Larue county commemorates their name. Isaac, who was born in New Jersey in 1712, removed in 1743 to the Valley, and established the Virginia branch of the family.

In Shenandoah county located the Servier, Roller and Boneauvent families, all of Huguenot ancestry. *Valentine Servier*, (father of John Servier, the famous Commonwealth builder), came from a family that had fled to England at the Revocation. About 1769 he accompanied his son and other Virginians to Tennessee, where they built Fort Watauga, and founded a new Commonwealth. John Peter Roller (2) and Jean Bonneauvant had both resided some years in Lancaster county, Pennsylvania, before their settlement here.

---

(1). See chapter VIII.
(2). Vide Chapt. XI.

The latter located on Mill creek, where he built the first mill in this region. From these families comes General John E. Roller. (1)

The *Disponnet* family soon after arrival in Pennsylvania (1739) removed to the Opequon, near Winchester. Here the father, Jacob, and several of his family, were cruelly massacred by the Indians during their bloody incursion into the Valley in 1756.

The *De Moss* (Dumas) family was likewise located on the Opequon at an early day. The father, Lewis Dumas, died in 1743, leaving a large posterity.

CHAPTER XVI.

Monuments of the Huguenots in America.

THEIR GREAT ACHIEVEMENTS AS STATESMEN—DIPLOMATS—SCHOLARS — SCIENTISTS AND PHILANTHROPISTS IN THE UNITED STATES.

> "*And while the races of mankind endure*
> *Let their great examples stand,*
> *Collossal, seen of every land;*
> *To keep the soldier firm—the statesman pure*
> *Till in all lands, and through all human story*
> *The path of duty be the way to glory.*"

IT was a remark of the Historian Bancroft, that America is full of monuments of the Huguenot emigration. This statement becomes apparent upon the most casual observation. The French Protestant exiles were among the most intelligent and enterprising of all the people who bore a part in laying the foundations of this great Nation. The "monuments" they have reared in the various fields of American enterprise and activity are indeed lofty and glorious, and form part of the distinctive elements of our National character. As it would be impractical to describe in detail all the monuments that stud the decisive field of Gettysburg, or the trophies of art at the Louvre at Paris, or the memorials of vanished empires in the British Museum, so is this brief recital ; we can call attention to only a few typical characters that stand out somewhat prominently, and pass by multitudes of almost equal greatness.

The intellectual force and personal worth of the Huguenot character is surprisingly illustrated in many important connections in the formative period of our Nation. Although but a handful as

---

(1). Gen. John E. Roller, (b, 1844), of Harrisonburg, Va., a distinguished Confederate officer, jurist, and historian, descends both from John Peter Roller and Jean Bonneauvant.

it were, during our Colonial period, yet scarcely any event of importance was consummated in our early history without receiving in some form the Huguenot impress.

In a preliminary way we may cite in this connection the following remarkable facts. The *first* session of the Continental Congress was opened at Philadelphia with prayer by Rev. Jacob Duche, the grandson of an eminent Huguenot refugee. *Three* of the presidents of the Continental Congress were Huguenots, namely John Jay, Henry Laurens, and Elias Boudinot. The first two were signatories to the Treaty of Peace with England, November 30th, 1782. This treaty was ratified by Congress, in April, 1783, but it did not become effective until signed by the Huguenot President of Congress, who was Elias Boudinot.

John Jay, as the American Plenopotentiary, signed the final Treaty of Paris, September 3rd, 1783. Thirty-one years later a Huguenot descendant again negotiated a Treaty of Peace with the Mother Country, namely James Bayard. This treaty remains unbroken to the present day, while Thomas F. Bayard, a descendant of the same family, as a cabinet officer and Embassador to England under President Cleveland's administration, has been a prominent factor in establishing the principles of International Arbitration, which bids fair to lay the foundations of a permanent Anglo-Saxon Union, which may change the course of the World's history during the coming century.

The *first treasurer* of our Nation was Michael Hillegas, who was the son of an Alsatian refugee. The sterling worth of this distinguished Philadelphian is shown in the many years of his incumbency in this responsible office, especially during the dark and trying period of the Revolution, (1776-1783).

Jay.—In the field of American *statesmanship* no name is more illustrious than that of John Jay. (1) His life work gave a distinct trend to our National history. As a member of the Continental Congress, and President of that body in 1778; as Minister to Spain in 1779; as one of the Plenipotentiaries for the Treaty of Peace at the close of the Revolutionary struggle ; as the first Chief Justice of the new born Nation ; and as one of the first anti-slavery advocates ; he not only illustrated the true nobility of his Hugue-

---

(1). John Jay was a descendant of Pierre Jay, a wealthy merchant of La Rochelle, France. At the Revocation he suffered the loss of almost his entire fortune, but succeeded in escaping with his family to Plymouth, England. His eldest son Auguste came to New York in 1686, where his grandson, John, was born in 1745. So highly did Washington esteem him that when he became President, he tendered him any office within his gift. Jay choose that of Chief Justice of the United States, being the first incumbent of that office. He died at Bedford, N. Y., 1829.

not ancestry, but bestowed also illustrious services to humanity. A character so useful to posterity well merited the enconium of Daniel Webster, when he said: *"When the spotless ermine of the judicial robe fell on John Jay, it touched nothing less spotless than himself."*

Boudinot.—Hardly less distinguished than Jay, stands Elias Boudinot, who descended from a prominent Huguenot family of De La Tremblade, France. He was born in Philadelphia, Apri 21, 1740. He was a member of the first convention, (June 11th, 1774), which called for a general congress. He was a member of the Colonial Congress, 1777-'79-'81-'82. Was elected President of Congress November 4th, 1782, and in that capacity he signed the Treaty of Peace with Great Britain, April 15th, 1783. In 1795 he was appointed Director of the Mint at Philadelphia by Washington, of whom he was a close personal friend. He was a ripe scholar and gave to the world a number of valuable histories. He was a patron and trustee of Princeton College, and a great promoter of literature. He was no less distinguished as a sincere Christian. In 1812 he became a commissioner for the American Board of Foreign Missions ; and in 1816 was one of the organizers of the American Bible Society, and was its first president.

In the great struggle by which American independence was achieved, the sons of the Huguenot exiles were in the van. South Carolina alone furnished an entire batallion composed of their descendants, some of whom rose to great distinction, and shed undying lustre on the page of their country's history. (1)

Laurens.—The name of Henry Laurens (1724-1792) shines as a star of the first magnitude amid the galaxy of the great. His parents were among the early Huguenot refugees to Charleston, S. C., where Henry was born. His services to his country were very great. He was president of the first Provincial Congress of South Carolina in 1775, and prepared the declaration against England. In 1777 he succeeded John Hancock as President of the Continental Congress. In 1780 he was sent as Plenopotentiary to Holland to negotiate a treaty and secure a loan. On this voyage he was captured by the British and held as a prisoner fourteen months. After his release he, with Benjamin Franklin and John Jay, negotiated the preliminary Treaty of Peace with Great Britain in November, 1782.

His son, Colonel John Laurens, (1755-1782). was a distinguished soldier and a member of Washington's staff. In 1781 he

---

(1). The Huguenot Batallion was organized 1779, and served to the close of the war. They were commanded by Marquis de Britagne, a distinguished officer who returned to France at the close of the war.

was sent to France to negotiate a loan for the Government, in which he was successful. Upon his return he again took the field in the South, where he unfortunately lost his life in action.

Marion.—During the Revolutionary struggle the great tower of strength in the South was Major General Francis Marion, (1) who with his undisciplined and poorly clad Provincials rendered such valuable services as to win a resolution of thanks from the Continental Congress and the universal gratitude of the Nation. Almost every state in the Union has a city or county named in his honor.

Huger.—Marion's worthy companions at arms were the Huger (2) brothers, five in number, and also from South Carolina. The chief of this quintett of heroes was Major General Isaac Huger, who served throughout the war, and was several times wounded in action. Next was his brother, Colonel Benjamin Huger, who fell in the battle of Charleston, S. C., in 1779. Then also Colonel Francis Huger, Deputy Quartermaster General, while the two younger brothers were of lesser rank.

Pickens.—To the list of South Carolina worthies we must also add the name of Andrew Pickens, (1) who rose from the rank of captain to that of Brigadier General during the Revolution. Always foremost in action, whether with British or Indian, is it safe to say that no American leader ever displayed greater gallantry, or ever achieved greater results with such limited resources. The Continental Congress presented him with a sword for his distinguished services.

Manigault.—The name of Gabriel Manigault (1704-1781) shines with a fadeless lustre on the escutcheon of South Carolina. His father, also Gabriel, was one of the Rochelles Refugees to Charleston, where Gabriel was born. He became one of the wealthy men of the South, and during the war of the Revolution loaned vast sums of money to his native state for the prosecution of the war. At the age of seventy-five years, with a grandson by his side, he took part in resisting the British attack upon Charleston in 1779.

Servier.—(3) (1745-1815). Perhaps no individual in the South left a more lasting impression on the civic institutions of that

---

(1). Gen. Francis Marion was born near Georgetown, S. C., 1732, and died in 1795. His grandfather Benjamin Marion was a refugee from La Chaume, France, from whence he fled to South Carolina after the Revocation.

(2). Grandsons of Daniel Huger, who fled from the Isle of Rhe to England in 1682, and from thence to Charleston, S. C., in 1696.

(3). Andrew Pickens was born of Huguenot parentage at Paxtang, Penna., 1739. His parents removed to S. C. in 1752. After a highly distinguished career he died in 1817. His son Andrew was also eminent, and was Governor of S. C. 1816-1818.

region than John Servier, "The Commonwealth Builder." His father, Valentine, was born in London, of Huguenot parentage, and emigrated to the Shenandoah Valley, Virginia, where his distinguished son was born. In 1769, he with other Virginians, including his aged father and brother, made a settlement on the Holsten river, in East Tennessee, where they built Fort Watuga. John Servier was an ardent patriot during the Revolution, placing himself at the head of his fellow frontiersmen he became a terror to the British.

His most brilliant achievement was at the battle of King's Mountain, October 7th, 1780. At this time the cause of the Colonists seemed lost in the South, when Gen. Servier, with fierce impetuosity, threw his little army against the seemingly impregnable position of the British, and in one hour annihilated the left wing of the army of Cornwallis, made his surrender at Yorktown imperative, and the glories of American Independence sure. Servier was practically the founder of Tennessee. Its first, and for three successive terms its Governor.

Le Conte.—The Le Conte family (2) affords a striking example of the intellectual virility of the Huguenot character, as they have furnished a very large number of distinguished names, especially in the field of Science. Among the most eminent may be mentioned *Dr. Lewis Le Conte*, born in New Jersey in 1782, and who settled in Georgia. He became famous for his work in mathematics, botany and zoology. He died in 1838. His son *John*, born in 1818, who as President of the University of California, has made for himself a name second to none in the special sphere of his labors. Another son of Lewis is *Prof. Joseph Le Conte*, born 1823, professor of geology and natural history in the University of California, and who has a world wide reputation as a Naturalist. His numerous works are considered standard authorities on the subjects on which they treat. *Major John Eaton Le Conte*, brother of Lewis first mentioned, was born in New Jersey in 1784, and died in Philadelphia in 1860. He was an eminent engineer, and for a long time in the service of the United States. Notwithstanding his arduous duties in the civil service, he made extensive researches in natural history. *John Lawrence Le Conte*, son of Major Le Conte, (b. 1825, d. 1883), was one of the greatest scientists of the century. He was for years the President of the American Entomological Society, and in 1873 was elected as President of the American Association for the Advancement of Science.

---

(1). See "John Servier as a Commonwealth Builder."
(2). Descendants of William Le Conte (b. 1659, d. 1728), who fled from Rouen, France, to New York, after the Revocation. On his mother's side he was descended from the Nobility.

Revere.—All the world has heard of Paul Revere and his famous ride. He was born in Boston, Massachusetts, of Huguenot parentage in 1735. He has the distinction of having been the founder of copper-plate engraving in America. He also rendered valuable services to his country as a Colonel in the War of the Revolution. His famous "ride," celebrated in song and story, was the carrying of the order of General Warren, at midnight, April 18th, 1775, through Charlestown to Concord and Lexington, warning the people of the approach of the British under General Gage, and displayed the signal lanterns in the steeple of Christ Church, in Boston.

Ravenel.—The history of the *Ravenel* family of South Carolina, is an honor both to the Huguenot character and the state of their adoption. The founder of the family was Rene Ravenel, of Vitre, France. The Ravenels are of noble rank, and figure honorably in the history of France. Rene Ravenel being a Protestant, was compelled to leave all his estates in 1686, and came with others to Charleston, S. C. His descendants were prominent already in colonial times. Only the briefest mention can be given a number of the present century.

Dr. St. Julien Ravenel (1819-1882) was one of the greatest agricultural chemists of the age, and his researches and discoveries have been of great value to mankind. *Henry W. Ravenel, LL. D.*, (1814-1887) was a botanist of world wide celebrity, and his great work on the Fungi of the South, (5 Vols., 1853-1860), was the first of its kind in America. Of him it was well said "The name of Ravenel will ever be perpetuated in the genus *Ravenelea* of the Uredinal, a genus so peculiar in its character that it is not probable that it will ever be reduced to a synonym." (1). The late *Dr. Edmund Ravenel* was an accomplished chemist and conchologist. *Dr. Mazyc Porcher Ravenel*, of the University of Pennsylvania, is a noted specialist. *Hon. H. E. Ravenel*, of Spartansburg, S. C., is an author of works on Jurisprudence, and has also written a valuable history of the Ravenel family. (2)

Dana.—The descendants of *Richard Dana*, who came as a refugee to Boston, Mass., prior to the Revocation, affords another notable example as that just illustrated. He has given us *Dr. Francis Dana*, (b. 1743, d. 1811), who was a delegate to the first Provincial Assembly, and our first Minister to Russia in 1781 ; delegate to the Convention that framed the Federal Constitution ; one of the founders of the American Academy of Fine Arts, besides many other notable connections.

---

(1). Botanical Gazette 1887.
(2). Ravenel Records.

Richard Henry Dana, (b. 1787), the distinguished poet and novelist, and his scarcely less distinguished son, *Richard Henry Jr.*, (b. 1815), *James Dwight Dana*, (b. 1813), of Yale College, the celebrated geologist, whose works are standard authorities; *Colonel Napoleon J. T. Dana*, (b. 1822), who served with distinction in the Mexican and Civil War; *Dr. Samuel Luther Dana, LL. D.*, (1795–1868), the eminent chemist; and lastly, *Charles Anderson Dana*, (1818–1897), who as a writer and editor, and Assistant Secretary of War under President Lincoln, and his confidential agent, proved himself to be one of the most resourceful of men.

Tourgee.—In literature we find but few more forceable writers than Judge A. W. Tourgee, while the musical world has no greater ornament than Prof. Eben Tourgee, (1) the leader of the New England Conservatory of Music in Boston, Mass.

Pumpelly.—Mention only can be made of *Professor Raphæl Pumpelly*, (2) of Harvard University, whose extensive researches, and valuable works, have done so much for the advancement of science.

Reference has already been made to the many eminent descendants of the Huguenot refugees to the South, the list of which would be incomplete without a reference to several more whose lives and services have contributed so largely to our country's greatness.

Poinsett.—To this number must be added *Joel Robert Poinsett*, (3) (1779–1851). This eminent American supplemented a thorough education by extensive travels in Europe and Asia before entering the public service. Among the numerous responsible positions he filled was that of Minister to Mexico and Secretary of War in President Van Buren's Cabinet. He was the founder of the Academy of Fine Arts in Charleston, S. C., and practically also of the National Museum at Washington.

Maury.—Undoubtedly one of the most eminent men of this age was *Matthew Fontain Maury*, (1806–1873), who eminated from the Huguenot colony on the James. Although Lieutenant Maury was in the service of the American Navy nearly all his life, yet his scientific researches, especially in astronomy and hydrography were world renowned, and epoch-making. In literature he is known as the "Philosopher of the Sea," and he is generally regarded as the Founder of Hydrographic Science. He was a member of many societies of learning both in America and Europe.

---

(1). Descendants of Pierre Tourgee, who came to Rhode Island in 1700.
(2). Descendant of Pierre Pumpelly, who came to Massachusetts in 1679.
(3). A descendant of Pierre Poinsett, a refugee to S. C. about 1686.

Perrine.—The *Perrine* family (1) has added a great list of distinguished names to the honor roll, and for almost two centuries has had its representatives in many important fields of action, where as ministers, jurists, scientists, and many other professions, they have added lustre to their ancestral name. The achievements in astronomy of Prof. E. D. Perrine, of the Lick Observatory, are especially noteworthy.

Soule.—It is well known that several Huguenot families came to New England with the Pilgrim Fathers in the "Mayflower." Of this number was *George Soule*, whose descendants have been especially distinguished as soldiers, ministers, and literary men.

Pintard.—One of the most progressive and public spirited men the Empire State has ever produced was *John Pintard*, whose ancestor, Antoine Pintard, came as a refugee to New York in 1690. John Pintard was distinguished in many spheres of activity, but his memory will be perpetuated chiefly for his noble philanthropy, and also as the Founder of the New York Historical Society.

Provoost.—Another distinguished descendant of the refugees to New York was the Right Reverend Samuel Provoost, (1742-1815), the first Protestant Episcopal bishop of New York. Among the notable services of this Divine was that of Chaplain to the Continental Congress in 1785, and Chaplain to the United States Senate in 1789.

In the further pursuit of this subject we find ourselves in the dilemma of Paul, in recounting his Bible Worthies as yet unmentioned, when he writes: "And what more shall I say, for the time would fail me to write."—*Heb. XI: 32.* We must content ourselves with the mere mention of some who have achieved a fame more lasting and honorable than the monarchs, whose blind bigotry drove their fathers across the seas.

Vincent Rougnion.—The ancestor of the *Runyon* family, of New Jersey, who came, prior to 1668, from Poitiers, has given to posterity many men of eminence, notably Hon. Theodore Runyon, (1822-1896), late United States Embassador to Germany.

The ancestor of the distinguished jurist, Gabriel Duval, (1752-1844), from 1811 to 1826 a Supreme Justice of the United States, was Mars Marien Duval, who fled from France in 1643, and came to Maryland.

---

(1). This family was mostly Protestant, was greatly scattered by persecution, some fled to England from whence John Perrine came to Braintree, Mass., in 1635-1640. Daniel Perrine from whom most of the name descended, came to New York in 1665; married in 1666. and settled on Staten Island. (See N. Y. Genealogical and Biographical Record, Vol. XIX and XX).

The ancestor of L. Q. C. Lamar, a member of President Cleveland's Cabinet, and later a member of the Supreme Court of the United States, likewise came to Maryland, from whence descendants went to Georgia, where the latter statesman was born in 1826.

The Hon. Columbus Delano, (1811–1896), Secretary of the Interior in President Grant's Cabinet, 1879–1875, descended from a refugee to New England.

The Hon. Richard Olney, late Secretary of State, descends from Andre Sigourney, also a refugee to New England.

Noted Institutions and Enterprises of Huguenot Origin.

In the more peaceful fields of learning the Huguenots of America have likewise erected lofty and most enduring "monuments." They have ever stood in the front ranks of art, science and literature, and in view of the smallness of their numbers compared with the other elements of our population, their achievements, to say the least, have been remarkable. Some of the greatest institutions of the New World have been founded by their munificence and philanthropy. Although Stephen Girard (1750–1831) can hardly fall under the designation of 'Huguenot," he was nevertheless an honor to the French race, and when he bequeathed his mighty fortune to Philadelphia, the city of his adoption, he enriched humanity as few men have ever done. *Girard College*, the offspring of his truly noble heart, is unriveled by any of its class in the world.

Faneuil Hall.—Next to Independence Hall, in Philadelphia, the cause of freedom has no more sacred shrine than Faneuil Hall, in Boston, and which has been aptly termed the "Cradle of Liberty." This historic edifice owes its existence to the munificence and public spirited character of a Huguenot merchant of that city, Peter Faneuil. (1) When he erected the structure as a market house and city hall, and presented it to the city, he "builded better than he knew." It would seem as though the Genius of Liberty, in vindication of the wrongs of the Huguenots, had singled out this building as the chief Forum for the discussion of principles and measures by which the torch of civil and religious freedom was lit, and which proved to be the harbinger of a new era in the history of the human race.

---

(1). Benjamine and Andrew Faneuil, merchants of La Rochelle, France, fled to New York at the Revocation, the former settled in New York City and the latter in Boston. Andrew died childless, and left his wealth to his brothers son Peter, who in 1741-42, erected the famous Faneuil Hall and presented it to the city of Boston.

Gallaudet College.—This institution, for the higher education of the deaf and dumb, and the first of its kind in the world, was founded at Washington, D. C., by the Gallaudets, whose services to this class of unfortunates have never been surpassed. The father, Rev. Thomas Hopkins Gallaudet, (1) of Philadelphia, (1787–1851), devoted his life to the improvement of the condition of the deaf and dumb, and originated many of the methods by means of which this unfortunate class of humanity are enabled to communicate with their fellow men. His sons are no less distinguished. Edward Miner Gallaudet, LL. D., (b. 1837), became an eminent authority on the instruction of the deaf and dumb, and was the Founder, and became the first President of the National Deaf-Mute College at Washington. His brother, Rev. Thomas Gallaudet, D. D., (b. 1822), has also become a successful author and worker in this humane field. In 1850 he became pastor of an Episcopal church in the city of New York, in which he established services in the Sign Language.

Bowdoin College.—Among the notable institutions in America founded by the Huguenots, is Bowdoin College, at Brunswick, in the state of Maine. It was named in honor of Governor James Bowdoin, (2) who was its patron, and who richly endowed it. Governor Bowdoin, was one of the foremost men of his times, not only in public affairs, but also in the field of learning. He was an intimate friend and correspondent of Benjamin Franklin, and the first President of the Academy of Arts and Sciences. His only son, James, was also a man of eminence and profound learning. In 1805 he was United States Minister to Spain. Dying childless in 1811, he also left a princely legacy to Bowdoin College.

It is no less a distinguished honor than a remarkable coincidence, that in 1895 three departments of our National Government were simultaneously under the presidency of Bowdoin graduates, namely, Thomas Reed, Speaker of the House of Representatives, Senator Frye, Chairman *pro tem* of the Senate, and Chief Justice Fuller, the head of the Judiciary Department.

Robert College.—This institution, situated at Constantinople, Turkey, is another notable Huguenot memorial. It was founded by the late C. R. Roberts, (3) of New York, whose princely muni-

---

(1). A descendant of Dr. Pierre Elisee Gallaudet, who came as a refugee to New Rochelle, N. Y., after the Revocation.

(2). Governor Bowdoin was born in Boston in 1726, and died in 1790. He was the grandson of Pierre Bowdoin, who came as a refugee to Boston soon after the Revocation. He died in 1706.

(3). The philanthrophist, Christopher R. Robert, was a descendent of Daniel Robert, of La Rochelle, who fled at the Revocation to Martinique, and from thence to New York.

ficence and tender sympathy for the unfortunate, not only led him to give with an unsparing hand to his countrymen, but also prompted him to provide the means for the elevation of his fellow-men in the benighted Orient.

Grinnell Polar Expedition.—In this connection it is worthy of record that the first promoters of Arctic Explorations in America were the Grinnell brothers, whose Huguenot ancestor came to New England at a very early day. These men were Hon. Henry Grinnell, (1799–1874), who was the first President of the American Geographical Society, and Moses Grinnell, (1807–1877). Their first venture was in 1850, when they sent an expedition in search of the lost Franklin party. The second under the leadership of the noted Dr. Elisha Kent Kane in 1853. By these expeditions our knowledge of the Polar Regions was vastly advanced.

GENERAL LIST OF HUGUENOT IMMIGRANTS TO PENNSYLVANIA.

The following list comprises the names of such immigrants to Pennsylvania during the Provincial period as are believed to have been of Huguenot origin. The list also includes the names of some Alsatians and Lorraines, and also a few whose ancestors had located in neighboring colonies. With the exception of the latter class, nearly all the immigrants in the subjoined list came to Pennsylvania as "foreigners" or non British subjects, and were compelled to be naturalized, and after 1727 all male foreigners above sixteen years of age were obliged to subscribe to an oath of allegiance. Fortunately for posterity, these lists are still extant and have been published by the State. (1).

Several volumes also contain lists of naturalizations of persons who arrived prior to 1727.

Should the reader fail to find the name of a supposed Huguenot immigrant to Pennsylvania in this list, he should not therefore conclude that such a supposed person did not arrive. Many things must be taken into consideration. Among others, the imperfections of the official records, arising from the fact that many names of immigrants were written phonetically. It should be remembered that French names abound in *silent* letters, and are not pronounced as the written name appears to the eye, and hence many names on

---

(1). Pa. Archives Vol. XVII., second series. See also Prof. Rupp's 30,000 names.

the official lists do not appear in their French form. We may cite a few examples. *Beauchamp* appears as *Bushong; Michelot* as *Mickley;* Wesco (Vasqueau) *Wesger; Voturin* as *Wotring,* and so on.

Again, in many instances where the original French name was preceded by the definite article *la*, *le* and *de* (the), and *du* (of, or from the), these prefixes have either been discarded or joined to the name. The following few examples will illustrate these changes. Many descendants of the *Du Fresne, De Cessna, De Saussier,* and many other immigrant families have dropped the prefix and write the name *Frehne, Cessna, Sausser,* etc. Of names where the article is now joined *to* the name we have *Dumont, Duhamel, Dubret, Lorange* (L'Orange), Lebo (Le Beau), Lesher (Le Char), *Devo* (De Veau), *Dilcamp* (De la Camp), *Dilabar* (De la Barre), etc.

Of names that have lost their French form entirely by phonetic transition we give the following examples: *Billow (Billeaux), Casho (Cacheau), Shadow (Chateau), Perrigo (Perrigeau), Boatman (Baudemon), Jacks (Jacques),* and so scores of others.

Then again, we find many honored French names now written in their English or German equivalent. A few examples must suffice. *Tonnelier* is *Kieffer* in German, and *Cooper* in English. *Pierre* is *Stein* in German and *Stone* in English, and so on. On this principle many French names have entirely disappeared. This list is the result of many years of careful research, during which time the Archives of the State have been thoroughly explored, church records of the Colonial period, and the records of many families have been searched with most gratifying results in many instances.

There are many families of French origin in Pennsylvania whose names do not appear in this list. In such cases we have failed to *find* traces of arrival or of Huguenot origin. No doubt many of these families come from the unfortunate Acadians, who were cruelly deported from Nova Scotia in 1755-'56 by the British government. The number who came to Pennsylvania was so large, and their distress so great, that the Provincial Assembly was necessitated to pass measures for their relief. (1) It will be remembered that Longfellow's touching poem, *Evangeline,* is based on an incident connected with these exiles.

---

(1). Vide Rupp's Hist. Lanc. Co., P. 301.

GENERAL LIST.

NOTE.—The dates following names indicate the time of arrival as derived from official records The names of counties where immigrants located are abbreviated. Immigrants from Alsace and Lorraine are mostly indicated by brackets.

Ache, John Ludwig—John George and Herman, 1752, Leb. Co.; John and George in Cocalico, Lanc. Co., prior to 1756.
Alleman, Jacob, Sr., Jacob, Jr., 1741—Stephen, 1749, (Lorraine)—Dorstius and Peter, 1752—John Christian, John Frederick, Christian and Hiram, 1753, Jean Jacques, 1754, (Lorraine), Lanc. and Leb.
Albert, see Chap. XIV.
Anganie, Nich., 1736, Dewalt, 1746, Theobald, 1733, Lanc.-Leb.
Amacher, Mich. 1754, (Lorraine).
Armeson, Pierre, (Armishong), 1753, Lanc.
Arnoul, Jean Pierre, 1751.
Aubertin, Pierre 1739.
Aune, Pierre 1744.
Aurand, Peter and Herman 1733, John 1733, Berks Co.
Balliet, Paul 1738, Lehigh, Joseph, 1749, Bucks.
Barberat, Jacques 1749, (Lorraine).
Barrett, Baldus 1738.
Baptiste, Jean Francois 1753, Jean 1770, Jean 1771, Jean 1771.
Baird, Francois and William, 1754, (Lorraine), Lanc.
Bach, Jacques 1754, (Lorraine).
Bachart, Geo. 1749, Lehigh.
Balme, Jacques 1753.
Balmas, Pierre 1757.
Baldy, Conrad, prior to 1740.
Baldus, John Leonard, 1749, John Peter 1753.
Bar, John, 1754, (Lorraine).
Barto, (Perdeau) John, 1730, Berks, Isaac, prior to 1750, Nicholas, 1773.
Barre, Jacob, Sr., Jacob, Jr., John Henry, Lanc.. prior to 1718.
Baron, John Philip 1747—Nich. 1752, Jacob 1753, Jonas 1763.
Bashore, (Le Baiseur), George, prior to 1733, Lanc., Jacob 1732, Ch. XIV, Daniel and Sebastian, 1749.

Batillion, (Bertillion), George, William, Christian, Frederick and Abraham, 1751.
Baudeman, Andri 1750, Jean and Isaac 1753, (Now Butman).
Bauer, John and Thomas 1754, (Lorraine).
Bayer, Chap. VII.
Bayard, Chap. VII. Bohemia Manor.
Bayle, Nich. 1729, Mich. 1748, Andrew, prior to 1745.
Bazillion, Peter Chap. XI, John Manwell 1732.
Berringer, Elias 1738, Paul 1743, Adam 1748, Henry 1750, Nich. and Bartholemew 1754.
Berrett, Jos. Berks, prior io 1753.
Beaver, Dieble 1741, Geo. Dewalt and John, (Alsace), John Geo. (Alsace) 1732, Mich., Val and John, (Beeber) 1768.
Beau, Jacques, Frans Carl 1768.
Beaumont, John Geo. 1764.
Beauchamp, Jean Lanc., prior to 1719. Jean 1731, died in Lanc. Co. 1749· John Mich. 1732, William 1741. (now Bushong).
Bernetz, John Leonard, John George Carl, Elias David, York, prior to 1737.
Bernot, Jacob 1751.
Belle, Jean Pierre 1754. (Lorraine).
Bernhart, John Thomas 1754. (Lorraine).
Bess, Christian 1754. (Lorraine).
Berge, Jacques 1754. (Lorraine).
Berot, Frans Ludwig 1738, York. Hellbarth 1751, Berks. Jacques 1752, Lanc.
Bertolet, Peter and Jean Chap. VIII.
Bertle, Nich. (Bertolet?) 1732, Lanc.
Bessonett, Richard, Bucks.
Benezette, John Stephen 1731, Phila.
Beaufort, Casper 1775.
Beuech, Martin and Simon 1732. John Mich. 1751. John Christian 1752.

Beggary, Vincent (Peckary), 1753.
Beidinger, John Adam and Peter 1736, (Alsace), York. Andrew 1752.
Beveneau, Anton 1749, York.
Bigonet, Jean 1752. Francis 1773, (Bigoney), Mont. Co.
Billet, Bosler, York.
Blocq, Albert, Del., prior to 1677.
Bodine, John, vide Conewago.
Boileau, Isaac, Bucks. Jacob, Berks prior to 1752.
Bouchee, Rudolf 1738, John 1749, Gregorius 1753.
Bohre, Peter 1750.
Borie, Laurens 1766, Mathew d. Lanc. 1780.
Bontaux, John and Joseph 1752.
Bourquin, Jean 1773.
Bourgeois, Benjamine—
Bouvard, Robert, Cumb., prior to 1740.
Bouton, Jean Daniel, 1739, Leonard Nat. Bucks Co. 1734, George Nat. Phila. 1754.
Bonnett, Jacques and fam. 1733, Jean Philipp, prior to 1736. Peter 1737, Lanc. Co., John Mich 1750, Jean 1753, Henry 1763.
Bouchell, vide Bohemia Manor.
Bouquet, Jacob 1743, Philip 1747.
Boschard, John 1738, Adam 1740, Bernard 1741, Fred 1750. John Daniel 1757.
Boyer, Alex 1648, Samuel 1710, John Phil. 1731, Gabriel, prior to 1732, James in Phila., prior to 1734, Carlos 1748, Vide Chap. VII.
Bonjour, And. 1754, Lanc.
Boudinot, Elias, Phila., Prior to 1731.
Boneauvent, Jean 1740, Va.
Bregonier, John Nich. 1740, Md.
Brant, Jos. Lanc.
Brevard—
Brunot, Felix 1732, John in Phila., prior to 1738, John 1752, Felix?
Buck, Nich. (Lorraine), Mont. Co. 1752.
Cacheau, (Casho), Jacob; early in Delaware. Samuel, Lanc., prior to 1752, Jacques 1772.
Cambourd, Jean 1732.
Carmeton, Fred 1742.
Cally, Christ (Lorraine), 1754.
Carel, Jacques, Sr,, Jacques, Jr., Peter and Jacob 1754.
Caquelin, Sebastian and sons Jean and Dietrich 1736, Felty "From the north of France" 1752, Lanc.
Carmane, John and Anthony 1756, Leb.
Caffarel, Paul, 1753.

Cazenove, de, Jean Antoine and Antoine Charles 1780.
Cazart, see Conewago.
Cellier, John 1727, Pierre 1748.
Chapelle, Eberhart 1757, Jeremiah and John Peter 1753.
Chamblin, John, York, prior to 1756.
Chasseur, Joseph 1764.
Chevelier, Philip Del., prior to 1677, Pierre C. Phila., prior to 1710.
Christien, Jean Francois from Rodan, Alsace, 1736, Christian and Peter 1757.
Charmeli, Simon 1749.
Chartier, Martin, prior to 1697.
Choape, Theors 1740.
Chars, And and fam. 1732.
Chateau, (Shadow) Jean Nich. 1739, Lanc.
Charett—?
Chedrone, (Shetron) Abr. 1749, York.
Clement, Mich. 1738.
Clevel, (Clewell), Francis and Geo. 1737, Northampton.
Claude, Charles 1738. Pierre 1770.
Clerq, Henri Del., prior to 1677.
Couvier, Jean Jacques 1754.
Cotineau.
Cochet, (now Gouche, Goshen), Daniel in Phila. prior to 1756. John Geo. Deitrich, Francis and Isaac 1768, Leb. Co.
Conte, John 1729.
Corbo, Jean 1737, Mont. Co.
Compos, Peter 1752.
Conrieu, Francois 1746.
Comer, Jean 1736, Lanc.
Conrad, John Mich (Lorraine), 1754.
Courteur, Joseph 1751.
Cossart, (Gr. Gossert), J. 1741, Henry 1749, Lanc.
Cossine, Peter and Cornelius, vide Conewago.
Coshune, Jean, Conewago.
Consul, Arenne 1746.
Cresson, Isaac, Phila., 1728. Conrad prior to 1728.
Crespin, Joseph 1753.
Creuccas, Jacques 1737.
Crownwalt, Jacob (Lorraine), 1754.
Cushwa, Isaac 1732, Leb. Co.
Darant, (Durant), Geo. Peter 1741.
Dacier, Daniel 1750. John Mich. and John Martin 1752. Paul 1753.
Daron, Mich. York Co.
Dasons, Francois 1734.
Dauny, Jean Louis, nat. 1732.
De Armand, James, Dauphin, prior to 1740. Henry 1756.
De Avier, Jean Louis, 1732, Lanc.

De Normandy, Andri 1706, Bucks.
De Bran, John 1690.
De Bertholet, John Phlilip, 1737.
De Mars, Jean 1741, Lanc.
De Belle, Jacob 1738.
De Bleame, ——? Mont.
De Benneville, Dr. Geo. 1741, Berks.
De Benoit, Humber prior to 1749,
De Cesna, Jean 1718, Lanc.
De Boileau, Isaac, Bucks.
De Beau, (De Bo, De Bus, Du Bus), Abraham and Philip 1732. Conrad, Lanc. prior to 1737. Christian 1740. Daniel and Jacob 1743.
De Dier, Jean Germantown early, Jean 1770.
De Dee, Jean 1712, Oley, Daniel 1750, David and John Geo. 1751, Abraham (Lorraine) 1754, Lanc., Josue, Jean Pierre and Jean, 1765.
De Fresne, (De Frain), 1731. Chap VII.
De France, John prior to 1740, Dauphin.
De Gann, Moris, Delaware, prior to 1677.
De Gomois, (Degoma), Adam, prior to 1754, York.
De Grange, Andre 1749; John, York Co., prior to 1750.
De Hass, Capt. John, Del., prior to 1660, Geo. Philip 1749, Leb.
De Longschamp, Chas. Julian.
De Lage, Pierre Phila. 1736, died 1766.
De Lancy, Francois, Lanc., prior to 1754.
De Long, Jacob 1743, Berks.
De Marcellain, Bucks.
De Morest, Gerrett, Conewago.
De Purcell, William, Bucks, 1734.
De Pree, Jacques 1764.
De Prefontain, Peter, Phila., prior to 1754.
De Pui, Nicholas, Minisink, 1697.
De Ring, Mat. Delaware, prior to 1677.
De Rimley, Nich. Francis, Bethlehem.
De Remo, Jacques, 1750.
De Sanno, Frederick, Bucks.
De Turk, Isaac 1712, Berks.
De Tar, John Lanc.
De Tray, Christian 1737, Bucks, Conrad, Nat. Phila. 1662.
De Veau, Pierre, 1736, Conrad 1754.
De Ville, John 1765.
De La Barrie, (Delabar), Jacob. Bucks, prior to 1745.
De La Bach, Val. and Peter, prior to 1757, Dauphin.
De La Cour,(Dellicker, Rev. Frederick)

De La Camp, Henry, Berks 1753.
De La Grange, Jost. Del. 1656.
De La Planch, Jacques, Berks, prior to 1720.
De La Plaine, Jacques, Phila. 1691.
De La Noe, Rev. Chas. Phila., prior to 1700.
De La Vall, John, Phila. 1682.
De La Ware, Isaac m. in Phila. 1735.
Decha, Edward 1752.
Deschong, (Des Champ), Diet. William 1752, Lanc., William and Mathias 1753.
Deque, Jacques, 1773.
Dessloch, Geo. (Lorraine) 1754.
Demje, Pierre 1773.
Deoux, Philip, prior to 1750.
Dilloe, Pierre, (Dillo) 1736, Lanc., Mich., prior to 1745.
Dillier, (Diller) Casper 1731, Lanc., Francis 1738,
Digeon, Daniel 1742, (Alsace), Northampton.
Dinkle, John Daniel 1750, (Alsace), York.
Dispionett, Jacques, (Des Bonnett), 1739, to Va.
Douthett—— York, prior to 1754.
Doz, Anthony 1685, Phila.
Dobler, Nicholas (Lorraine), 1752, Dauphin.
Dore, Antoine 1770.
Donderman, Jean Pierre 1773.
Dondore, Michael (Alsace), Lanc., prior to 1718, John and son Jacob, 1741, Berks.
Douay, Conrad 1740.
Donatt, Geo. nat. Chester Co. 1734.
Duey, John and John Christian 1750, Chester.
Doutell, Jacob 1738, Jacob, York Co., prior to 1746, Francois, Lanc., prior to 1750.
Doute, (Du Tay) David and John Geo. 1751, Lanc., Francois, Lanc., prior to 1758.
Dracot, Ralph—Bucks.
Drapet, Jean 1750.
Dravo, Anthony, Pittsburg.
Dupree, Jacob nat. 1734, Jacob in Phila., prior to 1693, Jacob nat. Berks Co. 1762, Geo. Berks Co. 1764.
Dupee, Danl, Phila., prior to 1754, Christian, Leb., prior to 1749.
Durye, Geo. 1733, Berks, Jacob 1738, Samuel, Conewago.
Duponceau, Peter Phila.
Duval, Daniel 1749.
Duche, Anthony Phila., prior to 1700.

Dufort, Philip, Sr., Philip, Jr., 1738.
Dubrett Jacques, 1763.
Duistro, Jean 1740.
Durell, Moses, Phil., prior to 1731.
Dushane—early in Delaware.
Duchand, Francis 1773.
Duton, Abraham 1754.
Du Simetere, Pierre Eugene 1764, Phil.
Du Corson, Benj., Bucks Co.
Du Keyness, Henry, Lanc., prior to 1762.
Du Castle, Edmund Phil., 1682.
Du Bach, Clement 1734.
Du Pont, Vide Chap. VI, George 1768.
Du Bois, Jean, New Castle, prior to 1694, Solomon 1718, Conrad 1728, (d. 1757), Abraham 1732, Philip—
Eckerline, Page 115.
Emilot, Nich. and Leonard 1732, Lanc.
Escogue, John Peter 1738.
Ekord, Phil. 1731.
Forney, Abraham age 64 y. 1734, Christian and Peter 1734, Lanc., Jacob 1752, John Adam 1747.
Femme, Geo., Jr., 1753.
Ferree, Vide Chap. XII.
Fidele, Mich. Mont., prior to 1740.
Fiscus, Gerhart (Alsace) 1744.
Fleury, Pierre-1732, Joseph and sons Joseph and John 1733, Abra. nat. in Phila. 1743, Adolphe and Geo. 1754.
Folquier, Jean Jacques 1754, married in Phila. 1755.
Fontain, Jacob, 1751, Dauphin.
Fortineaux, (Fortney) Jean Henri nat. 1727, Francois 1737, David 1739, Jean aged 56 and Samuel 1742, Mechoir d. 1754, Lanc.
Fournier, David York, prior to 1740.
Frentier, Jean 1755.
Frenier, Casper 1739, Lanc.
Frank, John Adam (Lorraine), 1754.
Frey, Henry, Altheim Alsace, to Phila., prior to 1685.
Garragues, Vide Ch. VI.
Garton, de, Abraham, Lanc., prior to 1736, Felix 1749.
Gasha, (Casho?) Peter 1749, York.
Gashon, Jean 1752.
Gannett, John Henry, prior to 1745, Berks.
Gateau, Nich. nat. Phil. 1704.
Gallo, Christian 1751, Jean 1768.
Gausfres, Jean 1738.
Gaigdon, Jean Henri, 1763.
Gautier, Pierre and Jacques 1753.

Gerra, Pierre and Joseph, 1746.
Gerard, Nich. 1736, David d. 1769, Berks Co., Peter nat. 1767.
Gerardin, (also Charetin, Sheradan), Jacob and fam. 1748, Berks.
Gennevine, Leonard York, prior to 1755.
Gehret, Geo. 1737, Frances 1744, Peter, 1749, Berks.
Gerber, Christian and Geo. Mich. (Alsace), 1738, Berks.
Gillion, Charle, 1738, Pierre 1752.
Gilbert, John 1757, John Wendel 1754, (Lorraine).
Gourrier, Pierre 1753, Lanc.
Grauel, (Crowell L. Dept. Rec), John Mich., Sr., (1683-1753), 1730, Berks, John Mich. 1733.
Gruwell, John (from France), Delaware after 1700.
Grimm, Egideus (Alsace) 1727, Lehigh.
Greine, Pierre, 1754, Lanc.
Gros Jean, Jacques (Groshong), 1756, Dauphin.
Granget, Jean 1738, Adrian 1767.
Grandaden, Francois and Adam, 1749, Lanc.
Grenoble, de, Jacob, 1743, Berks.
Gresamere, Casper, Peter and John Valentine 1730, Mont. and Berks.
Harcourt, Mich. 1751.
Haller, Henry (Alsace), 1733, Lanc.
Hathe, Jean Gaspard, 1771.
Hammand, Erasmus "from Nancy," 1739.
Hasslinger, Geo. (Lorraine), 1756.
Hauser, John Henry (Lorraine), 1754.
Hauser, Danl and Nich, (Lorraine,) 1754, Md.
Hay, John, Sr., John, Jr., 1757, (Alsace), York.
Herbein, Jonathan, prior to 1720, Peter and Abraham 1732, Berks.
Heyde, John Jost, prior to 1717, (Alsace), Pa. and Va., see Chap. XV.
Herring, John Geo. (Lorraine), 1754, Berks.
Heckendorn, Daniel and family (Alsace), 1736, Lanc.
Hoch, (High), Melchoir and Jonathan (Alsace), 1717, Berks.
Hillegas, John Fred 1727, Leopold 1730, John Adam 1732, Mich. and Peter, prior to 1745, Geo. Albrecht 1746, (Alsace).
Hogar, Antoine 1754, (Lorraine).
Hotel, John 1732.
Hobart, Adam, 1738.

Hodnett, John, Phila., prior to 1737.
Hoyer, Franc Carl (Alsace), 1738, Berks.
Hoshier, Laurans, Christian and Abraham 1741.
Hoschar, Theobald, John Peter and John Henry, 1749.
Hoozier, Geo. 1751.
Hotman, John 1755, Michael 1753.
Horry, William 1727, Martin, nat. York Co., 1763.
Hutier, Jean Jacques, prior to 1751. Lanc.
Hugo, John Daniel 1753.
Hubertson, Hubert 1709, Lanc.
Hubert, Geo. 1749, Andrew 1765.
Hubele, Joseph and sons Mich. and Barnard 1732, Jacob 1737, John Frederick 1743.
Huger, John Christ 1766.
Hueling, Lars, Geo. 1750, Vide Chap. VI.
Huidenbery, Val. (Lorraine), 1754.
Huguelet, Abr. and Charles (Lorraine), 1754.
Hugett, Francis (Hugus?), 1737, Lanc.
Huyett, Geo. Berks, prior to 1734, Franc Carl 1738, Mich. 1749, Peter 1746.
Imbert, Andrew, 1683, Phil.
Izard, Jean 1770.
Jardines, Dr. des, Del., prior to 1680.
Jacques, Jean (b. 1696, d. 1778, Lanc.), Abraham 1736, Lanc.
Jacquett, Jean Paul, Del. 1650.
Jacquard, Fred 1752, John Peter 1753, John Peter 1768.
Janvier, Thomas Del., prior to 1700.
Javin, Pierre—
Jeune, C. Jacques 1749, Henri 1751, Lanc.
Joho, John 1739, York.
Joch, (Schoch) John Jac. Sr., John Jacob, Jr., Mich. 1749. (Alsace).
Joray, (Jury) Jacques 1749, Abraham 1754, Dauphin.
Jourdan, Jean 1738.
Jommel, Mart. 1750.
Jurian, Mathias 1732.
Julian, Peter 1764.
Kauffman, John Jacob (Alsace). 1737.
Keppler, Simon (Lorraine), 1754.
Keim, Johannes 1697, Berks.
Kieffer, Casper and Abraham 1748, Nich. and Jacob 1750, Berks.
Klencke, Mich. (Lorraine), 1754.
Kuntzelman, John Jacob (Lorraine), 1754.
Lambing, Christopher (1720–1810), from Alsace.

Lachart, Barnard 1741, John Jacob 1753.
Lazelere, Nich. (1691 Long Island, N. Y.,) Nich., Jr., to Bucks Co.
Lantzinger, John (Alsace), 1738.
Lanbleau, Jean Jacques, 1752.
Latz, John Jacob, (Lorraine), 1754.
Laux, Pierre 1738, Lanc., Peter 1737, Bucks, John Jacob 1754.
Laschett, (Lawshe), John Jacob age 50, sons John Peter, age 25 and Christian, age 18, 1736, Lanc., John Wendel 1738, Daniel in Phila., prior to 1752.
Lallemand, Jacob 1757.
Laurans, Hubert Del., prior to 1677, John 1736, Henry 1738, Frances Peter, d. Lanc. 1758.
Laschelles, Geo., Vide Conewago.
Leasure, Abr. (Lorraine), 1754, Dauphin.
Levering, Wigard and Gerhart 1685, Phila.
Lingel, Paul and Jacob, 1737.
Lilou, James, prior to 1750, Cumb.
Linville, Henry, prior to 1740, Berks.
Loresh, Jacob, prior to 1751, Berks.
Lorraine, John, Phila.
Lorange, (L'Orange) Henry, Dauphin, prior to 1750.
Lorah, (Loreau) Phila., prior to 1715, John 1737, John Casper 1754.
Lorie, John Henry and John Melchoir 1749, John Peter 1753.
Lorisen, Geo. Mich. and Gabriel 1738.
Lovine, Abraham, Vide Conewago.
La Bar, Peter, Chas. and Abraham 1730, Danl. and Pnilip nat. in 1738, William nat. 1750.
La Belle, Simon, nat. 1762.
La Blanch, early in Phila.
La Bert, Michael 1729, Adam 1753.
Lapert, (Labert?) John 1739.
La Cellas, James Phila., prior to 1759.
La Gnau, Bartholomas 1754, York.
La Mar, Leonard 1741, Michael 1750, John, Nich. and Francis 1754, Berks.
La Mott, Jean Henri 1754, York.
La Place, Philip Peter 1765.
La Pierre, Jean Jacques 1753, Lanc.
La Port, Jean 1777.
La Roux, Jonas 1719, Lanc., John Phila., prior to 1739, George, prior to 1740, Dauphin, Abraham, Sr., and Abraham, Jr., in Bucks very early, Abraham, d. York Co. 1757.
La Rash, Ludwig (L. Dept). prior to 1757, Northampton.

LaRouse, Ephraim, prior to 1738.
La Rose, John Lewis 1740, Lehigh.
La Saul, Jacob 1738.
La Trine, Anna 1729.
La Tour, Herman and Jacob. 1749, Lanc.
La Wall, John Michael 1749, Daniel and John Ludwig, 1752.
LeBeau, (Lebo), John, prior to 1718, Lanc., Peter, prior to 1737, John, prior to 1734, John, prior to 1740, John Abr., prior io 1742, John Henry 1765.
Le Bot, Albert 1737.
Le Boyteau, John, early in Phila.
Le Blanch, Joseph Phila.
Le Boob, Mich. d. York Co. 1780.
Le Brant, John Conrad 1751, Lanc., George, Berks Co.
Le Brun, Ettine 1753.
Le Cene, Jean and Paul 1732, Lanc.
Le Colle, Pierre, prior to 1720, Phila.
Le Crone, Daniel d. Lanc. 1769, Jacob Lanc., prior to 1757, Jacob, Lanc., prior to 1757, Leonard, York Co.
Le Char. Vide Chap. VI.
Le Dieu, Lewis, Phila., prior to 1758.
Le Die, Jean 1772.
Lemont, Peter, Lanc., prior to 1718.
Le Drue, John 1718, Jos. and Noel in Phila.
Le Fevre, Hypolite, Jean and Jacques in Del. prior to 1685, Isaac, Lanc. Co. 1712, John in Mont. Co. 1778,
Le Gay, (Le Geau ?) early in Phila.
Le Maistre, John William, age 58, 1748
Le Moree, Jean Baptiste.
Le Roy, John Mich. and George 1738, Jean Jacques 1752, Abraham 1754, Abraham and Adam 1754.
Le Shemile, Peter prior to 1741., Phila.
Le Tort, James, prior to 1787.
Le Tellier, Peter— Phila.
Le Van, Abraham, Isaac and Jacob, prior to 1725, Daniell 727, Peter 1748.
Le Vassong, John Lewis, 1732.
Le Valleau, Chas. prior to 1695, Bucks Co.
Mackinett, Daniel, prior to 1739, Mont. Co., d. 1744.
Marchand, John Lewis and John Geo. 1737.
Marti, Laurans and John, 1749.
Mathiot, Jean and George 1754, Lanc.
Marionette, Jacques, 1738.
Mallo, John Michael (Alsace), 1749, John Geo. 1755.
Marot, Pierre and fam. 1733.

Martine, Mich. 1747, Yarra Emanuel 1744, John Theodore, Justus and Charles 1753, John Martin 1754.
Marett, Mich. 1736, Lanc. Mich. 1737, Abra. 1777.
Morett, Jean Dedier and Mattieu, 1757, Berks, Etienne, 1773.
Maier, Adam, (Lorraine), 1754.
Mallecot, Phillippe 1757.
Markie, Marcus 1736, Jacob 1745, Leb.
Marcoe, Abraham, Santa Cruz 1750, Phila.
Markley, John Christman (Alsace), John Jacob 1749, Jean Christopher 1752.
Marquetand, Laurans, Lanc.
Marquard, John Geo. and Martin 1743, John 1750.
Marquett, John Henry Lebanon, prior to 1743, Peter 1749, John Geo. 1752, John Geo. (2nd) 1752.
Marie, Casper 1732.
Merree, (Marie ?) Seb. 1729, James 1730, Christian 1733, Berks.
Morree, Wm. nat. in Bucks Co., 1734.
Mease, Henry, "late from France" 1749.
Melfort, John Casper, nat. Chester 1762.
Mercier, Augustine 1773.
Mestrezat, Charles Andre, Chap. XVI
Meurer, Rev. Philip (Alsace), 1742.
Mentjes, Francois, prior to 1750, Lanc.
Messakop, John 1754, Lanc.
Minuit, Peter, Del. 1738.
Mischele, John Geo. and Joseph 1749.
Michelot, (Mickley) John Jacob 1733, (Lorraine), Lehigh.
Missamer, John Mich. (Alsace), Mont.
Millot, Nich. 1749, Berks, Pierre 1749.
Moreau, (Morrow) Francois, Lanc., prior to 1750, John d. at Lanc. 1760, Philip m. at Bethlehem 1757.
Moser, 1720 Chap. IX.
Mottier, John Mich. 1749.
Molier, Etienne, 1773.
Monier, Jacques 1770.
Monel, Pierre, 1768.
Montmaton, Gulliaume, 1770.
Montieth, John, Conewago.
Morell, Matthieu, prior to 1770, Berks.
Molan, Jacques 1752.
Molin, Mathew 1752.
Moris, Jacques, 1749.
Monin, Jean Pierre Se., and Jean Pierre, Jr.. (Lorraine). 1754.
Montandon, David 1729, Phila.
Montfort, John, Conewago.

Momma, John Conrad and Hermanus, (Lorraine), 1747, Lanc, Christian d. Lanc. 1755, Jacob 1737, Lanc., Leonard 1737 Lanc., Peter 1748 Lanc. Laurens d. Lanc. 1752.
Muni, (Le Moyne), Jacob, Sr., Jacob, Jr., Conrad, Andrew and Christopher 1570, Dauphin.
Mylander, John Daniel, (Lorraine) 1754.
Naudin, Elie. Del. 1698.
Neron, Lorie 1750.
Noble, Anthony, Sr., Anthony, Jr., 1734.
Noel, Enas and Joseph with families, 1736, Killian 1738, John m. at Bethlehem 1746, Philip, prior to 1740, Jean prior to 1750, in York Co.
Oberlin, Martin and John Adam (Alsace), prior to 1730 Lanc., Israel 1752 Lanc.
Ozias, Henry, prior to 1750, Phila.
Paca, John, prior to 1758, Phila.
Pallio, Peter, prior to 1730, Berks.
Palin, Laz., 1738,
Paris, Pierre, Isaac, Sr., Isaac, Jr., 1750, Isaac 1750, Pierre, George and Nicola 1770.
Parat, Cornelius 1734.
Paire, Jacob 1736, Lanc., Jacob 1747.
Pavon, Jean Pierre 1744.
Patier, Louis 1770.
Parent, John 1727.
Parshing. Nich. 1732.
Paushon, John Nich. 1733.
Perzonze, John Jac. 1740, Leb., d. 1749.
Pierson, Laurans 1738, Lanc.
Perrett, Henry 1777.
Perretier, Jean Henri, Sr., and Jr., 1754, (Lorraine).
Perlett, John 1732, John Fred 1751, Perqua, Adam, 1749.
Pechin, Pierre, and sons Jean Nicholas and Jean Christopher 1754, (Lorraine), Chester.
Pettit, John York, prior to 1749, Jona. than, Northampton, prior to 1759.
Perrine, Thomas, Lanc., prior to 1718,
Pershing, Frederick, 1749, (Alsace), Westmoreland.
Pigonie, (Bigony-Pigoney) Jean 1752, Francois 1773, Montgomery.
Pievex, Laurans, 1739.
Pinnard, Jos. Phila., prior to 1703.
erre, Nicholas 1727, York, Christian, nat. in Chester 1750, Martin 1750, Jean Henri 1757.

Picquart, James d. Lancaster 1749. Henry prior to 1744, John Gottfried in Phila., prior to 1754.
Pons, Jacques 1727, Augustus 1728, Abra. 1751, John Sr. and Jr., 1768.
Poponet, Pierre Carl, 1773.
Porreau Jean Daniel, 1773.
Pontius, John 1738, (Alsace), Nicholas, Martin and David 1768, Berks.
Purviance, Saml, Phila., prior to 1693, David (Lorraine), 1754, Dauphin.
Purdieu, William, Phila., prior to 1738.
Pyatt, Chap. XV.
Pythan, Jean Gulliaume 1769.
Querrier, John Nich., 1752, Berks.
Qua, (le.) John and Frederick 1753, Chester.
Quepic, Jeania (Lorraine) 1754.
Rausier, Fred, Phila., prior to 1748.
Raboteau, Chas. Cornelius, Mont. prior to 1750.
Rappe, Gabriel 1683. Phila.
Raiguel, Jean Jacques 1754, Dauphin.
Rayer, (Royer) Sebastian 1718, John Jacob 1729, John Martin 1729, John Mich. 1732, J. Nicholas and Jacob 1749.
Raquet, Henry, Lanc. prior to 1752, John Nich. and John Christopher 1764.
Ramey, Pierre, (Lorraine) 1754.
Ranc, (Ranck) John, Mich. 1728, John Philip, 1729, Lanc.
Remey, Bartol and son Jacob 1737, Daniel, prior to 1754, Northampton.
Revere, Geo, 1773.
Remley, (de) Ambrose and Jacob 1741, Northampton, Conrad in Phi la.
Renoudet, James, Phila., prior to 1733.
Receau, Thomas, Phila., prior to 1716.
Retteu, William, prior to 1726, Chester.
Renart, John Adam, 1741.
Reusal, John Peter, 1751.
Renan, Joseph 1764.
Relan, Nicola 1749.
Renolle, Daniel, 1749, York.
Renau, (Reno) Claude 1749, Isaac, 1751, Peter and Francis 1752, Joseph, 1764.
Riehl, Simon 1729, Nicholas, Berks, prior to 1732, John Philip 1738, Jonas 1742, John George 1751.
Ritner, Abr. (Alsace), 1750 Berks, Laurans, 1754.
Ridett, Benj. and John, Conewago.
Ribolett, Christian 1733, Abraham, Jacob and John Peter 1749.
Richardeu, Pierre and Jean 1754.
Riboleau, Nicholas, Phila. 1683.

Rochia, Laurans, Delaware, Adam 1752.
Roller, John and John Jacob 1750, John Geo. and John, Mich. 1753, John Peter, 1752.
Ronner, John Rinehart 1743.
Roberdieu, Isaac, Phila.
Rosier, Laurans, 1732, De Beau Rosier, in Lanc. prior to 1753.
Roshong, Adam, Phila., prior to 1733, Henri and Pierre (Lorraine) 1753, Philip 1754.
Robinett, Samuel, Phila. 1684.
Rosher, Gabriel, 1731. Lanc, John 1764.
Routte, Daniel, New Castle, prior to 1683.
Rottie, Jean Pierre, 1754.
Rutan, Gerritt, NewCastle, 1660.
Rubishong, Septimus, Lanc. 1712. Mathias, Lanc. 1732, John, Berks 1732, John 1734.
Rumont, Vernier 1753.
Ruhlin, John Geo., Berks 1754.
Rutselia, (Rudesill), Philip M. at Conestoga 1734, d. 1754, Weirick 1737, York Co., John Jacob 1752, York Co., Andrew 1749.
Rubie, (Ruby), Peter 1738, Casper 1748, York.
Santee, Isaac, Bucks.
Santeau, (Sando), Jacques, 1754, Lanc.
Sauvet, Henri 1773.
Sanguinet, Jacob 1753.
Sauvage, John 1738, Berks.
Sausser, (De Saussier), David 1743, John Jacob 1749.
Saurian, Philip 1754.
Sarijons, Philippi 1754.
Sangree, Christian, York, prior to 1738, John Ludwig 1749.
Saye, Richard, Delaware, prior to 1686, Bernet 1740.
Savoy, Jean, Delaware, prior to 1700.
Sallada, Jacob 1749, Peter 1750, Frederick 1751, d. 1770, Nicholas 1752, Thomas 1764.
Scharille, Christian, (Lorraine), 1754.
Schnellbach, John, (Lorraine), 1754.
Schendt, Mathew (Lorraine), 1754.
Schilling, John, (Lorraine), 1754.
Schreiner, Adam, (Lorraine), 1754.
Schuett, Carl. Val Mich., prior to 1734.
Schora, Jacob 1753, Nich. and John Adam 1768.
Sevier, Philip 1733.
Servier, Jean Jacques 1753.
Secore, Mathew 1749.
Seiz, Jean Louis 1763.

Seubert, John and Andrew, (Alsace), 1752.
Serieux, Jean 1770.
Seyzer, John, (Lorraine), 1754.
Seal, John Paul, (Lorraine), 1751, Dauphin.
Sensinia, (Sensiny), Jacob Lanc., prior to 1737, Christian d. Lanc. 1753.
Shultz, Ch. Otto, (Alsace), 1734.
Shuey, Daniel and Ludwig 1732, Leb., John 1748, John Fred 1749, John Philip 1764.
Showa, Frederick, (Lorraine), 1754, John, Sr. and John, Jr., prior to 1745.
Shetron, (Chedron), Abraham 1749, York.
Sibrick, Guilliaume 1752.
Simonett, (Simony), Jacques 1727, Lanc.
Sieur, Philip 1752.
Sochonet, Henri 1733.
Souplies, (Supplee), Andre 1684, Phila.
Soloman, Abra., (Alsace), 1739.
Soule, John and Francis 1749,
Somaine, Vide p. 60.
Sponselier, Philip, (Lorraine), 1732, Lanc., Philip 1754, Geo. nat. York Co.. 1761.
Spurior, Nich. 1741.
Steubesant, John Geo., (Lorraine), 1754.
Steg, Albert Otto, (Lorraine), 1754.
Suffrance, John 1732, Phila.
Sumois, (Summey), John Peter, Sr., and sons John Peter, Jr., John Jacob, John and John Michael 1733, Lancaster.
Talman, Jacques, (Lorraine), 1754.
Thebaut, (Tebo), Philip 1714.
Thoulozan, Jean 1749.
Tien, Jean Henri, 1751.
Tiesser, Etienne 1770, Etienne 1771.
Torson, F. Christopher 1752.
Tomel, Paul 1750.
Tournay, Daniel 1740. Peter 1741, John 1750.
Trasbart, Nicola 1736.
Travenger, Peter nat. Lanc. Co., 1727.
Transue, Abr. 1730, Mont. Co.
Trippeo, Fred, prior to 1713, Phila.
Trego, Pierre, Delaware Co., prior to 1684.
Trevillier, Jos., Phila., prior to 1745,
Trebert, Justus, Lanc., prior to 1755.
Trevett, Christian 1738.
Trylopare, Jacob, (Alsace) 1732.
Udree, Henry 1741, Phila.
Urner, Ulrich, (Alsace), 1708, Chester.
Urffer, Mich., (Alsace), 1765.

Ull, John, (Lorraine), 1754.
Varlet, C. 1773.
Valin, Gabrial 1773.
Vasqueau, (Wesco), Philip 1754, Lehigh.
Vassar, Jacob 1751.
Vallerchamp, Simon, Vide p. 35.
Vautie, Pierre, (Lorraine), 1754.
Vandalin, H. Martin 1754.
Verdieux, Jacques, York;prior to 1755.
Vertrie, (Verdries), John with fam. to Lanc. Co., prior to 1733.
Vidal, Stephen, Phila., prior to 1754.
Vincent, Louis 1738.
Viellard, ("Willer"), Casperius 1732, Lanc., John Peter, Lanc., prior to 1733.
Vintvas, Jean Pierre, 1746.
Viersard, Jean Richard 1764.
Vielleman, Francois 1773.
Viebert, Geo. 1732.
Vishang, Conrad and Philip, 1740.

Voturin, (Woodring), Abraham, (Lorraine), 1733, Northampton, John 1739, York, Nicholas?
Vosin, Jean Pierre 1738, Jean Pierre 1754, Abraham 1768.
Voyer, Peter, Phila., prior to 1713.
Voshell, Wm., "Delaware near 1700."
Votaw, Paul, Isaac and John, near Phila., prior to 1744, John to Va.
Wendling, (Vandalin), Peter and Dewalt, (Bushweiler, Alsace), 1752, Lanc.
Welschans, (Velschang), Peter, Abra. and Joseph 1739, Lanc.
Werley, Dietrich, (Alsace), 1736, York.
Welle, Jean Pierre 1768.
Wiershang, (Viershang), Conrad and Philip 1740, Peter 1741, Casper 1753, Lanc.
Weimer, Barnard 1732, (Alsace), John 1747.
Willeman, (Vielleman), Alphonse, (Lorraine), 1754.
Willard, Christian and Martin, 1749.

LIST OF THE FRENCH NOBILITY.

Families of Patrician rank, the names of which occur among the immigrants to America, compiled from "The Nobility of Normandy."—(*Nobiliaire de Normandie.*) Date A. D., 1688.

Ache (Aughe)
Achard
Allemand, le
Baille
Baron
Barre, de la
Baudoin
Bauquet (Bouquet,)
Benard
Benoist (Benoit,)
Berranger
Bernard
Bisaye (Bisse?,)
Blanc, le
Bois, du
Boiteau, le
Bonnett
Bonneville
Bos, du
Boucher
Bourgeois
Bourget
Boutillier, le
Bouton
Boyer
Bouyer
Brosses, des
Brunot
Buisson, du
Cacheux (Casho,)
Carmone
Carre
Cavelier
Cesne, de
Champs, des (Deshong,)
Chapelle
Chartier
Chateau
Chesne, du
Chevelier, le
Chrestien
Clerc, le
Cochart
Cointe, le (Le Conte,)
Compte, le
Cossart (Cassatt,)
Coursey, du
Consine
Croismare (Griesamer?,)
Daudet (Douty,)
Darie

Durand
Duret
Espee, le
Febvre, le
Ferree
Fevre, le (Lefever,)
Fountain
Four, du
Fournier
Franc, le
Francios
Fresne, du (de Frain, etc.,)
Garnier
Gaudin
Girard
Guyon
Haas, des (de Hass,)
Harcourt, de
Hubert
Huett
Hullin (Huling,)
Hurel
Imbert
Jardins, des
Jourdain
Lamy
Lanoy, de
Lasseur, de
Lescalles
Long Champ, de
Loureux (Lorah)
Lucas
Maheu Mahew,
Maistre, le (Lemaster,)
Mallet
Marchand, le
Mare, de la
Marets, des
Marie
Martel, de
Martigny (Martine,)
Masnry, du
Maurey
Mellun
Menard
Mercier, le
Merle, du
Merlet, du
Millet
Moine, le
Morret

Mounier, le
Mont, du
Montagne, de
Montfort
Marant, de
Morel, de
Morin
Motte, de la
Moyne, le
Noble, le
Noe, de la (Delano,)
Noel
Parc, du
Pardien, de
Parent, du
Pere, le
Perier, du
Petit, le
Picquet (Pickett,)
Picony
Pierre, du
Pierrepont,
Place, la
Pont, du
Prevost
Puis, du
Regnalt
Remy, de
Renouard
Ridel
Roche, la
Romilly, de
Roux, le
Roy, le (Larou,)
Royer
Rou, de la
Sauvage
Secart
Sellier
Sublet
Sueur, le (Lesure,)
Tellier, le
Val, du
Valleau, le
Vasseur
Vaux, de
Viellard
Vieux, de
Villers, du
Vosin
Voyer, le

THE FRENCH NOBILITY, Con.

Familes of noble rank described in de Maigney's Science of Heraldry (1) and which appear in name among the Huguenot immigrants to America.

Ache, de
Astier
Auber, de (Dauber,)
Astorg, de (Astor,)
Autre, de Utree,
Baron
Barral
Baudin
Farrel, de la
Beau, de
Beauchamp
Beaufort
Bechonnet (Pechonet ?,)
Behrent
Benoist (Benoit,)
Bernetz
Bernon
Boutellier
Bouvet
Bouvier
Boyer
Brun, le
Cazenave
Cellier
Chapelle, de la
Chardon
Chavlier
Charrett
Chateau
Conte, le
Courson, du
Courtenay, de
Consine
Crozier, de
Dassier
Dautry
Ferneau

Ferree
Fleury
Garnett
Garrigues
Hugo
Huelin
Hurel
Imbert
Jacquett
Julien
Lambin
Lancy, de
Laneau, de
Laplace
Laurens, de
Laurent, du
Lery, de
Longchamp, de
Long, de
Marchant
Marien
Marquet
Martel
Martineau
Maurey, du
Mayaud (Mayo,
Mere, de
Monier, de
Mont, du
Moreau
Morret
Morel
Motte, de la
Mounier
Orth, d'
Palliot
Paris, de

Perrier
Perrin
Pierre, de la
Pingre
Pibard
Planch, de la
Ponce, de
Ponceau, du
Pons
Porchier, du
Prevost
Puis, du
Puy, du
Ramey
Raguet, du
Remy
Robert
Roche, de la
Rohan
Roux
Royer
Rumont
Soule
Tellier, le
Tricaud, de (Trego,)
Tru, de
Trion, de
Val, du
Vallee
Vasseur, le
Vastan, de
Vaux, de
Villars
Vincent
Vosin
Voyer

(1.) Claude D. du Maigney was one of the greatest authorites on Heraldry. He established the Heraldic College at Paris in 1841. His work on the French Nobility "Science des Armoiries," published in Paris in 1856 is a grand work, and the descriptions and engravings of the arms of the families treated of are very fine.

MEMORIALS OF THE HUGUENOTS. 161

GENERAL INDEX. (1)

Acadia colonized, 29, inhabitants deported	148
Achey fam. hist.	120
Abbadie, Jacques	24
Albert fam. hist.	122
Alsace, devastation of 72, 112, emigration from	72
Antillies, Huguenot colony of	32
Antoine de Bourbon renounces Prot. faith	5
Antes fam. ref. to	86
Asylum, Pa., founded	34
Audubon, John James	36
Aurand fam. hist.	119
Bayard fam. hist. 45–46, Col. John and Stephen	41
Bailiet fam. hist., 83, Col. Stephen	41, 83
Baldy fam. hist.	59
Bashore fam. hist.	119
Barnitz fam. hist.	128
Barree, Jacob	90
Bancroft, historian, quoted	137
Benezette fam. hist.	49
Berrott fam. hist.	126
Bezillion Peter	89
Bessonett fam. hist.	78
Beau Jacques, F. C.	124
Benoit, Elias, historian	24
Besnage [Benage] 23–24, fam hist.	120
Bertolet fam. hist.	41, 63
Beaver fam. hist 76, Gen. James A	41
Beeber 76, Hon. Dimmer	41
Bittenger fam. hist. 128, Hon. J. W	41
Bigony fam	59
Blenheim battle of	72
Bleim, Christian	58
Bouquet, Gen. Henry	134
Bonnett fam. hist.	96
Bordieu de, fam	28
Bochart, Dr. Samuel	23
Bonneauvant, Jean	136
Bonrepos de, Rev. David	32
Boston, Huguenot church of	32
Bondet, Rev. Daniel	32
Boudinot Elias	40, 48, 138–139
Bowdoin fam. and college	146
Boyer fam hist	43, 54, 89
Bohemia, Manor	46
Bouchell fam. hist.	46
Brashier, Judith	87
Bushong fam. hist.	58, 98, 134
Bucher, Hon. Joseph C.	70
Brunot fam. hist.	132
Bruno, St.	132
Bregunier fam. hist.	135
Calvin, John, Reformer	2
Corree, Rev. Ezechiel	32
Casho fam. hist.	43
Cassatt fam. hist.	131
Charleston, S. C., founded	27
Charleston, S. C., colony of	123
Chartier, Martin	88
Chevallier fam	48
Chamier, Dr. Daniel	24
Charles IX dies	8
Clewell fam. hist.	86
Coligney, Duke de, a Huguenot leader 2, 5, murdered	7
Conde, Prince of, a Huguenot leader	3–9
Court, Antoine	20
Cochet fam hist.	120
Conewago colony	130
Conyngham, Redmond, quoted	89
Conestoga, Valley of the	88
Cresson fam. hist.	52
Creyfels, a refuge	112
Crousillat, Louis	35
Daille, Rev. Pierre	32
Dasser, Paul	50
Dana fam. hist.	142
Desert, church of the	19
Decatur, Stephen	VII
Dewy, Admiral Geo.	VII
Dedier, Jean	51
Desha fam.	82
De Monts founds New France	29
De Medici, Queen Catherine	306
De Beza, Rev. Theodore	4, 23
De Sanno, Frederick	36
De Albret, Jeanne 6, death of	7
De, Hass Gen. Philip 40, fam. hist.	124
De Cessna fam. hist.	41, 129
De Graffenreid, Ch.	112
De Forrest, Jesse, colonizer	41
De Frehn fam. hist.	56
De Turk fam. hist.	62
De Harcourt fam	64
De Benneville, Dr. George	66
De Long fam. hist.	74
De Normandy fam. hist.	79

(1) For names that do not appear in this index the reader is referred to the General List of Huguenot Immigrants in this work.

De Boileau fam. hist...............	80
De Tray fam..........................	80
De Schweintz fam. of.............	80
De Pew fam. of......................	81
De Avier, Jean.......................	121
De Bow fam...........................	97
Delano, Hon. Columbus.........	145
Delaware, Huguenot families of	41, 44
De La Grange, Joost 43, Arnoldus...............................	45
De La Vall, John....................	48
De la Plaine fam. hist.............	57
De la Plank fam. hist..............	69
Delliker, Rev. Frederick.........	38
Dillier fam. hist.....................	96
Dinkle, John Daniel................	126
Disponnett fam......................	137
Dodderer, Henry S., quoted.....	7
Douty fam. hist......................	87
Doutel fam. hist.....................	126
Dragonades, the.....................	16
Dravo, Anthony.....................	133
Du Corson fam.......................	80
Du Castle, Edmund................	48
Du Bois. Louis founds New Paltz 30, hist. of 58, Rev. Laurent 32, John 43, Abraham........	114
Du Pont fam. hist...................	46
Duval, Gabriel.......................	144
Duponceau, Peter...................	35
Duche fam. hist 48, Jacob.......	138
Dundore fam. hist...................	122
Dunkards, persecuted come to America.............................	113
England refugees to........ 19, 39,	118
Egle, Dr. W. H. biog..............	IX
Edict of Nantes 11, Revocation of 18, Edict of toleration.......	22
Esopus, N. Y..........................	31
Ephrata community................	115
Eckerline fam. hist.................	115
Feneuil fam. hist., 145, Hall......	145
Fenelon pleads for toleration....	19
Ferree fam. hist............ 41, 100,	106
Forney fam. hist.....................	92
Fortney fam. hist....................	97
Francis I. favorable to reform...	2
Garfield Pres. James A............	IV
Gallaudet fam. 146, college.....	146
Gallatin, Albert mentioned......	132
Garrigues fam........................	50
Galley slaves..........................	37
Germantown, settlement of.....	51
Girard, Stephen 36, college.....	144
Girardin fam. hist...................	74
Gobin, Gen. J. P. S................	74
Goshahoppen church..............	53
Grimm fam. hist.....................	77
Grinnell brothers 147, Polar expedition............................	147
Griesemer fam. hist................	77
Groff fam. hist. 117, Prof. Geo. G...................................	77
Gruwell fam..........................	43
Grubb, Bishop N. B...............	66
Guise fam. oppose reformation 3, Duke of—killed..............	9
Hauer, Rev. Daniel.................	134
Hamilton, Hon. Alex. N.........	
Hay, Col. John............... 41,	126
Haller, Col. Henry........ 41,	48
Heydt, Jost.............................	125
Herbein fam. hist....................	77
Herrman, Augustine...............	45
Hillegas, Mich. 40, 138, fam. hist....................................	54
Horry................................. 1,	135
Hoch fam...............................	77
Hubley fam hist............... 41,	93
Huger fam..............................	140
Hubertson, Huber...................	90
Huelings fam. hist..................	44
Huguenots character of, VII, strength of 5, wars of the 3, 6, 9. 11, massacre of—Vassey 5. St. Bartholemew 7, churches destroyed 16, invited to foreign lands 17, flight of 18, last persecution of 21, eminent characters 23, colleges of 24, settlements in America 25, 39, "monuments" of........................	137
Imbert, Andrew......................	48
Jay, John................................	138
Javin, Pierre...........................	35
Jacquett, Jean Paul.................	42
Jacques, Jean 90. Lancelot......	135
Jessup, Jos.............................	87
Julian, De St. fam. of.............	28
Kauffman, John Jacob............	77
Keim fam. hist.......................	61
Kelpius, Johannis...................	34
Kieffer fam. hist.............. 73,	123
Kocherthal, Rev. Josiah colony of	39
Lanier, poet...........................	IV
Landis fam. persecuted..........	110
Lawshe fam. hist	114
Laux fam. hist.......................	121
Laurans, Hon. Henry...... 138,	139
Lafayette, favors toleration.....	22
Lancaster church records 90, French services in...............	90
Lazelere fam. hist...................	80
Labadie, Jean.........................	45
La Bar....................... 41, 58,	85
La Mar, 41, 85, L. Q, C.........	145
La Rou, fam. hist......... 123, 130,	136
La Mott. fam., hist.................	127
La Rose, fam. hist..................	84
La Trobe, Benjamin................	86
La Wall fam...........................	85

La Tour fam.............................. 99
Leiden, city of, a place of refuge 29
Levering fam. hist..................... 51
Leasure fam. hist..................... 124
Lesher fam.............................. 59
League of the Holy Union......... 9
Lemont, Peter......................... 90
Le Beau fam. hist..................... 121
Le Brun, Jean.......................... 51
Le Clerc, Jean, martyr. 3
Le Colle, Pierre....................... 50
Le Doux fam. exiled................ 86
Le Fever, Jacques, reformer 1,
  fam. in Delaware 43, in New
  York 31, John 58, Isaac 107,
  Col. Daniel............................ 108
Le Conte fam.......................... 141
Le Roy fam.............................. 94
Le Tort, Capt. James................ 89
Le Van fam. hist.................. 41, 68
Le Valleau fam........................ 80
Lingel fam. hist....................... 124
Lischey, Rev. Jacob list of........ 129
Lorraine, devastation of 72, house
  of... 3
Lorah fam. hist.................... 41, 59
Louis XIV revokes edict of
  Nantes 18
Longfellow's Evangeline, mention of............................. 148
Luther, Martin reformer............ 1
Manigault, Gabriel................... 140
Marion, Gen. Francis................ 140
Marchand fam. hist.................. 96
Mathiot fam. hist..................... 91
Marquett fam. hist................... 78
Manakintown, Va., settled........, 28
Mazarine 14
Margaret Queen of Navarre...... 2
Markley fam. hist..................... 74
Maury, Prof. Matthew Fontain... 143
Mercier, Rev. Andre................. 32
Mestrezat, Jean 23. fam hist. 132,
  Hon. S. Leslie........................ 41
Mentges, Col. Francis.......... 41, 96
Meurer, Rev. John Philip.......... 87
Mennonites, persecution of 108,
  martyrs 109, migrate to
  Alsace 111, to Pennsylvania
  112, Pioneers............... 113, 116
Missamer fam. hist................... 58
Minnuit, Peter, Gov. of New
  Sweden................................. 42
Minnisink settlement................ 81
Mickley fam. hist..................... 83
Michelle, Lewis, prospector,... 89, 112
Millot, Col. Daniel.................... 135
Moravians 34, church 85, synod.. 70
Montandon, David................... 50
Nantes edict of 11, abridged 13,
  revoked'................................ 18

Navarre, house of Protestant 2,
  Henry de, abjurates 8, becomes King 10, promulgates
  the edict of Nantes 11, assassinated 11, Catherine de,
  dies....................................... 11
National synod 12, 13, 14, restored 21
Names of immigrants changed... 148
Naudin, Elie............................ 43
New France, settlement of....... 28
New Netherlands founded......... 29
New Paltz, N. Y....................... 30
New Rochelle, N. Y.................. 31
New Oxford, Mass................... 32
Neff fam. hist.......................... 117
"Nipmuck country" settlement
  of... 32
Noel, Hon. D. K....................... 125
Nobility favorable to reform...... 2
Olney, Hon. Richard................ 145
Oberlin fam. hist..................... 99
Otterbein, Rev. P. W................ 94
Oley valley, the....................... 61
Ohenbach, tower of................. 109
Patentees of New Paltz............ 31
Palatinate, devastation of 72,
  101, 112, 118, immigration
  from.................... 34, 112, 118
Parett, Nicholas....................... 98
Paris treaty of......................... 138
Pastorius, Francis Daniel mentioned.................................. 34
Pennsylvania, emigration to 33,
  a place of refuge................... 34
Pechin fam. hist...................... 57
Pettit, Dr. Samuel 25, James, 130
Penn, William, Holy experiment
  of... 34
Pershing, Hon. Cyrus L............ 132
Perdeau, William 50, fam.......... 60
Perrine, Thomas 90, John 135,
  fam 144
Philadelphia Huguenots in 48,
  church records of............. 50–51
Philippi, King Louis, mentioned............................ 35, 133
Pickens 36. Gen. Andrew......... 140
Piatt fam. hist......................... 129
Piedmontese martyrs................ 38
Possey, debate at....................
Pons fam. hist.................... 98, 133
Port Royal, settlement of......... 26
Pontius fam. hist..................... 119
Poinsett, Joel Robert............... 143
Prioleau, Eli............................. 27
Prevoost, Bishop Samuel..........
Priestly, Dr. Joseph a refugee.... 35
Puritans at Leyden................... 29
Purviance fam. hist.................. 57
Pumpelly, Prof. Raphael........... 143

Quay, Matthew Stanley	58
Ravenal fam. hist	28, 142
Raiguel, Abraham	124
Racine, poet	19
Ranc, Louis martyr 20, fam. hist	98
Rapp, Gabriel	48
Revocation, the	18
Reformation, French I, character of	2
Reidenour fam. hist	76
Reed, Hon. Thomas	146
Rettew fam. hist	66
Reynolds, Gen. John F	106
Reboteau, Mich.	48
Richards, Hon. John	54
Ribaut, Jean colonist	26
Ritner, Gov. Joseph	74
Roberdeau, Gen. Daniel	40, 50
Rohan, Duke de	11, 13
Roosevelt, Pres. Theodore	IV
Royer fam hist	114
Roller fam. hist	95, 136
Ronner, Rev. John R	87
Rochia, Lauraus	44
Robinett, Samuel	38
Routte, Daniel	43
Robert college	146
Rutan, Gerritt	43
Rupp, Prof. I. Daniel	120
Rudesill fam	127
Runyan fam	144
Rosecrucians mentioned	34
Ryswick peace of	72, 112
Saurin, Jacques	28
Sachse, Prof. Julius works of	34, 115
Santee fam. 79, colony	28
Sangree fam. hist	127
Sallada fam. hist	127
Scotch Irish, notice of	34
Schwenkfelders, the	34
Schley, Admiral W. S.	107
Servier, John "the commonwealth builder"	136, 140
Shreiver fam the	134
Shetrone fam	127
Shuey fam. hist	122
Sigourney, Andre	145
Simetere du, Piere E	36
Simonette, Jacques	98
Slaymaker fam	3 117
Smalkaldic League	2
Somaine	60
Sower, Christopher	67, 117
States general, favorable to reform	4
Supplee fam	49
Sumois fam	97
Thoreau, poet	IV
Trego fam	57
Tourgee fam	143
Toleration granted	5, 22
Touton, Dr. John, petition of	31
Tohickon, church at	82
Tulpehocken, settlement of	118
Tyler, Pres. John	IV
Utree, Gen Daniel	41, 70
Universalism, preaching of	67
Urner fam hist	113
Vallerchamp, Simon	35
Voshell fam	43
Votaw fam	60
Voturin fam	126
Walloons. migration of	29
Waldensians, come to America	30, 42
Wesco fam	84
Weiser, Conrad interpreter	118
Whittier, poet IV, quoted	75
Woodring fam	126
Zeller fam	119
Zinzendorf, Count Von	85
Zimmerman fam	118
Zug fam	III

www.ingramcontent.com/pod-product-compliance
Lightning Source LLC
Chambersburg PA
CBHW050816160426
43192CB00010B/1785